A WEAVER NAMED

French Studies in South Asian Culture and Society VI

A WEAVER NAMED KABIR

Selected Verses With a Detailed Biographical and Historical Introduction

by

CHARLOTTE VAUDEVILLE

DELHI
OXFORD UNIVERSITY PRESS
CALCUTTA CHENNAI MUMBAI

Oxford University Press, Great Clarendon Street, Oxford OX2 6DP

Oxford New York
Athens Auckland Bangkok Calcutta
Cape Town Chennai Dar es Salaam Delhi
Florence Hong Kong Istanbul Karachi
Kuala Lumpur Madrid Melbourne Mexico City
Mumbai Nairobi Paris Singapore
Taipei Tokyo Toronto

and associates in

Berlin Ibadan

Oxford India Paperbacks 1997

ISBN 0 19 563933 2

The publisher acknowledges with thanks the support given by the Maison des Sciences de l'Homme, Paris.

Printed at Rekha Printers Pvt. Ltd., New Delhi 110 020
and published by Manzar Khan, Oxford University Press
YMCA Library Building, Jai Singh Road, New Delhi 110 001

Foreword

Charlotte Vaudeville's rendering of Kabīr's verse and her assessment of his work are an authoritative statement of a perception of Kabīr which has evolved over many years of intense involvement and study. Though the figure of Kabīr, as the nineteenth century perceived him, has come to exist in its own right as standing for the unity of Hindu and Muslim, and though there is need, in this dark period in the history of the subcontinent when communal tensions make daily headlines, to invoke Kabīr once again, there is need also that this tradition be reviewed. For Kabīr, a low-caste weaver, stood in the market place, *kabīrā khaṛā bazār mẽ*, as he himself specified his own location, to preach not the synthesis of Hinduism and Islam, but to rail at the bigotry of both Hindu and Turk. Bitingly satirical, he was equally striking in his religious fervour and the intensity of his convictions and his search. In the following centuries he was claimed by many and at least three distinct traditions were to form, that of the *pīr* Kabīr, the *vaiṣṇava* Kabīr, apart from that of the Kabīr of the sectarian Kabīrpanth. All these traditions were to come together and be moulded into yet another, in the course of the nineteenth century, by the enthusiasm of Indian and British scholars (a number of them Protestant missionaries) for this prophet of 'eclectic monotheism'—as George Grierson termed it. There was near consensus regarding this vision of the religious and social reformer who, by attacking the orthodoxies of both religions, Hinduism and Islam, had broken down the barriers that separated the two.

The nationalist devotion for this—as they had come to consider—almost secular apostle of Hindu-Muslim unity was, however, soon to be followed by a spate of intensive research by modern Indian scholars. After the mid-thirties there were a series of important publications by P.D. Barthwal, Hazari Prasad

Dwivedi and Parshuram Chaturvedi. All three concerned themselves with the wider devotional tradition in which Kabīr was embedded and which till then had remained largely unknown in the West. From this point on it was Charlotte Vaudeville who provided the decisive impetus in 'Kabirian' studies. In her introduction to the present volume she has traced the evolution of the varied strands of tradition enfolding Kabīr, untangling thereby the web woven in the nineteenth century, while at the same time assessing and incorporating the results of modern Indian scholarship in her research.

The present volume has its own history, which I should like to recount briefly. Mme. Vaudeville's study of Kabīr, comprising an English translation of Kabīr's most popular verse, his distichs or *sākhī*s, and a long introductory essay, was published originally in 1974 by Clarendon Press, Oxford. The book soon became a classic and inspired a whole generation of scholars to take up work on the *nirgun* school of medieval devotional poetry. Yet the scholarly world waited in vain for the promised second volume of Kabīr, which was to contain translations of the remaining verse, the longer *pad*s, *śabda*s and the *ramainī*s.

While discussing the publication of Mme. Vaudeville's *Selected Essays*, Oxford University Press, Delhi, asked me whether she would consider an Indian paperback edition of *Kabīr I*, which in its time had been accessible to few in the country and had in the meantime gone out of print. When I approached her with this request, it became apparent why the second volume had not followed. For the 1974 edition of her *Kabīr* Mme. Vaudeville had undertaken the translation of the *sākhī*s as accessible in the critical edition of Kabīr's verse, *Kabīr Granthāvalī* (Allahabad, 1965) prepared by Dr P.N. Tiwari. After sifting the enormous mass of verses attributed to Kabīr, Tiwari had selected 744 *sākhī*s, 200 *pad*s and 20 *ramainī*s as approximating to what might have been the original size of Kabīr's text. Later reflection was to show that much spurious material had been included even after his cautious winnowing. I shall not go into the details of her reasons for reaching this conclusion, which she has enumerated in her present introduction. Since, however, the first volume no longer satisfied her own criteria, the second did not follow, and for the same reason she refused to consider a reprint. She undertook instead the task of revising the whole of her material on Kabīr in order to present in one new volume, alongside the introductory essay, the *sākhī*s, *pad*s, *śabda*s and *ramainī*s she considered authentically '*Kabirian*'. The *sākhī*s have now been reduced to a fifth of the original number, a revised selection from the *Gurū Granth* verses has been added, along with a selection of the poetry of the Bhagats who were Kabīr's forerunners and contemporaries. The Hindi originals of the three Western traditions, which are the primary source of Tiwari's edition of the *Kabīr Granthāvalī*—which latter in its turn had been out of print for some time now—are accessible in her own edition of 1982: *Kabīr-Vānī*, recension occidentale, published by the French Indological Institute in Pondicherry.

The following have participated in the process of making an intricate text appear in print, and deserve warm thanks: Françoise Mallison, Monika Thiel-Horstmann, Denis Matringe, Angelika Malinar and Gert Lüderitz for help in various ways, including the sending of the manuscript to and fro between Paris, Tübingen, Leuven and Delhi; Oxford University Press for its patience in securing the financial support needed to get the camera-ready copy prepared; Mrs. N. Vannieuwenhoven, Leuven, for the typing; Winand Callewaert for his enthusiasm and energy in undertaking to supervise the typing, inspite of a load of other work; Françoise Delvoye 'Nalini' for patiently correcting the proofs twice over in between numerous pressures, and Nicole Merkel for her care in the final proof-reading.

Tübingen VASUDHA DALMIA-LÜDERITZ
November 1991

Abbreviations

BSOS	*Bulletin of the School of Oriental Studies.*
Gu	*Śrī Gurū Granth Sāhib,* Amritsar, 1952.
GB	*Gorakh Bānī,* ed. P.D. Barthwal, Prayāg, 3rd ed., Vi.S. 2017
GKY	G.W. Briggs, *Goraknāth and the Kānphaṭa Jogīs,* Calcutta, 1938.
HLHH	Garcin de Tassy, *Histoire de la littérature hindouie et hindoustanie,* 1st ed., vol. i, Paris, 1939.
IM	Y. Husain, *L'Inde mystique au Moyen-Age,* Paris, 1929.
IS	G.S. Ghurye, *Indian Sadhus,* 2nd ed., Bombay, 1964.
JA	Journal Asiatique.
JASBE	Journal of the Asiatic Society of Bengal.
JRAS	Journal of the Royal Asiatic Society.
KB	Mohan Singh, *Kabir, His Biography,* Lahore, 1934.
KF	F.E. Keay, *Kabīr and his Followers,* Calcutta, 1931.
KG	*Kabīr Granthāvalī,* ed. P.N. Tiwari, Prayāg, 1961.
KKP	G.H. Westcott, *Kabir and the Kabir Panth,* 2nd ed., Calcutta, 1943.
KSP	P. Chaturvedi, *Kabīr sāhitya kī parakh,* Prayāg, Vi.S. 2011
NSHP	P.D. Barthwal, *The Nirguṇa School of Hindi Poetry,* Benares, 1936.
ODBL	S.K. Chatterji, *The Origin and Development of the Bengali Language,* 2 vols., Calcutta, 1926.
ORC	S.B. Dasgupta, *Obscure Religious Cults,* 2nd ed., Calcutta, 1962.
ORLI	J.N. Farquhar, *An Outline of the Religious Literature of India,* repr. Delhi, 1967.
Rāj.	Rājasthānī tradition of Kabīr's verses.
RSH	H.H. Wilson, *Religious Sects of the Hindus,* 2nd ed., Calcutta, 1958.
SR	Macauliffe, *The Sikh Religion,* 6 vols., repr. New Delhi, 1963.
UBSP	P. Chaturvedi, *Uttarī bhārat mė sant-paramparā,* Prayāg, Vi.S. 2008
VS	R.G. Bhandarkar, *Vaiṣṇavism, Śaivism and Minor Religious systems,* Collected Works, iv, Poona, 1929.

Contents

Part One: Introduction

The Discovery of Kabīr

Kabīr is one of the best-known and most revered names in Indian tradition. From the Panjab to Bengal and from the Himalayan frontiers to South India, he has long been hailed by Hindus and Muslims alike as a great mystic and bold religious reformer. His name has travelled far and wide in the Indian subcontinent and, thanks to the admiration of Mahātmā Gandhi and Rabindranath Tagore, he is not completely unknown even in the West today. In the literary field too, Kabīr ranks very high: he has been hailed as 'the father of Hindī literature' and even sometimes placed on a par with the greatest Hindī poet, Tulsīdās, the author of the Hindī *Rāmāyaṇ,* 'the Bible of Northern India'.

In Indian religious history, Kabīr is unique: to the Hindus, he is a Vaishnav *bhakta,* to the Muslims a *pīr,* to the Sikhs a *bhagat,* to the sectarian Kabīr-panthīs an *avatār* of the supreme Being. To modern patriots, Kabīr is the champion of Hindu-Muslim unity, to neo-Vedantists a promoter of the Universal Religion or the 'Religion of Man', he who steadfastly opposed the superstitious beliefs and empty ritualism of orthodox Hinduism as well as the dogmatic pride and bigotry of orthodox Islam. In modern, progressive circles today, Kabīr is held in high esteem as a social reformer, a bold enemy of Brahmanical pride and caste distinctions, a revolutionary whose scathing attacks on caste prejudices, the principle of untouchability and all forms of social discriminations are for ever famous and comforting to the enlightened Indian mind, like a breeze of fresh air. To modern India, Kabīr appears as a symbol of nonconformity, of all that is free, noble and challenging in the Indian tradition. Some contemporary Indian writers have not hesitated to compare him to the Buddha Gautam for the fearlessness of his character, the loftiness of his views, and his extraordinary hold on the common masses of India.

But Kabīr, unlike the Buddha, was not born a prince: he was neither scholar nor aristocrat, but at the same time a *Shūdra* (of non-Aryan, impure descent) and a *mleccha,* a 'barbarian', since the social group to which he belonged was already islamized.

Both tradition and Kabīr's own words attest that he was born a poor *Julāhā,* - a Muhammedan weaver of the ancient Kashi, the modern Benares. He never had access to Sanskrit scriptures or Sanskrit knowledge and he was most probably illiterate. Kabīr's *bānīs*, or 'sayings', so popular among the Indian masses, are expressed in the vulgar tongue, a rough idiom which appears as a form of old *Hindui* or Hindī: the very roughness of his idiom enhances the striking forcefulness of his style and reveals the fervour of his conviction, the depth of his mystical awareness. The British scholar J.N. Farquhar was surely not far from the mark when he said of Kabīr: "His best utterances are probably the loftiest work in the Hindī language and hundreds of his couplets have laid hold of the common heart of Hindustan".[1]

The impact of Kabīr's sayings on the masses of Northern India has been profound and not to be disregarded by historians of Hinduism. In *Medieval Mysticism of India,* a work

(1) J.N. Farquhar, *Outline of the Religious Literature of India,* p. 333.

largely based on the popular sayings and songs carried by the itinerant sadhus of Northern India, the Bengali scholar Kshiti Mohan Sen had testified to the depth of Kabīr's impact on the common folk: "Kabīr's superior spiritual achievements came to have a sovereign influence on the people of the Indian medieval times. Kabīr's influence, direct or indirect, on all liberal movements which occurred in the medieval times after him is uncommonly deep".[2]

Kabīr's great voice and remarkable hold on the Northern Indian masses did not pass unnoticed by western scholars who, from the end of the eighteenth century, applied themselves to the study of Indian traditions and literature. Their attention seems to have been early attracted by the existence of a well-developed sect bearing his name, the Kabīr-panthī sect, who claims to be followers of the *panth,* or the spiritual 'path' shown by Kabīr himself.

The Kabīr-panthīs own a number of religious establishments or *maṭh*s, spread over Northern and Central India, one of their main centres being in Benares itself, at 'Kabīr Chaurā'.[3] Though they consider themselves as Hindus, the Kabīr-panthīs are remarkable for their opposition to idol-

(2) *Medieval Mysticism of India,* London, 1930, p. 87. This is the English version of the *Adyar Mookerji Lectures,* delivered in Bengali, Calcutta University, 1929.

(3) The Kabīr-panthīs are divided into several branches: the Surat-Gopāl branch whose centre is at Kabīr Chaurā, Benares, with a sub-branch at Magahar, sixteen miles from Gorakhpur, and the well-developed Dharmadās branch, established in Chattīsgarh (Madhya Pradesh), which has its centre at Damakhera. According to Wilson, *RSH,* p. 53, the Surat-Gopāl (i.e. Kabīr Chaurā) branch had an establishment at Puri-Jagannath in Orissa and another at Dvarka, which suggests a Krishnaite influence. Another important branch of the Kabīr-panth claims descent from Bhaggodās, *alias*

worship, their strong monotheism, the uprightness of their moral code, as well as their opposition to caste distinctions. Those characteristics earned them the respect and attention of a small number of Protestant missionaries and British officials who came into contact with them. From the beginning of the nineteenth century onwards, the interest in the Kabīr-panthīs, as well as in the mysterious personality of their purported founder, steadily increased in missionary circles, as western scholars began to recognize in Kabīr one of the greatest mystics and religious reformers in India.

The real pioneer in 'Kabirian' studies, however, seems to have been an Italian Capuchin monk, Padre Marco della Tomba, who arrived in India in 1758 and returned to Rome in 1775. Padre Marco travelled in Northern India, Nepal and Tibet, but spent most of his Indian years at Bettia, in Northern Bihar, close to the Nepalese frontier, where he applied himself assiduously to the study of Sanskrit as well as of the vernaculars. He also studied carefully the various traditions of the inhabitants of the region, one of them - and not the least remarkable in Padre Marco's eyes - being that of the Cabiristi':

> I saw a sect or kind of religion called *Cabiristi,* descended from a certain Cabir, a man considered as a great saint, who had performed many miracles: it is said he was the spiritual Master of Alexander the Great. On this sect, we would have to say much, as they are in great credit and number.[4]

Bhagavān Sāhib, *alias* Bhaggojī, established at Dhanauti, in the Saran district of Bihar; he is the purported compiler of the *Bījak.*

(4) Angelo de Gubernatis, *Gli scritti del Padre Marco della Tomba,* Florence, 1878, p. 94.

Padre Marco did in fact translate into Italian the *Satnaus Cabir,* i.e. *Satnām Kabīr* (also known as *Gyān-sāgar*), and another book called *Mūlpancī (mūlpanthī?)*[5] - besides a particular *Rāmaen* (*Rāmāyaṇ*) in eight books, which appears to be a Cabirist' (i.e. Kabīr-panthī) version of the *Rāmāyaṇ* legend, in which Rām appears as a great penitent and ascetic resembling the Buddha.

Of the 'Cabiristi Fachiri' (Faqīrs), Marco notes that they are *secolari* (married), wear a particular rosary (*mālā*) made of small beads, are strict vegetarians and careful in the practice of ahimsa (non-violence), taking care not to crush insects etc. According to Padre Marco, they believe in 'no god in particular', the supreme Deity being for them the impersonal Force at work in the universe. Nevertheless, they recognize a visible god called 'Naraen' (*Nārāyaṇ*) and another one whom they call 'Niranjen' (*Nirañjan*) and who is the instrument through which 'Naraen' creates the world - a creation in which the great eight-armed Bavani (*Bhavānī*) goddess plays the main part.[6] Seen through Padre Marco's eyes, the Kabīr-panthīs of Bettia appear to have accepted a strange mixture of Buddhist and Vaishnav beliefs, besides allowing a place for the popular cult of the Devī (Bhavāṇī or Durgā-devī), who was and remains to this day the principal deity of the inferior castes.

In the Introduction to his edition of a part of Padre Marco's papers, Angelo de Gubernatis attempts a synthesis of Kabīr's doctrine. In the chapter entitled 'Kabīr et la sua riforma', he remarks that Kabīr's ideas are fundamentally Buddhist and that his rejection of caste, scripture and Brahmanical practices

(5) This work was found among the papers left by Padre Marco in the Borgia Collection of the Vatican; an abstract of the Italian translation was published by Angelo de Gubernatis in vol. III of *Mines of the East*.

(6) Angelo de Gubernatis, *op.cit.*, p. 96.

and ritual had their source in Buddhism, which had survived for a long time in the Eastern region of Tirhut and the Nepalese border, where Bettia is situated.

Remarking on the strange attempts found in the *Gyān sāgar* to 'Kabīrize' local cults and beliefs and to roll Vishnu, Rām and the Buddha into one divine Being identified with Kabīr, de Gubernatis nevertheless suspected the authenticity of the evidence collected by Padre Marco della Tomba. He warns that we should not try to derive all Kabīr's doctrines from it, but wait for more evidence.[7]

In the last years of the eighteenth century, in Calcutta, Dr. J.B. Gilchrist had already heard of Kabīr's outstanding personality and of his famous utterances, as he mentions him in his 'Hindostanee Grammar': "That famous Indian sage who lived in the humble condition of a weaver expressed sentiments and did actions which would have honoured the most illustrious men".[8]

In Calcutta again, in 1812, Malcolm published his *Sketch of the Sikhs,* largely based on the material he had collected in the Panjab. According to his Sikh sources, Nānak, the founder of Sikhism, "constantly referred to the admired writings of the celebrated Muhammedan Kabīr".[9] Malcolm sums up his information on Kabīr in this way:

> This celebrated Sufi or philosophical deist lived in the time of the emperor Sher Shah. He was, by trade, a weaver, but he has written several admired works. They are all composed in a strain of universal

---

(7) Referring to Padre Marco's pioneer work on the subject, de Gubernatis concludes: "Blessed be his memory!"

(8) J.B. Gilchrist, *A Grammar of the Hindostanee Language,* Calcutta, 1796.

(9) Malcolm, *Sketch of the Sikhs,* London, p. 146.

philanthropy and benevolence; and, above all, he inculcated religious toleration, particularly between the Muhammedans and Hindus, by both of whom his memory is held in high esteem and veneration".[10]

If Kabīr is, in fact, much revered by the Sikhs, the opinion that he was a 'professed Sufi' could hardly have been expressed by Malcolm's Sikh informants: he would probably have heard it from Muslim circles, either in Panjab itself, or even in Bengal, where Kabīr had always been held in high esteem, especially as a symbol of religious toleration.[11]

In 1827, the first lithographed edition of W. Price's *Hindee and Hindoostanee Selections* appeared. The first volume includes *The Rekhtus of Kabeer,* plus a few small sectarian works concerning Kabīr - besides the stanza devoted to him in the *Bhaktamāl* of Nābhājī and a long anonymous *ṭīkā* (commentary), giving a legendary account of Kabīr's life, which was later to be translated by Garcin de Tassy.

In his *Mémoire sur les Kabīr-panthī*s, published in 1832 (in French), General Harriott compares them with the Quakers: "... Des sectaires qui, de même que les Quakers, sont remarquables par la simplicité de leurs moeurs et leur bonne conduite mais que personne ne semble bien connaître...".[12]

---

(10) The connection between Kabīr and Bengal is not clear. There is a Kabīr-maṭh at Puri in Orissa, where, according to the local Kabīr-panthī tradition (mentioned by Keay, *KF,* pp. 107-8), Kabīr prevented the sea from submerging the Jagannāth temple. One of the two tombs of Kabīr mentioned by Abū'l Fazl is at Puri in Orissa. Actually, there are few Kabīr-panthīs in Bengal, but Kabīr's name is famous throughout the province and wandering minstrels sing a number of songs attributed to him. A number of early collections of Kabīr *bānī*s were published in Bengal.

(11) W. Price, *Hindee and Hindoostanee Selections,* vol. 1, Calcutta, 1827.

(12) *JA,* 9 (1832), 169.

Harriott reports that he had many conversations with them in Bihar and Malwa. He praises their pleasant manner and notes that "ils aiment à raisonner". He calls Kabīr "ce philosophe grossier mais libéral et éclairé" and several verses attributed to him are quoted in French. General Harriott seems to have been the first western scholar to note a resemblance between the *śabda* doctrine of Kabīr and the platonic *logos*[13] - an idea which was to be developed later by Westcott and Grierson. Comparing the Kabīr-panthīs with the Sikhs, Harriott expresses the opinion that the principal object of Kabīr's as well as of Nānak's reform was to exclude all forms of idol-worship.

In H.H. Wilson's *Sketch of the Religious Sects of the Hindus,* which appeared in 1862 but was based on previous essays published in 1828 and 1832 in *Asiatic Researches,* we find the first serious attempt to disentangle the mass of legendary traditions surrounding Kabīr. Quoting from the narrative of Kabīr's biography as it appears in Nābhājī's *Bhaktamāl* and in its commentary published by W. Price, Wilson gives a brief account of Kabīr's life in the Hindu tradition:[14] how he was miraculously born from a Brahmin virgin widow by saint Rāmānand's blessing; how he was exposed on a lake, then later found by the wife of a Mohammedan weaver and brought up by the couple as their own child; inflamed with the love of Rām, Kabīr used a stratagem to become Rāmānand's disciple, in spite of his being accounted as an

---

(13) "Ce *Śabda* ou verbe ressemble au *logos* de Platon: une étude de trente ans me fut nécessaire pour les comprendre; et lorsque je montrai cette interprétation à feu mon ami le Dr. A. Nicol [...] il eut de la peine à croire qu'elle vînt d'une secte aussi illettrée que sont les Kabīr-panthīs de l'Hindoustan".

(14) Wilson, *RSH,* pp. 36-41. Wilson quotes Malcolm and Price. He does not appear to have consulted Harriott's paper, published a few months earlier.

'impure Muhammedan'; he was persecuted by the cruel emperor Sikander Lodī, who nevertheless failed in his attempts to have him put to death, owing to Kabīr's display of his own supernatural powers.

The most remarkable story - and by far the most famous - concerns Kabīr's passing away and his double funeral: feeling his end at hand, the saint demanded to be left alone in a hut where he lay covered with a single cloth, whilst his Hindu and Muhammedan disciples hotly contested the right to dispose of his body according to the rites of their respective religions. But, when the cloth which concealed Kabīr's mortal remains was lifted, nothing was found but a spray of flowers. One half of the flowers went to the Rājā of Benares, Vīr Singh, who had them cremated in the Hindu fashion, whilst the other half went to the Pathan noble Bijlī Khān, the head of the Muhammedan party, who buried them on the spot, at Magahar, near Gorakhpur. Magahar is generally acknowledged to be the place of Kabīr's *samādhi,* or memorial, built over the ashes of the flowers secured by the Hindu Rājā.

Wilson approaches his sources with caution and expresses great doubt as to the historical character of the stories.[15] But he also rejects Malcolm's assertion that Kabīr had been a Muhammedan and a Sufi. According to Wilson, "his (Kabīr's) conversancy with the Hindu *śāstra*s and his evidently limited knowledge of the Muhammedan authorities in matters of religion renders such a supposition perfectly unwarrantable". For Wilson, therefore, Kabīr must have been a Hindu. On Kabīr's dates, Wilson's guess is that he flourished about the beginning

(15) Wilson even goes so far as to doubt Kabīr's existence altogether: "I think that it is not at all improbable that no such person as Kabīr ever existed and that his name is a mere cover to the innovations of some free thinkers among the Hindus..." *RSH,* p. 36, n. 25.

of the fifteenth century and that his religious innovations were connected with the previous exertions of Rāmānand, whom he tentatively places in the fourteenth century.

1. THE BĪJAK OR EASTERN TRADITION OF KABĪR'S WORKS

Wilson's account shows that he was fairly well acquainted with the Kabīr-panthī traditions, especially with those found in the *Kabīr Chaurā maṭh* in Benares. He gives a list of works attributed to Kabīr which are found in the large compilation called *Khās Granth* and preserved there. The latest work on the list, and by far the most important, is the *Bījak*. Wilson gives a rough account of the contents and remarks on its obscurity. But he rightly accords much importance to the collection of distichs or *sākhī*s it contains, because of their popularity "even among those who are not Kabīr's followers". Wilson's account and his English translations of one hundred *sākhī*s from the *Bījak* were the source of most of what was known and said about Kabīr, at least in the western world, till the first decade of the twentieth century.

In the first edition of his famous *Histoire de la littérature Hindouie et Hindoustanie,* Garcin de Tassy[16] gave a brief account of Kabīr, quoting Harriott, Price and Wilson. In the second edition, he added a French translation of the verse about Kabīr in Nābhājī's *Bhaktamāl* and its commentary as given by Price.[17] In spite of the legendary character of the narrative, Garcin clearly discerned the importance of Kabīr in Indian religious history. He also referred to the testimony of Abū'l Fazl who had mentioned Kabīr in the *Ā* ͨīn-i-Akbarī.

(16) Garcin de Tassy, *HLHH,* Paris, 1st ed., vol. I (1939), 274 ff.

(17) *Ibid.,* 2nd ed. (1870), 120 ff.

Garcin admits with Malcolm - and against Wilson - that Kabīr was born a Muhammedan, though he was venerated by Hindus and Muslims alike, a unique distinction.

In his *Indian Empire,*[18] Hunter mentions Kabīr only briefly, relying on Wilson, but with the curious addition that Kabīr had carried Rāmānand's doctrine throughout Bengal. According to Hunter, Kabīr, who lived about the fifteenth century, "had tried to build up a religion that should embrace Hindus and Muslims alike". Hunter, therefore, goes one step further than Malcolm in asserting that Kabīr not only "inculcated religious toleration", but that he actually strove for the building up of some syncretic religion. Hunter's source here appears to be a tradition already current in Bengal in the nineteenth century.

2. THE ĀDI GRANTH OF THE SIKHS

In 1877, a German missionary, E. Trumpp, published the first (incomplete) translation of the sacred book of the Sikhs, the *Ādi Granth*[19] or *Gurū Granth,* including a part of the *pads* of the Bhagats (*bhakta*) or 'Saints', which are found in the *Granth,* and the *saloks* (*śloks*) of Kabīr and Shaykh Farīd.[20] In his preface, Trumpp details the extreme difficulties he encountered in deciphering the holy Granth, with the help of two Sikh Granthīs.[21] Though he passed severe judgments on the

(18) W.W. Hunter, *Indian Empire,* London, 1882, p. 273.

(19) The *Ādi Granth* or *The holy scriptures of the Sikhs,* translated from the original Gurmukhī with Introductory Essays by Dr. Ernest Trumpp, London, 1877.

(20) See below, Part 6: The Śloks of Shaykh Farīd in the *Gurū Granth.*

(21) "After I had succeeded in engaging two Sikh Granthis at Lahore, I was not a little surprised when they declared to me that the Granth could

Sikhs of the time, who, according to him "had lost all learning", Trumpp clearly recognized the importance of the Granth in the linguistic line "as being the treasury of old Hindui dialects". He also showed a partiality towards the poems of Kabīr, which he judged "far superior in form as well as in originality of thought to the versifications of the Sikh Gurus". It must be said that Trumpp's painstaking attempt at translating the Granth does not read too well in English, and his translations of Kabīr's *pad*s and *salok*s are very often wrong. Yet, he did some pioneering work in the field in so far as he revealed a collection of Kabīr's sayings not found in the *Bījak*.

Towards the end of the nineteenth century and during the first two decades of the twentieth century, not only the Kabīr-panthīs but Kabīr himself, his message and his personality, became an object of growing interest on the part of a new group of Indian and British scholars who were mostly Protestant missionaries. All Kabīr's utterances which they

---

not be translated in the literal grammatical way I desired. I soon convinced myself that, though they professed to understand the Granth, they had no knowledge either of the old grammatical forms or of the obsolete words; they could only give me some traditional explanations, as I found them contradicted by other passages, and now and then they could give me no explanation whatever; they had not even a clear insight into the real doctrines of the Granth. Other persons, who were recommended to me for their learning, I found equally ignorant...". (Trumpp, *op.cit.,* Preface, pp. v and vi).

Trumpp's appraisal not only of Sikh learning of the time, but also of the compositions of the Sikh Gurus themselves, is bluntly depreciatory and contemptuous. The Sikh Granth, according to him, "is incoherent and shallow in the extreme... It is for us, Occidentals, a most painful and almost stupefying task to read only a single *rāg,* and I doubt if any ordinary reader will have the patience to proceed to the second *rāg* after he shall have perused the first..". This is why Trumpp left the work incomplete.

came to hear of struck them as having a decidedly Christian ring, and his spiritual message aroused their enthusiasm. In this group were the Revd. Prem Chand, the Revd. Ahmed Shah, Bishop Westcott, and the great linguist George Grierson. In 1890, the Revd. Prem Chand, a Baptist missionary of Monghyr in Bengal, brought out an edition of the *Bījak;* in the short English Preface to that edition, he alludes to the possibility of a Christian influence on Kabīr. Prem Chand held that Kabīr "had some knowledge of Christian truth, which made him think of the brotherhood of man", and "that his moral teachings correspond with the teachings of the Bible". Moreover, he expressed the opinion that the *Bījak* was corrupted "by the Vaishnavas and pantheists", who had inserted in it dogmas peculiar to their sect.

It is interesting to note that Prem Chand was not alone in holding such views. In 1881, Pandit Walji Bhai, Pastor of a small Irish Presbyterian Congregation in Gujarat, had published in Gujarati an exposition of his views on Kabīr under the title of *Kabīr caritra.*[22] According to him, not only were current Kabīr-panthī doctrines quite similar to Christian beliefs and practices, but the Kabīr-Panth itself was actually instituted by Jesuits! Bishop Westcott, who admits that he had "some interesting correspondence with Walji Bhai", wryly adds that "the Pandit's writings are not marked by any great critical acumen"[23] This trend of thought must have been fairly common among Indian clergymen, who were familiar with Kabīr's words as quoted by the people and naturally inclined to take a Christian view of their meaning. In 1903, in Allahabad, a Hindī work called *Kabīrjñān ṭikā-sahit,* was published by one

(22) Walji Bhai, *Kabīr caritra,* Surat, 1881.

(23) On Walji Bhai's views and Bishop Westcott's reactions, cf. Westcott, *KKP,* pp. 144-145.

Sukhdev Prasād, giving some extracts of Kabīr's teachings with brief commentaries showing the corresponding teachings in the Christian Holy Scriptures. The book was re-edited several times: the appearance of a fifth edition in 1914, in Lucknow, testifies to its success. In 1911, the Revd. Prem Chand himself brought out the first complete English translation in his own edition of the *Bījak*[24] - a commendable if not a very successful effort.

In his well-known study on *Kabīr and the Kabīr-panth,* first published in 1907 from the Christ Church Mission Press, Kanpur, Bishop Westcott expresses a view of Kabīr which comes near to that of Malcolm:

> We are inclined to accept both of the theories advanced by Malcolm and to believe that not only Kabīr was a Muhammedan by birth but also that he was associated with the Sufi order; and that the great object of his life was to break down the barriers that separated Hindus from Muhammedans.

In the Preface to the same edition, Westcott ventures the opinion that "we have probably in the Kabīr Panth a religious system that owes something to Hindu, Muhammedan and Christian influences". This judgment apparently reflects the views held by the Indian clergymen quoted above, and it may also have been influenced by the opinion of Grierson, expressed in an article on *Modern Hinduism and its Debt to the Nestorians,*[25] upon the development of Indian Bhakti. In the same article, Grierson declares that "Kabīr's doctrine of the Word (*śabda*) is a remarkable copy of the opening verses of St. John's Gospel". Westcott himself, however, seems to have been

(24) *A Translation of Kabīr's Complete Bījak into English,* by Prem Chand, Calcutta, 1911.

(25) *JRAS,* 1907, p. 311.

reluctant to accept those views. In the chapter entitled 'Early Christian influences in Northern India', he readily acknowledges that he knows nothing about the work accomplished by Christian missionaries in Northern India, prior to the dispatch of the Emperor Akbar's famous embassy to Goa in 1579. Referring to Grierson's paper, Westcott merely ventures to say that "Christian thought in varying degrees of purity may have penetrated regions unvisited by professing Christians".[26] Later, however, he may have come closer to accepting Grierson's view. In an additional note to the fourth chapter of the same work, after exposing briefly 'the doctrine of Śabda', he adds: "It is not improbable that this doctrine, as set forth in the literature on the Kabīr-Panth, has been influenced by the writings of St. John".[27]

The question of the Christian influences that might have affected certain aspects of Kabīr's thought or might explain certain Kabīr-panthī practices was again discussed briefly by Macnicol in his book, *Indian Theism*.[28]

Macauliffe himself was not a missionary like Trumpp or Westcott, but he had long served in India as a magistrate and his avowed aim was to soothe the injured feelings of the orthodox Sikhs, who had rejected Trumpp's translation as "not

(26) Westcott, *KKP*, p. 90.

(27) *Ibid.*, p. 50.

(28) Nicol Macnicol, *Indian Theism from the Vedic to the Muhammedan Period*, 1st ed., 1915, 2nd ed., Delhi, 1968, pp. 135 ff. Macnicol refers to Grierson's claim (*op.cit.*, p. 326) to find similarities between the Christian Eucharistic celebration and some of the Kabīr-panthī practices; but he is of the opinion that such similarities, though striking, are not conclusive, and the question of the Kabīr-panthīs' indebtedness to Christianity "is a matter upon which we cannot dogmatize".

only generally incorrect but injurious to our religion".[29] Macauliffe, therefore, has taken great care to follow the interpretations of the Gyānīs, the representatives of Sikh orthodoxy. His avowed aim was to foster the loyalty of the Sikh soldiery to Her Majesty the Queen and Empress of India, by acquainting the British officers with their subordinates' religion. It is curious to see the superior interests of the British Rāj concurring with Protestant missionary zeal in fostering 'Kabirian' research...[30] A close examination of Macauliffe's translations of Kabīr's verses in the *Granth,* however, shows numerous errors and the translations are only slightly more reliable, though a little more readable, than those of his unhappy predecessor, in spite of the Gyānīs' guidance and the Sikh Sabhā's enthusiastic approval. Nevertheless, Macauliffe's translation of the *Ādi Granth* or *Gurū Granth* did remain to this day the only complete translation of the Sikh scriptures.[31]

---

(29) According to a letter written by Bhāī Hazāra Singh Gyānī, quoted by Macauliffe in *SR,* Preface, p. xiii; in the same letter, Hazāra Singh Gyānī congratulates the author on having "taken great care in keeping the rendering in accordance with the *sampardai arthas* (the traditional interpretations) of the Sikh Gurus".

(30) "It is admitted that knowledge of the religion of the people of India is a desideratum for the British Officials who administer the affairs, and indirectly for the people who are governed by them so that mutual sympathy may be produced. It seems, at any rate, politic to place before the Sikh soldiery their Guru's prophecies in favour of the English and the texts of their sacred writings which foster their loyalty" (*SR,* Preface, p. xxii).

(31) *The Sacred Writings of the Sikhs,* translated by a group of Sikh scholars under the auspices of the National Academy of Letters, which first appeared in 1960, is only a short anthology; it consists of selections from the *Ādi Gurū Granth* and the *Dasm Granth,* with a few pages of Introduction by S. Radhakrishnan.

Besides the spreading of western thought and ideals through the study of the English language and the preaching of Christian missionaries, another force was at play in nineteenth century India, especially in Bengal: the religious revival known as 'the Indian Renaissance' or 'Neo-Hinduism', which encompassed several movements and was itself deeply influenced by Christian religious ideals and ethics. The aim of the reformers was to salvage Hinduism from the morass of superstition, polytheism and idol-worship, and to make it into a strongly monotheistic faith, spiritually and ethically acceptable to the new western-educated Hindu elite.

At first Sufi, and later Christian influences were at play in the reform initiated by Rām Mohan Roy, which gave birth to the *Brahmo-samāj,* an eclectic religious movement with deistic theology and Christian ethics. The most notable among Rām Mohan Roy's first collaborators was Prince Dvarkanath Tagore, Rabindranath Tagore's great-grandfather. Neo-Hinduism under various forms developed during the first quarter of the twentieth century, a period which saw the rise of the great poet Rabindranath Tagore.[32]

Tagore himself largely drew his inspiration from the Vaishnav lyrics in Bengali - especially the Baül songs - and also from the words of Kabīr, for whom he professed a deep admiration.[33] It was Tagore who suggested to his friend Kshiti

(32) For these movements and the development of neo-Hinduism in the nineteenth century, see J.N. Farquhar, *Modern Religious Movements in India,* 1st ed. Oxford, 1914; repr. Delhi, 1867. The period studied by Farquhar extends from 1803 to 1913.

(33) There are various testimonies to Tagore's deep admiration for Kabīr, whose poetical utterances the great Bengali writer considered as the highest achievements of all vernacular literatures. In *Saritā Pattrikā* (Sept. 1959), a certain Bhagavandin Jī recalls a conversation with Tagore on Kabīr, in which

Mohan Sen to undertake a collection of poems attributed to Kabīr and sung by itinerant sadhus all over India (especially in Bengal) and their translation into Bengali. The work was published in Calcutta in 1910-11.[34] Tagore himself selected a hundred poems out of K.M. Sen's collection and translated them into beautiful English in 1914, under the title *One Hundred Poems of Kabīr,* with an Introduction by Miss Evelyn Underhill.[35]

Unfortunately, the authenticity of those poems is very questionable: it does appear that most of them were probably not composed by Kabīr. And, the Introduction written by Miss Underhill contains some baffling statements.[36] But the whole book clearly shows the considerable prestige Kabīr had acquired in the eyes of those westernized Bengali intellectuals: they tended to consider him not only as a great mystic, but also as the herald of the 'Universal Religion', a champion of the unity of mankind, and a bold social reformer. The exaltation of Kabīr by Hindu patriots - and generally by the Hindu intelligentsia of the twentieth century - dates from that period. Unfortunately, Tagore's version of the Words of Kabīr re-

---

Tagore told him that what the Bengali language could not achieve in the expression of mysticism had been achieved in Hindī by Kabīr. (Quoted in *Sadgranth Bījak,* with a Hindī commentary by Abhilasdas, Gonda, 1969).

(34) *Kabīr ke pad,* ed. K.M. Sen, Hindī text with a Bengali translation, 4 vols., Underhill, London, 1910-11.

(35) *One hundred poems of Kabīr,* translated by R. Tagore assisted by Evelyn Underhill, London, 1914.

(36) Evelyn Underhill - and probably Tagore himself - both of them uninitiated in the old Hindui language, show a surprising ignorance of the tenets held by Kabīr; e.g. on p. xiv of her Introduction, Miss Underhill writes: "Again and again he (Kabīr) extols the life of home, the value and the reality of diurnal existence...". Nothing could be further from the truth!

mained for a long time the only available document accessible to the westernized public.[37] The question of authenticity was apparently never raised, either by Tagore himself or by his Indian and western admirers.

3. THE KABĪR-GRANTHĀVALĪ

Some ten years after Macauliffe's translation of the Sikh *Granth,* a third important collection of Kabīr's verses came to light: this collection, known as *Kabīr-granthāvalī,* represented the tradition preserved by the *Dādū-panthī* sect of Rajasthan, whose founder, Dādū-Dayāl, was known as a close follower of Kabīr. That collection was published in 1928 at Benares by an Indian scholar, Shyam Sundar Das, under the title *Kabīr-granthāvalī,* with a fairly long introduction in Hindī.[38] The Indian scholars were taking over.

The S.S. Das edition is based on two manuscripts preserved in the library of the *Nāgarī Prachāriṇī Sabhā* in Benares, one of them dated Vi.S. 1561 (AD 1504), a very early date indeed, which was accepted by the editor. But the colophon which gives this date is written by a different hand from that of the manuscript and could not, therefore, be accepted as genuine,

(37) It was widely read in the West, and even retranslated into French by Madame Mirabaud-Thorens. *Cent poèmes de Kabīr,* translated by Mme Mirabaud-Thorens, Paris, Gallimard. Tagore's English translation was also adapted into Russian: Rabindranath Tagore, *Poems of Kabīr,* translated by B. Vasin, Moscow, n.d., *Collected Works of Tagore,* vol. VI.

(38) *Kabīr-granthāvalī,* ed. Shyam Sundar Das, N.P.S. Kashi, 1st ed. 1928; 5th ed. Vi.S. 2011, AD 1964. The text printed is that of the first manuscript (*ka*). Some variants found in the second manuscript (*kha*) are given in the foot-notes. Our references are to the 5th edition. This edition, known as the 'Sabhā edition' has been constantly reprinted since.

as shown by the great Indologist Jules Bloch in one of his Forlong Lectures, delivered in 1929. In the same lecture, Bloch deplores the lack of attention shown to the philological problems raised by medieval Hindī and New Indo-Aryan literatures and the extreme paucity of well-established texts.[39]

Even if the date ascribed to the Benares manuscript by S.S. Das could not be accepted, the collection published under the name of *Kabīr-granthāvalī* was of great importance. It was, nevertheless, overlooked by British scholars of the time. In 1931, the last of the Christian missionaries to write on Kabīr, the Revd. F.E. Keay, in *Kabīr and his Followers,* gives a fairly exhaustive compendium of what was then known about Kabīr: though apparently well informed of the Kabīr-panthī tradition and of other sources of Indian biography, Keay mentions only two compilations of Kabīr's verses, namely the *Bījak* and the *Ādi Granth.* Quoting from the partial translations by Ahmed Shah and Macauliffe, Keay's surprising ignorance of the existence of the *Kabīr-granthāvalī* collection of Kabīr's verses exemplifies the kind of divorce existing between the old school of British scholars-cum-missionaries and the new 'native' scholarship.

In his long Hindī Introduction to the first edition of the *Kabīr-granthāvalī,* S.S. Das attempts a critical appraisal of Kabīr's origins, personality and spiritual message. He accepts on the whole, though not without some reservations, the traditional account of Kabīr's life as already recorded by Wilson

---

(39) Jules Bloch, *Some Problems of Indo-Aryan Philology,* Forlong Lectures for 1929, publ. in *BSOS,* 5, pp. 719 ff. The date attributed by S.S. Das to the Vi.S. 1501 manuscript is criticized by Bloch in his third Lecture, pp. 747. For Bloch, Kabīr is an example of a very popular Hindī poet whose verses had never been critically edited; cf. also Barthwal, *NSHP,* pp. 276-277; H.P. Dvivedi, *Kabīr,* p. 20; P. Chaturvedi, *KSP,* pp. 76-77.

and others - an account mostly based on Kabīr-panthī sectarian literature. He takes sides, however, in the old controversy about Kabīr's social origin and adduces some curious arguments to demonstrate that Kabīr could not have been brought up in a Muslim family and that, even if he had, he could hardly have been influenced by his upbringing! Kabīr, according to S.S. Das, was so imbued "in his whole body" with "Hindu thought" that "there was a great probability that he was of Brahmin blood, at least of Hindu blood...".[40] According to the same author, Kabīr was at one and the same time a pious Vaishnav and a staunch partisan of *advaita,* the monist interpretation of the Upanishads! Though non-sectarian in his approach, the evident anxiety displayed by S.S. Das to 'hinduize' Kabīr appears somewhat coloured by the rising Hindu patriotism of the time.

The first scholar to take into account the *Kabīr-granthāvalī* recension was Mohan Singh, an Indian Professor at the Oriental College of Lahore and a well-known specialist of Urdū and Panjabi literatures. Mohan Singh's book on Kabīr, *Kabīr, His Biography,* published at Lahore in 1934 and dedicated to Dr. T. Graham Bailey, does not read too well in English and it is badly composed: yet, the book constitutes a mine of information, bringing out a mass of little-known facts mostly culled from unpublished works.

In his earnest search for the 'historical Kabīr', Mohan Singh peevishly criticizes his predecessors in the field, his main targets being Keay and S.S. Das. Mohan Singh also sets about destroying the myth of Kabīr's eminent role as a 'reformer' or initiator of a new form of religion. Newly coined epithets

(40) S.S. Das, *op.cit.,* Introd., p. 24. The fact is that most Indian scholars of that time consistently tried to convince themselves and others that Kabīr could not have been born in a Muslim family!

flourish under his pen, such as 'mythographers' and even 'Kabirolatry'. And it is not only the sectarian Kabīr-panthīs (who see in Kabīr an *avatār* of the Supreme Being) who stand accused of 'Kabirolatry', but the whole new legion of Kabīr's fervent Hindu admirers - and some of their western counterparts.

In spite of Mohan Singh's solitary protest, enthusiasm for Kabīr as 'a social reformer' and herald of a new religion, appears to have been rising among the Hindu intelligentsia in the thirties and forties, and this enthusiasm seems to have followed the curve of the powerful movement towards political and cultural independence led by Mahatma Gandhi.[41] In the Introduction to his edition of Kabīr's verses as found in the *Gurū Granth* (published under the title of *Sant-Kabīr*), R.K. Varma expresses his personal opinion as much as that of his contemporaries when he writes:

---

(41) Mahatma Gandhi's deep respect for Kabīr is well known; some of Kabīr's popular poems used to be sung regularly in his own Ashram. It is also known that, in 1935, when Gandhi was at Benares, he paid a visit to the Kabīr Chaurā Maṭh, where he saluted Kabīr's image. According to the testimony of the Mahant of the *maṭh,* Gandhi refused the seat prepared for him in front of Kabīr's *samādhi* and humbly sat on the ground instead. Gandhi also declared, to the surprise of those present, that his own mother was a Kabīr-panthī. Barthwal, who refers to this episode in *Gāndhī aur Kabīr,* asserts that, of all influences that may have played upon Gandhi's mind, the strongest and deepest was that of Kabīr. According to Barthwal, the 'Gangā of *gāndhitva*' (i.e. Gandhism) had its source in Kabīr's teachings, which he had absorbed with his mother's milk. Gandhi, like Kabīr, was a dedicated seeker of Truth (*satya*) and had made his whole life an exercise in the practice of Truth.

> Kabīr opens a new era ... He introduces a critical judgment on the religious and social life of his time ... He stands for the abolition of traditions and a new social awakening. He originates a new religion, *sant-mat*. This new religion is a simple living religion, open to all, it is a truly spiritual religion, a religion based on personal feelings...[42]

According to R.K. Varma, through Kabīr, human society as a whole discovered "the true nature of religion". Varma calls Kabīr "the saviour of Hinduism" and he presumes that it was solely owing to the great mystic's teaching and influence that the Hindus of his time did not lose heart altogether and abandon *en masse* their own religion for Islam. "In the new awakening brought about by Kabīr", he says, "Hinduism found strength".

Similar statements, which often smack of communalism under the guise of Hindu patriotism, can be found in other works and articles published in Hindī during that period. They were mostly expressed by people who did not care to study Kabīr or his verses in an objective, critical way, but found it easy to enlist him as an ally in what was primarily a political struggle.

4. NEO-HINDUISM AND KABĪR

The judgment on Kabīr found in the 'Publishers Note' prefaced to the 1953 Sushil Gupta's reprint of Westcott's well-known work on- *Kabīr and the Kabīr-panthīs* is characteristic of the way most modern, educated Hindus look at Kabīr:

> Kabīr is the Indian Luther of the 15th century who may rightly be regarded as the creator of sacred literature in Hindī. He and his successors endeavoured to combine strict monotheism of Islam with its abhorrence

(42) R.C. Varma, *Sant-Kabīr,* 4th ed., 1957, pp. 29 ff.

> of idolatry with whatever was best and most deeply rooted in the creed of Hinduism. Like Raja Rām Mohan Roy, he attempted to form a composite creed out of the best elements of Hinduism and Islam. He based his teachings on the monotheism of the Upanishads. He was a great singer, an *avadhūt,* an advocate of *advaitavāda,* who placed the Law of the Universe in the heart of man as his higher self, where alone the soul can discover it...

An echo of Rabindranath Tagore's judgments on Kabīr is noticeable in this passage, and the reference to Luther and Rām Mohan Roy is also characteristic. The neo-Hindu view of Kabīr somehow synthesizes the views of the Christian missionaries of the nineteenth and early twentieth centuries with the re-appraisal brought about by the neo-Vedantist movement and the political struggle for Indian independence. In a similar way, even a Muslim author like Yusuf Husain writes that "Kabīr was primarily prompted by a desire to bring about a synthesis between Islam and Hinduism" and that, in so doing, he indicated "the way leading to the establishment of a national cult".[43]

Though all those efforts, in different ways, helped to give impetus to 'Kabirian' research, they at the same time prevented such a research from being carried out in an objective, dispassionate manner. The attempt to annex Kabīr in support of one's own religious convictions or social preferences was made all the easier as Kabīr's personality was clouded in mystery and the contents of his message remained uncertain. As we have seen, the first European scholars to write about Kabīr knew him only through the traditions of the Kabīr-panthī sect - and the authenticity of that tradition was not questioned for quite a long time. Even though Wilson and other scholars were well aware of the legendary character of Kabīr's biography current in their time, they had no means of checking the authenticity of Kabīr's sayings either as recorded in the *Bījak* or in the *Gurū Granth* or as quoted by the common people of Hindustan. As a result, the interpretation of Kabīr's message remained for a long time a 'free for all' and to some extent it remains so, even today. No Indian mystic was so much quoted and misquoted, so lavishly praised - and so misunderstood.

From the end of the eighteenth century onwards, popular editions of so-called Kabīr's verses proliferated all over India, principally in Bengal, but also in Gujarat and Maharashtra.[44] The very abundance of those editions testify to Kabīr's growing prestige among the literate - and also to the extreme confusion prevailing as to what could be admitted as his authentic teachings. The interpretation of many verses attributed to Kabīr, found in the *Bījak* or in other collections, raised many difficulties, due partly to the uncertainties of the text and partly to the strange, allusive, esoteric language in which many

(44) The earliest printed text attributed to Kabīr is found in the first lithographed edition of Price's *Hindee and Hindoostanee Selections*. The oldest of the popular editions of Kabīr was a book described in the Supplementary Catalogue in the British Museum for 1893-1912, as a collection of 'Poems by Kabīr and other Vaishnav Poets' in Gujarati script, edited by Shankar Haribhai in 1888. During that period, a number of editions or paraphrases of Kabīr's verses in various vernaculars appeared: not only in Bengali and Gujarati, but also in Panjabi, Sindhi, Tamil and Telugu. Today cheap editions of Kabīr's words can be found in all those languages; they are very common in Marathi. The author herself found such 'bazaar' editions of poems attributed to Kabīr in a strange half-Hindī, half Marathi jargon, sold in the form of cheap booklets in the Vaishnav pilgrimage city of Pandharpur in Maharashtra.

of his utterances - or sometimes imitations of his utterances - were couched. Kabīr's first translators: Prem Chand, Ahmed Shah and Trumpp, had rightly pointed out those difficulties, adding that commentaries, whenever they existed, as in the case of the *Bījak,* were of little help. A valid interpretation of Kabīr's sayings also depended on some reliable information concerning the poet's origins and milieu, his own religious and literary tradition - information which had to be painstakingly retrieved from a mass of legendary material, in the face of preconceived ideas and judgments which, as they mainly depended on sectarian affiliations, were often mutually contradictory.

That Kabīr was born a low-caste Muhammedan weaver is undoubtable. Yet he is generally considered in India - at least by Hindus - as a Vaishnav, though 'a liberal one'.[45] More specifically, he is represented as the chief exponent of a particular form of *bhakti* (devotion) centered on the invisible, 'non-qualified' (*nirguṇ*) Deity, distinct from the 'qualified' (*saguṇ*) Deity, i.e. the incarnate and visible manifestations of the supreme Lord, *Bhagavān.* In India, so-called 'Vaishnav *bhakta*s' (devotees) worshipping a *nirguṇ* supreme God and opposed to caste distinctions, or at least very liberal on matter of caste, are generally called 'Sants' (lit. 'saints'), both in Northern India and in Maharashtra. The original appartenance of Kabīr with the Muhammedan faith, or his Shaiva connexions are either rejected or ignored. He belongs to the category of 'Sant', lit. 'a holy man', whatever his background. In Northern India, the

(45) K.M. Sen, in *Medieval Mysticism in India,* classifies Kabīr among the 'liberals' as opposed to the 'Orthodox Thinkers'; Farquhar, *ORLI,* pp. 330 ff., considers him as a 'reformed Vaishnava'; so does R.G. Bhandarkar, *Vaiṣṇavism, Śaivism and Minor Religious Systems,* Collected Works, iv, Poona, 1929, pp. 95 ff.

promoter of the 'Sant' school is said to have been Rāmāṇand, about whom little is known: he is said to have been Kabīr's own 'Guru', since to be a *nirguru* ('one without a guru') is disreputable in India. Nevertheless, Kabīr is considered the first and foremost of all Sants, the *Ādi-Sant*.

The Northern Sant tradition was critically studied by a group of modern Indian scholars, under the leadership of P.D. Barthwal, a pioneer in the field. In 1936, Barthwal published *The Nirguṇa School of Hindi poetry*, a study which showed remarkable insight.[46] A few days earlier, in a communication to the Kāśī Nāgarī Pracāriṇī Sabhā, a scholarly organization, Barthwal had brilliantly demonstrated the close link between the so-called 'Sants' and the medieval Tantric sect of the *Nāths*, also known as Kānphaṭa or Gorakhnāthī Yogīs. Barthwal had worthy successors in H.P. Dvivedi[47] and Parashuram Chaturvedi,[48] whose writings on the Nāth and Sant traditions constituted an important contribution to the religious and cultural history of medieval India.

As far as most of the writers of that period were concerned, however, and especially in the case of Kabīr, an important hurdle remained, as already noted by Jules Bloch: an imperfect knowledge of facts and documents, lack of indexes and dictionaries. Said Jules Bloch: "What is worse, the texts are in-

(46) P.D. Barthwal, *Hindī kāvya mẽ yog-pravāh,* NSPS, (Vi.S. 1987, AD 1930), p. 385.

(47) H.P. Dvivedi, *Nāth saṁpradāy,* Allahabad, 1950; *Hindī sāhitya kā ādikāl,* 3rd ed., Patna, 1961; *Kabīr,* 6th ed., Bombay, 1964.

(48) P. Chaturvedi, *Uttarī bhārat mẽ sant-paraṁparā,* Allahabad, Vi.S. 2008, AD 1951 (UBSP); *Kabīr-sāhitya kī parakh,* Allabahad, 1961 (KSP). Actually, in the *Gurū Granth* tradition, though Kabīr himself is not called 'a Vaishnav', Vaishnavas as a whole are presented as 'holy men', opposite to the 'despicable' Shāktas; cf. *Gurū Granth, śloks* 16; 52; 88; 100; et *passim.*

trinsically open to suspicion and editors generally take no heed of their duties in that matter".[49] The *Bījak* itself, which was twice translated into English and abundantly commented upon in Hindī, was never critically edited. Of the *Kabīr granthāvalī,* the third great compilation of the words attributed to Kabīr, no translation or analysis, not even an entirely reliable Hindī commentary were so far available. A great need, therefore, was felt for a critical edition of Kabīr's words, based on a systematic study and comparison of all the main recensions and compilations of the verses attributed to him.

This difficult task was attempted in 1961 by a young scholar of the University of Allahabad, Shri P.N. Tiwārī, under the guidance of Dr Mata Prasad Gupta. The title, *Kabīr granthāvalī* was justified in so far as the collection was based on the Dādū-panthī tradition, and had already been published under that title by S.S. Das in 1928. Tiwārī's edition, therefore, was the first basis of our translations. Though, unfortunately, the author gives no Concordances, a close scrutiny of the variants and the comparison of his amended text with the *Gurū Granth* and the *Bījak* texts so far available, made it possible to guess, at least with a fair amount of probability, the substance of Kabīr's teachings. Tiwārī's labours were not in vain: his Hindī translation encouraged further studies in textual criticism and medieval Hindī poetry. In his efforts to retrieve the old *sākhī*s or *ślok*s spoken by Kabīr, he also brought out the extraordinarily attractive figure of the greatest Indian mystic who ever spoke and sang in the vulgar tongue, and whose utterances, in the words of Farquhar, "have laid hold of the common heart of Hindustan".

(49) Jules Bloch, *op. cit.,* 1828-9.

2

Kabīr's biography in history and legend

According to Westcott, one of the causes of the prevailing confusion about Kabīr's biography and dates, is the existence of several 'Kabīrs' in the Indian tradition.[1] The name itself is undisputably Muhammedan, meaning 'Great' in Arabic: 'Al Kabīr' is one of the ninety-nine titles applied to God in the Qur'ān. Yet the Hindī poet Kabīr cannot be confused with any other 'Kabīrs' quoted by Westcott, though Indian Muslims have sometimes referred to him respectfully as 'Kabīr Shāh'.[2] Others called him 'Bābājī Kabīr', *bābā* being a familiar appellation given to a holy man, especially a Sufi or a Yogi.[3]

Hindus often refer to our Kabīr as 'Kabīrdās'. The word *dās* (Skt *dāsa*), meaning 'slave' or 'servant' is commonly added to the names of pious Hindu devotees, from medieval times to the present day, with the meaning of 'servant of God': *dās* applies generally, though not exclusively, to Vaishnav Bhaktas, who regard themselves as humble servants or 'slaves' of the supreme Lord, Vishnu-Hari.[4] According to the Kabīr-panthī

(1) Westcott, *KKP*, pp. 15-17.

(2) H.R. Nevill, in the *Basti Dictrict Gazetteer*, Allahabad, 1907, p. 225, says that Magahar contains the shrine 'of the prophet Kabir Shah'.

(3) *bābā* means 'father, grandfather, old man'; it also refers to a *faqīr*.

(4) The Vaishnav devotees of Karnatak are known as *haridāsas*; yet, in Karnatak, some *Vīrashaiva* or *Lingāyat* names also end in *dās:* Mohan

tradition, Bhagavāndās, (alias Bhaggodās or Bhaggojī) and Dharmadās - names with a distinguished Hindu ring, - were Kabīr's main disciples. Yet it seems that Kabīr - and not Kabīrdās - was the real name of the poet.

Most modern accounts of Kabīr's life are based on two Kabīr-panthī works: the *Kabīr-kasauṭī* and the *Kabīr-caritra*,[5] both full of wonders and miracles: their legendary character is evident. References to Kabīr in older Hindī or Persian works, however, are not lacking. Among the Hindu sources, the most important are the *Ādi Granth* (or *Gurū Granth*) of the Sikhs and the *Bhaktamāl*, or Garland of Saints of Nābhājī.

The *Gurū Granth*, compiled in the Panjab on the order of the fifth Guru of the sect, Arjun Dev, was completed in 1604. The work brought together the compositions of the first four Sikh Gurus and those of the old Bhagats (*bhakta*) or 'saints', predecessors of Nānak, from the ancient Sufi Shaykh Farīd, to Rāmānand and Nāmdev. Among the Bhagats, Kabīr held the place of honour, the number of poems and couplets attributed to him being particularly large.[6] The tenth Guru, Gobind

---

Singh, *KB*, p. 29, remarks that the names of the Aughar section of Gorakhnāthī Jogīs also end in *dās*.

(5) *Kabīr-kasauṭī*, or 'the Touchstone of Kabīr', and *Kabīr-caritra* or *Kabīr-kā jīvan-caritra*, are the most often quoted of the Kabīr-panthī narratives on Kabīr's life and the main basis of popular biographies of the saint. Keay remarks that the *Kabīr-caritra* seems to gather most of its material from the *Kabīr-i-Manshūr*, originally written in Urdū by Paramānand-dās of Ferozepur (Panjab) in 1887, of which a Hindī edition is also in existence. Both *Kabīr-caritra* and *Kabīr-kasauṭī* quote from a biography in verse composed by Sant *Garībdās* (1777-82). The Garībdāsīs are one of the numerous sects found in Northern India owing their inspiration to Kabīr.

(6) No less than 225 *pads* and 243 *salokus* (*śloks*), (elsewhere called *sākhīs*) are attributed to Kabīr. The *Granth* also attributes to Kabīr some

Singh, made a few additions to the work of Guru Arjun and proclaimed that there would be no more 'Gurus'. At the end of the seventeenth century, he compiled the final version of the *Granth,* henceforth known as *Śrī Gurū Granth Sāhib* and regarded as the living voice of the 'Gurus' or Prophets of the Sikhs.[7]

Nānak himself, the founder and first Guru of the Sikhs, though he was sometimes wrongly considered as a disciple of Kabīr, never mentions him in the *Granth.* Yet Kabīr is held in high esteem among the Sikhs and a meeting between Kabīr and Nānak is described in various *Janam-sākhī*s, or 'life-stories' of Guru Nānak. But the Janam-sākhīs contain much legendary material and there is no reason to believe that Nānak ever met Kabīr.[8] A mention of Kabīr, however, is found in the writings of the third Guru, Amardās (1479-1574), who was the Emperor Akbar's contemporary. Says Amardās: "Nāmā was a

---

compositions called *Bāvan akharī, Tithi* and *Vār.* Similar compositions based on months and days were also made in the Panjabi language by Indian Sufis; cf. Mujeeb, *The Indian Muslims,* London, 1967, p.325.

(7) The text of the *Granth* has remained fixed since, and it has been reprinted many times in Amritsar, both in the original *gurmukhī* and in the *nāgarī* character. Our references are to the *nāgarī* edition, repr. 1951. As to Macauliffe's translations, our references are to *The Sikh Religion,* repr. New Delhi, 1963.

(8) According to W.H. McLeod (*Guru Nānak and the Sikh Religion,* Oxford, 1968, pp. 85-6) "Kabīr-panthī traditions concerning the life of Kabīr are notoriously unreliable and can be accepted only when confirmed by other evidence (...) There is no authentic tradition (in Sikh writings) concerning a meeting between Guru Nānak and Kabīr".

calico-printer (*chībā*) and Kabīr a weaver (*jolāhā*), yet from the Perfect Guru, they obtained salvation".[9]

Among the Bhagats whose poems are preserved in the *Granth,* 'Ravidās' or 'Raidās' (fl. 1450?) is generally believed to have been Kabīr's younger contemporary, but he more probably belonged to the following generation. Raidās mentions Kabīr three times in the *Granth* and his testimony is probably the most ancient of all:

> (1) The lowly dost Thou exalt, my Govind (God),
> and none dost Thou fear:
> Nāmdev, Kabīr, Trilocan, Sadhanā, and Sain were saved...[10]

> (2) In whose family on the occasion of Id and Bakr Id, the cow is butchered; in whose family Shaykh, Shahīd and Pīr are reverenced, Whose father acted in this way, the son following him - he, Kabīr, became reverenced in the three worlds.[11]

These two testimonies would be enough to prove that Kabīr was indeed born a Muslim. In another *pad,* Ravidās mentions Kabīr, together with Nāmdev, in connection with the redeeming power of Hari's Name:

> (3) Through the Name of Hari, Kabīr became renowned
> And the accounts of his sins of many births were torn up.[12]

In the *Granth,* another of the old 'Bhagats', 'Dhannā', a Jāṭ by birth, from Rajputana, also mentions Kabīr together with Nāmdev, Raidās and Sain, among the 'low-born' saints:

> In Gobind, Gobind, Gobind was Nāmdev's heart absorbed:

---

(9) *nāmā chībā Kabīru jolāhā pure gura te gati pāī* (*Gurū Granth, sirī rāg, mah.* 3; *aṣṭh.* 5, v. 3, p. 67).

(10) *mārū* vv. 1-2 (p. 1106).

(11) *malār* 2, v. 2 (p. 1293).

(12) *āsā* 5, v. 1 (p. 487).

A calico-printer worth half a cowrie[13] became worth many thousands

Giving up weaving and stretching thread, Kabīr devoted his love to God's feet:

Though a poor weaver of low family, he obtained untold virtues...[14]

In the *Bhaktamāl* of Nābhājī, a Vaishnav poet who flourished c. 1600,[15] a whole stanza (*chappay*) is devoted to Kabīr. Though Nābhājī himself is sometimes described as a *Rāmānandī* (a follower of saint Rāmānand) his work is non-sectarian in outlook and it constitutes a very valuable source of information. Nābhājī's statement about Kabīr is as follows:

Kabīr refused to acknowledge caste distinctions or to recognize the authority of the six Hindu schools of philosophy nor did he set any store by the four states of life (*āśramas*) prescribed for Brahmans. He held that religion (*dharma*) without devotion (*bhakti*) was no religion at all (*adharma*) and that asceticism, fasting and alms-giving had no value if not accompanied by adoration (*bhajan*). By means of *ramainīs*, *śabdīs* and *sākhīs*, he imparted religious instruction to Hindus and Turks alike. He showed no partiality to either but gave teaching beneficial to all. With determination he spoke and never tried to please the world. Kabīr refused to acknowledge caste distinctions and the six systems of philosophy.[16]

This stanza of Nābhājī contains very remarkable - and apparently objective - statements. The author of the *Bhaktamāl* does

(13) A cowrie is a small shell, worth one *paisā,* or less.

(14) *āsā* 2, *rahāū,* the name given to the refrain in the *Gurū Granth* *pad*-singing.

(15) According to Farquhar, *ORLI,* p. 317, the *Bhaktamāl* was composed between 1585 and 1623. The date most usually ascribed to it is 1585: cf. Grierson, *'Gleanings on the Bhaktamāl', JRAS,* 1909, p. 607; 1910, pp. 87, 169. Our references are to the edition by S.B. Rupkala, with *Bhaktisudhāsvād ṭīkā,* Lucknow, 2nd ed., 1962.

(16) *Bhaktamāl (mūl), chappay* 60, p. 479.

not say whether Kabīr was (or was not) born a Muslim: he simply asserts that Kabīr had rejected the whole Brahmanical tradition, including the division of society into castes, and that he judged both religions, Hinduism and Islam, with total impartiality. Nothing is said about Kabīr's life, but his extraordinary independence of character is stressed. Nor is anything said about Kabīr's guru. Yet, in another stanza of the *Bhaktamāl*,[17] the name of Kabīr occurs in the enumeration of the disciples attributed to Rāmānand. But the contents cannot be considered as 'historical', since those disciples attributed to Rāmānand are either unknown or belong to different times and cannot have been his contemporaries. The information about Rāmānand in the *Bhaktamāl* is particularily vague: Nābhājī simply states that Rāmānand lived to a very old age and he enumerates his twelve disciples, the number twelve being apparently conventional.

A commentary in verse on the original (*mūl*) of the *Bhaktamāl* was composed by Priyādās in 1712, under the name of *Bhaktirasabodhinī.* In a long development, the commentary introduces the legendary biography of Kabīr.[18] The most remarkable episode concerns the way Kabīr, though a 'Turk' (i.e. a Muslim), managed to become Rāmānand's disciple: warned by a heavenly voice, he lay on the steps of the *ghāṭ* where Rāmānand used to come down for his first dip in the Ganges before daybreak.[19] The saint stumbled over Kabīr's body in the dark and the sacred invocation: *Rām, Rām!* involuntarily es-

(17) *Bhaktamāl, chappay* 36, p. 282.

(18) *Bhaktamāl, ṭīkā kavitta* 28-41, pp. 480-91.

(19) According to tradition, the *ghāt* was the *Pañcagaṅgā ghāṭ*.

caped him: this was the sacred *mantra,* through which Kabīr received the so-called *nāmadīkṣā* from the guru.[20]

Besides this unconventional way of initiation, other miraculous events are narrated by Priyādās. One of the most notable incidents concerns the denunciation of Kabīr by the Kashi Brahmins to the Muslim judge and administrator, the Qāzī. Kabīr was accused of fomenting sedition and imprisoned. He was later brought in chains before the Sultān Sikander Lodī himself, who happened to be visiting Kashi at the time. In spite of the Qāzī's injunction, Kabir refused to bow to the Sultan, as he would only bow to Rām. He was, therefore, condemned to death. Three successive attempts were made to execute the sentence: he was first bound and thrown into the Ganges, then into a blazing fire, and finally in front of a furious elephant, to be trampled to death - but each time he had a miraculous escape. In the end, it was the Sultan who bowed to Kabīr. On another occasion it is said that some Apsarās (heavenly damsels of radiant beauty) vainly attempted to seduce him; he was then favoured by a vision of the Lord Vishnu-Hari in His *Caturbhuj* (four-armed) form. Kabīr resolved to go to Magahar to die: he was then said to be 120 years old.

Priyādās' narrative presents Kabīr as Muslim born, but converted to Vaishnav Bhakti through the influence of Rāmānand. The famous story of the double funeral, however, appears only in late commentaries. The main shrine at

(20) In Vaishnav sects, the *dīkṣā* is performed by the Guru or Āchārya in front of the image of the divinity; besides the *mantra,* the ritual includes the imposition of a string of holy beads (*mālā*) and the sectarian frontal mark (*tilak*). During the sixteenth century, a number of Vaishnav sects did accept Muslim candidates (converts) - but the latter could only receive *nām-dīkṣā,* 'the *dīkṣā* of the Name', and usually were not allowed entrance into the shrine.

Magahar is still in Muhammedan hands, and Kabīr is honoured there not as a Vaishnava but as a *pīr*. The Muhammedan Julāhās in charge of the Kabīr shrine strongly deny the legend of the flowers and assert that 'Kabīr Shah' was buried on the spot in accordance with Muslim custom.[21] It is said that Kabīr's cenotaph at Magahar was built by Nawāb Bijlī Khān in 1450, two years after the Sant's death, and that it was repaired by Nawāb Fidāī Khān who was garrisoned at Magahar with an imperial force, c. 1567. The smaller Hindu shrine now found at Magahar near the Muslim shrine was built much later: only Hindus visit it.[22] Both monuments are described in detail by Keay.[23]

Up to the time of Priyādās, at the beginning of the eighteenth century, the fact that Kabīr was born a Muhammedan was apparently never questioned. It is only in later commentaries, and in popular biographies composed by Kabīr-panthīs, that Kabīr himself is represented as the son of a Brahmin virgin widow: he was born without a human father, as a result of the blessing of saint Rāmānand on the child

(21) Cf. Nevill, *op.cit.*, p. 226.

(22) The main Kabīr *rauẓa* has been described by A. Führer in *Monumental Antiquities and Inscriptions in the North-Western Provinces and Oudh,* vol. ii, p. 224: "To the east of the town, on the right bank of the Ami river, there is the cenotaph (*rauẓa*) of the famous reformer Kabīr-Das or Kabīr Shah, erected in 1450 by Bijli Khan and restored in 1567 by Nawab Fidai Khan. A little further stands another shrine, dedicated to Kabīr-Das and frequented by Hindus only".

(23) *KF,* pp. 95-97. If Führer's information is correct, the year 1450 would be the *terminus ad quem* for Kabīr's death. Strangely, another Kabīr cenotaph is found in Jagannāth Puri, in Orissa, not far from the great temple: the strange object representing Kabīr looks like a stone covered with dark-blue clothes with a conical cap. It has not been investigated so far.

widow... Later the baby was exposed on a lake and was then picked by a Muslim Julāhā couple called Nīru and Nīmā who were the child Kabīr's foster parents.[24] Evidently the fact that Kabīr was a Julāhā by birth was too well established, both by tradition and by his own utterances, to be denied. Yet, according to a Hindu tradition, the child Kabīr "had refused circumcision". The intricate legend woven around his miraculous birth aims to establish that Kabīr was not a *mleccha* - but that his origins were 'pure' according to Brahmanical views. This story clearly marks a further step towards the hinduization of Kabīr in modern times. In this case, as in the case of Kabīr's *dīkṣā,* saint Rāmānand appears as the 'historical' link between Kabīr and traditional Hinduism.

Another ancient Hindu source is often quoted in connection with Kabīr's life: the *Śrī Kabīr sāhibjī kī parcaī* written by Anantadās, an author generally considered to have lived during the later part of the sixteenth century.[25] According to Anantadās, Kabīr was a Julāhā of Kashi who did become a disciple of Rāmānand. Having spent his childhood 'in error' (i.e. as a Muhammedan) he received spiritual enlightenment when he was twenty years old. He was persecuted by the emperor Sikander Lodī when the latter visited Kashi. He reached *mukti* at the age of one hundred. The miracle of the

(24) About the names attributed to Kabīr's foster parents, Mohan Singh (*KB,* pp. 4-5), remarks that, in Panjab, a Muslim Julāhā is called *nīrawaf* and a Muslim woman of low caste is called *nīmā;* Ahmed Shah (*The Bijak of Kabīr,* Intr. p. 4) mentions *nurbaf* and *neiman* as the common names of a Muhammedan weaver and a low-born Muhammedan woman in the Panjab.

(25) S.K. Varma gives c. 1600 as Anantadās's *floruit;* Mohan Singh (*KB,* pp. 4-5) accepts the date 1588 for the composition of the *Kabīr kī parcaī*; Chaturvedi (KSP, pp. 276) discusses the problem in detail and also concludes that Anantadās must have lived c. Vi.S. 1645 (AD 1588).

flowers and Kabīr's double funeral are also mentioned by Anantadās, a pious Vaishnav.[26]

The Muslim tradition knows Kabīr not only as a Julāhā, but also as a *muwāhhid,* i.e. a believer of the unity of God. The first testimony is found in the *Ā* ᶜīn-i-Akbarī compiled by Abū'l-Fazl-i-Allamī, the emperor Akbar's friend and chronicler, in 1598. Abū'l Fazl mentions Kabīr on two occasions. In the section dealing with the Konarak temples in Orissa, the author of the *Ā* ᶜīn-i-Akbarī says of Jagannāth-Puri:

> Some affirm that the believer Kabīr reposes here and to this day many authentic traditions are related regarding his sayings and doings. He was revered by both Hindus and Muhammedans for his catholicity of doctrine and the illumination of his mind, and when he died the Brahmans wanted to burn his body and the Muhammedans to bury it.[27]

In another passage, describing the famous places in the province of Oudh (Ayodhya, in Eastern Uttar Pradesh), Abū'l Fazl mentions Kabīr again:

> Some say that at Ratanpur is the tomb of Kabīr the Believer. The portals of spiritual discernment were partly open to him and he discarded the effete doctrines of the time. Numerous verses in the Hindī language are still extant of him, containing important theological truths.[28]

---

(26) Other references to Kabīr are found in various works composed at the end of the sixteenth or the beginning of the seventeenth century - as in the *Vinay-Pattrikā* of Tulsīdās and the *Eknāthī Bhāgavat* composed by the Maharashtrian poet Eknāth: though no new information is given by those poets, both stress the fact that Kabīr was low-born.

(27) *Ā* ᶜīn-i-Akbarī, Engl. trans. by H.S. Jarett, 2nd ed., vol. 2, p. 141; about Kabīr's double cenotaphs, cf. supra.

(28) *Ā* ᶜīn-i-Akbarī, 2nd edition, vol. 2, p. 182. The mausoleum at Ratanpur is also mentioned by Sujan Rae, who draws upon Abū'l Fazl in

Though the author of the *Ā*ᶜīn-i-Akbarī asserts that Kabīr was a *muwāḥḥid,* both statements are remarkably cautious and their wording suggests that at the end of the sixteenth century there were already conflicting opinions in Muslim circles about the substance of the doctrines taught by Kabīr: such doctrines may not have been completely acceptable to some staunch Muhammedans, and this is probably the reason why Abū'l-Fazl does not clearly state that Kabīr was a *musalmān.* On the other hand, the testimony of ᶜAbdul Ḥaq Dihlawī, in his Persian work *Akhbār-al-Akhyār,*[29] composed some years later, shows that Kabīr's verses were already being read or quoted in Sufi circles in Delhi and Agra at the beginning of the sixteenth century. It also shows that questions were raised about his teaching and his true theological position - some divines not being sure whether Kabīr was to be reckoned as a *musalmān* or as a *kāfir.*

The testimony of the *Dabistān-i-Mazāhib,* ascribed to Muḥsin Fānī of Kashmir and probably written in the mid-seventeenth century, testifies to the continuous prestige of Kabīr among Indian Muslims, especially among those who shared the liberal tendencies of Akbar and Abū'l Fazl. The unknown author of the *Dabistān* shows a mind inclined to religious syncretism and he is fairly well informed about Hindu

his *Khulāsat-ut-Tawarīkh* (Delhi ed., p. 43): "At Ratanpur is the grave (or shrine, *mazār*) of Kabīr the Julāhā who, at the time of Sultan Sikander Lodī, had gone to the capital of Reality from the town of Appearance". The mausoleum at Puri-Jagannāth is also mentioned by the French traveller, Tavernier; cf. *Les six voyages de J.B. Tavernier,* vol. 2, Paris, 1642, p. 441.

(29) A collection of short biographies of Sufi saints composed in 1590-99. ᶜAbdul Ḥaq Dihlawī's testimony in *Akhbār-al-Akhyār* (ed. Delhi, 1853) is summarized and discussed in Mohan Singh, *KB,* p. 28, fn.

beliefs. In the eighth section of the second book, dealing with 'the opinions and ceremonies of the worshippers of Vishnu' (i.e. the Vaishnavas), it is said that the ascetics among them are called *Vairāgīs* - and Kabīr himself is represented as one: "Kabīr, a weaver by birth, celebrated among those Hindus who profess their belief in the unity of God, was a 'Vairāgī'..." (or Bairāgī).

The account of Kabīr's life given in the *Dabistān*[30] is rather confused and it reflects some late Hindu traditions and interpretations of Kabīr's sayings; at the same time, a rather absurd story is introduced to show Kabīr's extreme devotion towards 'the Faqīrs'. A Faqīr again is brought in to interfere in the quarrel between Hindus and Muslims over Kabīr's mortal remains and to remind both parties that "Kabīr was independent of both religions". The *Dabistān* also mentions the tomb of Kabīr at Purī-Jagannāth: "In Jagernath, at the place where they burn the dead, is the form and simulacre of a tomb which they call Kabīr's".[31]

It is interesting to note that, whereas in the seventeenth century, a Muslim author did not hesitate to call Kabīr 'a Vaishnav' and 'a Bairagi' (i.e. a Vaishnav ascetic), the late Persian work *Khazinat-ul-Asāfiyā* (c. 1868) is probably the first treatise composed by an Indian Muslim to mention Kabīr as a 'Sufi' and even as a disciple of a famous Shaykh, known as

---

(30) *Dabistān* or *School of Manners,* Engl. trans. by D. Shea and A. Troyer, Paris, 1843, vol. 2, pp. 186-91. The *Dabistān* does not distinguish clearly between the Vaishnavas, the Bairagis and the Ramanandīs. According to McLeod, (*op.cit.* p. 9), the author of the *Dabistān* relied largely upon his Sikh informants.

(31) *Ibid.,* p. 191. A Kabīr tomb is still to be seen at Puri-Jagannāth. Its origin is not clear.

Shaykh Taqqī.[32] Since the *Khazinat* was composed in Panjab some sixty years after Malcolm published his *Sketch of the Sikhs,* in which he refers to Kabīr as a Sufi, it is possible that both did draw on the same tradition, then current among Panjabi Muslims.

Kabīr-panthī sectarian literature, on which, as we have shown, most modern popular biographies of Kabīr are based, presents Kabīr as an *avatār* of the supreme Being, 'Sat Purush': the latter is supposed to have successively taken birth in each one of the four *yug*as - and Kabīr, or Sat-Kabīr - is the name he had assumed in the present *Kali-yug.*[33]

Besides Kabīr's legendary biographies, Kabīr-panthī literature includes a number of imaginary dialogues called *bodh,* (enlightenment),[34] *guṣṭ, guṣṭi, goṣṭi* (Skt *goṣṭhī,* or conversa-

---

(32) Cf. Westcott, *KKP,* pp. 15-16.

(33) The enumeration of Kabīr's *avatāras* is found in the *Granth-bhavatāran,* 'the crossing of the Ocean of Existence' (ed. Narsinghpur, 1908), a Kabīr-panthī work in the form of a dialogue between Kabīr and his disciple Dharmadās: the contents are briefly analyzed by Keay (KF, pp. 125-6). Though composed in Braj verse, the *Granth-bhavatāraṇ* imitates the *Bhagavad-gītā,* with *Sat-Kabīr* holding the role of Krishna: "In every age (*yug*), I incarnate myself and I am always present in a manifested (i.e. visible) form in the world. In the *Sat-yug,* my name was *Sat-sukṛt,* in the Treta age, it was *Munendra,* in the Dvāpar age, I was called *Karuṇam* and in the Kali age, I was *Kabīr*". Reminiscences of the Jaina and Buddhist faiths are noticeable in this passage, as 'Munendra' refers to the Jin Mahavīr and Karuṇam to *karuṇā,* the principle of universal compassion, which is one of the two elements to be united together for the production of the *bodhicitta* in Tantric Mahāyān Buddhism.

(34) A compilation of such works was published by the Kabīr-panthī Svami Yugalananda under the title *Bodh-sāgar,* Bombay, Vi.S. 1963 (AD 1956).

tion), in which Kabīr is made either to answer a trusted disciple's questions or to argue victoriously with a famed saint or Yogi, such as Guru Gorakhnāth, or even the Prophet of Islam, Muhammad himself. Such works as *Rāmānand-goṣṭ, Gorakh kī guṣṭi,*[35] *Muhammad-bodh,* are evidently meant to establish the superiority of the Kabīr-panthī tenets over the Jain faith.[36] Westcott's list of Kabīr-panthī works also includes a *Nānak gushṭ,* but the existence of such a work is doubtful.[37] Yet Sikh literature includes Kabīr-Nānak dialogues, composed with a view to establish Nānak's superiority over Kabīr.

1. THE PROBLEM OF KABĪR'S DATES

Kabīr's dates are uncertain and have been the subject of endless controversy. Wilson quotes a Kabīr-panthī source according to which Kabīr was born in Vi.S. 1205 (AD 1149) and died in Vi.S. 1505 (AD 1449) - so that he would have lived 300 years![38] In Kabīr-panthī literature and Hindu tradition in general, the date of Kabīr's birth is given as 1398 and that of his death as 1518.[39] It is said that the first date would make it possible for Kabīr actually to have been Rāmānand's disciple,

---

(35) The *Gorakh kī guṣṭī* has been analyzed by Keay, *KB,* pp. 115-17. The poem ends with Gorakhnāth laying down his cap, wallet and banner at Kabīr's feet.

(36) Keay, *KF,* p. 130.

(37) Westcott, *KKP,* pp. 112-14; the *Nānak gushṭ* is among the works that the author knows only 'by hearsay'.

(38) McLeod, *op.cit.,* pp. 85-6.

(39) The choice of the eleventh day of the dark *ekādashī* of the month of Māgh as the day on which Kabīr entered into *samādhi* is evidently dictated by the Vaishnav preference of the author, the *ekādashī* being, for Vaishnavas, the most sacred of all *tithis*.

since the latest date assigned to Rāmānand's death is 1410:[40] Kabīr, therefore, would have been twelve years old when he met Rāmānand, who was then 111 years old! This *tour de force* is credited to the boy Kabīr's 'exceptional precocity'.[41] On the other hand, since the Sikhs generally believe that their founder, Nānak, who was born in 1469, did meet Kabīr, Westcott delays Kabīr's purported birth till 1440, so that he would have been only twenty-nine when Nānak was born.[42] Macauliffe and Carpenter, however, quote some 'native works' which place Kabīr's death as early as 1448.[43] Bhandarkar provisionally accepts the Hindu traditional dates, whereas Farquhar proposes to bring down Rāmānand's dates to 1400-70 and Kabīr's to 1440-1518.[44] He is supported by Keay, who accepts these dates, since, according to him, they fit in with the dates of Rāmānand, Sikander Lodī and Nānak - all of whom Kabīr is supposed to have met. Keay believes that King Sikander, who

(40) Rāmānand's dates are uncertain and very little is known about his actual teachings. He would have been more than 118 years in order to be the real guru of all the twelve disciples attributed to him in the *Bhaktamāl.*

(41) See Carpenter, *Theism in Medieval India* (Hibbert Lectures, 2nd series, 1919), quoted by Westcott, *KKP,* p. 117.

(42) Westcott, in *Kabīr and the Kabīr-panth,* p. vii, gives no evidence to justify that date, in his Chronological table; the table is not found in the 2nd edition of the same work.

(43) Macauliffe (*SR* vi. 140, n. 1) mentions a work called *Bharat khanda cha arvachin* (in Marathi?) in which the date of Kabīr's death is given as Śak 1370 (AD 1448); Carpenter, *op.cit.,* p. 88, mentions another work, *Bhārat brahmaṇ,* which gives Kabīr's dates as 1398-1448.

(44) R.G. Bhandarkar, *Vaiṣṇavism, Śaivism and Minor Religious Systems,* Collected Works, iv, Poona, 1929, p. 98.

reigned from 1488 to 1512, did visit the town of Jaunpur, and possibly Kashi in 1495.[45]

The whole controversy over Kabīr's dates appears to be linked with the saint's Hindu biographers' conviction that Kabīr was Rāmānand's actual disciple and also that he was persecuted by Sikander Lodī in person. Some authors, influenced by Sikh popular beliefs, also wanted to make Kabīr a contemporary of Guru Nānak - but, as we have seen, such an encounter was highly improbable, and the first two are very doubtful. Western scholars have been inclined to doubt the fact that Kabīr was actually Rāmānand's disciple, but they have generally accepted his being a contemporary of King Sikander Lodī: of the two traditional dates, that of Kabīr's birth (1398) and that of his death (1518), they tended to deny the first and to admit the second. Yet there is no historical evidence - not even any probability - that Kabīr was Sikander Lodī's contemporary, as shown by Mohan Singh, Barthwal and Parashuram Chaturvedi.[46]

It has been argued that the pushing back of the date of Kabīr's birth to 1398 was motivated by a desire to uphold the belief concerning the relationship of Kabīr to Rāmānand: but it might just as well be argued that the date of Kabīr's death was pushed forward to 1518 to make it possible for him to

---

(45) Keay, *KF*, p. 28.

(46) Cf. Mohan Singh, *KB, p. 25;* Barthwal, *NSHP*, p. 253; Chaturvedi, *UBSP*, pp. 708. Mohan Singh denies it on the evidence of the *Firishta* I. 333-4. Abū'l Fazl is silent about the persecution of Kabīr by Sikander Lodī. He mentions the persecution of a holy man, a Hindu called Bodhan, who was put to death by Sikander Lodī. The latter's reputation for cruelty is so well established in India that a fate similar to Bodhan's could have been attributed to Kabīr: the latter would have escaped by means of his supernatural powers.

have been persecuted by Sikander Lodī. According to another tradition, Kabīr would have lived in the sixteenth century.[47]

The various arguments brought forward by the debaters concerning the date of Kabīr's death were reviewed in detail by Chaturvedi in an Appendix to his work on the tradition of the Northern Sant or Nirguni poets. The author concludes that the available material simply does not allow one to draw definite conclusions about Kabīr's dates; there is a probability that Kabīr was born in 1398 and died in 1448. We can provisionally accept the first half of the fifteenth century AD as Kabīr's *floruit*. If this is the case, Kabīr would not have lived during the reign of Sikander Lodī, but under the Sayyed dynasty at Delhi and the independent Sharqi dynasty at Jaunpur. Jaunpur was the capital of the 'Eastern' Muslim kingdom which includes the ancient city of Kashi, also known as Varanasi, the modern Benares.

2. KABĪR'S AUTOBIOGRAPHICAL VERSES

Traditional accounts of Kabīr's life refer to a number of verses which are interpreted as autobiographical, but such accounts are not always reliable. While reading the popular accounts of Kabīr's life, one often gets the impression that such-and-such anecdote has been clumsily concocted to explain the peculiar circumstances in which the saint uttered such-and-such verse. Conversely, some sayings appear to have been attributed to Kabīr in order to justify a common belief about him. Such is the case with the often quoted line: "I was born in Kashi and

(47) That tradition was accepted by Ghulam Sarvar in the *Khazinat-ul-Asafiyā,* also by S.W. Fallon in *A New Hindustani-English Dictionary,* London 1879, Preface, p. viii; also Malcolm, according to whom Kabīr "lived in the time of the emperor Sher Shah".

Rāmānand instructed me"[48] - an utterance which is not found in any of the main traditions and for which manuscript evidence does not exist. Actually, Rāmānand himself is mentioned only once in the three compilations - in the *Bījak* - and in this particular line Kabīr does not say that Rāmānand was his guru, but he refers to him as a saint 'who drank deep of Rām's Liquor'.[49]

Kabīr frequently refers to himself as a simple Julāhā, i.e. a Muslim weaver, of Kashi. Nothing is said about the place of his birth: he may have been in Kashi, or, as Barthwal believes, at Magahar near Kashi, a particularly wretched place; various opinions have been expressed on this matter. In the *Gurū Granth* compilation of Kabīr's sayings, we find a number of so-called 'autobiographical *pada*s' which both in tenor and style have a look of authenticity. One such verse concerns Kabīr's experience in Magahar:

> Confiding in Thee, I dwelt in Magahar and the tormenting fire of my body was quenched:
> First I had a vision of Thee in Magahar and then I went to dwell in Kashi".[50]

The question of Kabīr's birth place has also been much discussed. Barthwal believes that more probably Kabīr was

(48) *kāśī mẽ hama pragaṭa bhaye haĩ rāmānanda citāe*: the line is found in the *Kabīr Śabdāvalī*, Allahabad, 1908, Pt 2, p. 47 - but this work, which was published in four parts by the Belvedere Press in 1903-1914, is a mere compilation of verses collected from very uncertain sources.

(49) *rāmananda rāmarasa māte*: these words are found in the *Bījak;* ed. Vicardas Shastri, Allahabad, 1928, *śabda* 77, 4.

(50) *tore bharose magahara basio, mere tana kī tapati bujhāi,*
pahile darasanu magahara pāio, phuni kāsī base āī.
(*Gu. Rāmkalī* 3, v. 2).

born at Magahar 'which is preeminently a place of weavers'. The Kabīr-panthīs of Benares believe that he was born at Lahartārā, only two miles from the famous *Kabīr Chaurā maṭh*. According to H.R. Nevill[51] Kabīr was born in Belharā in the Azamgarh district. Subhadra Jha,[52] relying on one line in the *Bījak* (*śabda* 103), tried to establish that Kabīr was born in Mithila... P.N. Tiwārī[53] suggests that Kabīr may have been born at Candvār, in the Ballia district of Eastern Uttar Pradesh, basing his opinion on several little-known Kabīr-panthī works, all of which mention Candvār: the search for Kabīr's birth-place had become a 'querelle de clocher'.[54]

Born in Magahar or not, the poet exalts the 'Vision' of the supreme reality which is not tied to any place. So the poet says in the following line:

Just as Magahar, so is Kashi (to me): I have known both as the same,[55]

meaning that 'Holy' Kashi is no better than 'impure' Magahar. The intention of the poet is clearly to demonstrate that Hindu prejudice about 'holy places' is mere phantasy, since the attainment of spiritual experience does not depend on the reputed sanctity of any given spot.

That supreme Reality, which can be contemplated 'within', Kabīr mostly calls 'Rām' - which is a Hindu name for God. From a Muslim point of view, this must have been felt as an unwelcome innovation. That Kabīr's 'Julāhā' family may have

(51) *Benares Gazetteer*, Allahabad, 1909.

(52) *Journal of the University of Bihar*, Pt 2, Nov. 1956.

(53) *Kabīr kā janmasthān*, Sammelan Pattrikā, 54, 1-2, p. 17; see also *Kabīr-granthāvalī*, Allahabad, 1970, pp. 9 ff.

(54) The whole confused discussion is dismissed by P. Chaturvedi, *UBSP*, 139-43.

(55) *jaisā magaharu taisī kāsī, hama ekai kari jānī.*

resented it, is implied in the words put into the mouth of his mother in the *Granth*:

> Who, in our family has ever invoked 'Rām'?[56]

An often-quoted *pad* found in the *Granth* tells of Kabīr's mother's sorrow because her son had given up his ancestral trade, weaving, to devote himself to the cult of 'Rām'. Another complaint of the same type is put in the mouth of Kabīr's wife. Such verses seem to corroborate the testimony of Saint Dhannā, according to which Kabīr, when he took up 'the name of Rām', gave up his weaving.

One should not, however, infer from such isolated quotations that when Kabīr took 'to the Name of Rām', he renounced his ancestral trade once and for all and became some kind of wandering ascetic. In spite of what the *Dabistān* says, Kabīr certainly did not take ascetic vows, nor did he become a *bairāgī* or 'renouncer'. Kabīr's often-expressed contempt for family ties and family 'honour' is only equated by his disdain and aversion for 'professional' ascetics: Yogīs, sadhus, sannyasis and the like, whom he constantly ridicules. The general tenor of his verses makes it certain that he himself never donned ascetic garb, nor did he put on *tilak* and *mālā,* or any of the various paraphernalia used by any particular sect, as he held all such 'disguises' in utter contempt.

References to Kabīr's family are scanty, except for the *pad* quoted above, which mentions his mother. In one line found in the *Granth,* Kabīr refers to his father calling him 'a great Gosain' (*gosvāmī*); the term 'Gosain', often applied to a Hindu saintly man, can be variously interpreted and the reference is isolated. In an often-quoted couplet from the *Granth,* (sal.

---

(56) *Gurū Granth, Bilāval* 4, v. 1.

115) Kabīr expresses disappointment and disgust at his own son, Kamāl's, behaviour:

> Kabīr's lineage was lost (lit. 'drowned') when his son Kamāl was born:
>
> He forgets to invoke Hari while he brings wealth into the house...

a verse which seems to indicate that Kamāl preferred practicing his trade and bringing home his earnings rather than following in his father's steps.

In spite of the view held by a number of Kabīr-panthīs, there is hardly a doubt that Kabīr was married. The Sikh tradition calls his wife 'Loī' and attributes two sons to him: 'Kamāl' and 'Nihāl', and also two daughters, 'Kamālī' and 'Nihālī'. It is probable that Kabīr had several children, as suggested in the *Granth,* but, apart from the couplet quoted above, nothing is known about it. All that can be said with certainty is that Kabīr's view of family life and family relationship was pessimistic in the extreme. Yet, somehow, the memory of Kamāl, Kabīr's son, lingers: at Magahar, at the back of the Muslim shrine built over Kabīr's tomb, a smaller shrine is found, which is said to be the tomb of Kamāl.

In a poem found only in the *Granth,* Kabīr's mother curses some 'shaven ascetics' who have changed her little daughter-in-law's name from 'Dhanīā' to 'Rām Janīā':

> My little daughter-in-law's name is 'Dhanīā'
>
> But they have called her 'Rām Janīā' -
>
> Those shaven ascetics have darkened my house:
>
> They have attached my son to Rām-Rāmaüā! (*āsā* 33, v. 1)

There is a pun on Dhanīā, which means either 'wealth' or 'wife'. The *mumḍia,* literally the 'shaven ones', most probably refer to the Vaishnav ascetics known as *Bairāgīs*.[57] Ghurye[58] says that the Bairāgīs are not cleanshaven; actually, today, most of them keep their hair long and some keep it mattèd like the sannyasis.

Like all Indian saints, Kabīr is supposed to have travelled far and wide, not only in Northern India and the Deccan as far as Pandharpur, but even abroad to Mecca and other far-away places.[59] There are, in fact, a number of allusions to the Mecca and the Kaaba pilgrimage in Kabīr's verses - but the allusions are either disparaging or ironical:

> *Kabīr,* I was on my way to the Kaaba
> when God came in front of me,
> But the Lord frowned on me saying:
> "Who ordered you to go there?"[60]

Apart from his imaginary confrontation with the Sultan Sikander Lodī, in which he emerges victorious, Kabīr keeps

---

(57) The early stages of Vaishnav asceticism in Northern India have not been fully investigated. It seems that, for a long time, the Bairāgīs were also called *muṁḍīs*. Similarly, Marco della Tomba describes the Rāmānandī 'Fachiri' (*fakīr*) as shaven. On the close relationship between the early Vaishnav sects in ancient India and the remnants of the ancient Buddhist orders, called *neṛā-neṛī* (shaven ones) of Bengal, cf. D.C. Sen, *History of Bengali Language and Literature,* Calcutta, 1911; M.T. Kennedy, *The Chaitanya movement,* Calcutta, 1925.

(58) *IS,* p. 151)

(59) On Kabīr's travels, cf. K.M. Sen, *op.cit.,* p. 98; Keay, *KF,* p. 17. On Kabīr's visit to Pandharpur, cf. C.A. Kincaid and D.B. Parasnis, *A History of the Maratha people,* London vol. ii, 1922, p. 107. According to the *Kabīr-i-Manshūr,* Kabīr met *sādhakas*, i.e. 'Seekers of the Absolute', in such places as Mecca, Baghdad, Samarkand and Bokhara!

(60) *Gurū Granth, sal.* 197.

away from royalties. Simplicity is for him the *sine qua non* of true Bhakti. His own quarrels and polemics seem to have taken place at the local level, with the Qāzīs and Mullas who represented Islamic law and orthodoxy and who persecuted him. Two *pada*s, found both in the *Gurū Granth* and in the Rajasthani tradition allude to the attempts made on Kabīr's life. According to the first, Kabīr was bound with chains and thrown into the Ganges[61] - but he had a miraculous escape when the 'Holy Ganga' brought him up again "seated on a deer's skin"; according to the second,[62] Kabīr was condemned by the Qāzī to be trampled down by a furious elephant - but the holy beast would not oblige.[63]

Some of Kabīr's most famous utterances concern Magahar near Gorakhpur, the place where he departed from this world and where, according to Muslim tradition, he was buried.[64] Magahar is an ancient site, reputed to have been the seat of the Buddhist hierarchs for some time after the city of Kapilavastu was destroyed. According to local traditions, the first inhabitants of Magahar were a non-Aryan tribe belonging to the inferior Ḍom race, called Ḍomkatars. Nowadays, Magahar has a large Muslim population, the main group being precisely that of the Julāhās, who in that area are either cultivators or weavers, like Kabīr. The Hindus of Kashi held Magahar in contempt; moreover, according to popular belief, whilst those who die in holy Kashi reach salvation through Lord Shiva's

(61) *Gurū Granth, bhairaū* 18 (*pad* 24 in KG 2).

(62) *Gurū Granth, Gauṇḍ* 4 (*pad* 23 in KG 2).

(63) Mohan Singh, *KB,* p. 43.

(64) Cf. Führer, *op.cit.,* p. 224; A.C.L. Carlleyle, *Arch. Surv. of India,* vol. xxii, p. 72; H.R. Nevill, *Jaunpur Gazetteer,* Allahabad, 1908, p. 227. Magahar, which is situated only thirteen and a half miles from Gorakhpur, is now in the Basti district.

grace, those who die in Magahar are reborn as asses! Magahar's ill repute, in opposition to Kashi, a stronghold of orthodox Brahmanism is easily explained, as noted by Mohan Singh, by "the prominent association of the place with Buddhism, with Doms, low-caste Śūdras, and also with Mussalmāns, among whom first came Julāhās".[65] In Brahmanical eyes, impure Magahar was the very antithesis of holy Kashi: a place of perdition as against a place of salvation. But it is easy to surmise that the Julāhās themselves, who had their stronghold in Magahar, held the opposite opinion. We have already referred to a line of Kabīr's which seems to imply that he had received enlightenment in Magahar. Anyhow, the tradition according to which Kabīr died there is reinforced by several verses, found both in the *Gurū Granth* and in the *Bījak*. In the *Granth* Kabīr says:

> My whole life I have wasted in Kashi
> But, at the time of death, I have risen and come to Magahar.
> For many years I had practised austerities at Kashi,
> But, in death, I have made my dwelling in Magahar.
> For him who thinks, Kashi and Magahar are one:
> With such scanty devotion, how could man be saved?[66]

Those famous lines were variously interpreted, especially the line *maranu bhaïa magahara kī bāsī,* which Trumpp translates: 'Death has come to me, dwelling in Magahar'[67] and Macauliffe: But now that death is at hand, I have come to dwell in

(65) Mohan Singh, *KB,* p. 43.

(66) *sagala janamu sivapurī gavāïā marati bāra magahari uṭhi āïā*
bahutu baras tapu kīā kāsī maranu bhaïa magahara kī bāsī
kāsī magahara sama bīcārī ochī bhagati kaise utarai pārī.
gaürī 15, vv. 2-4.

(67) Trumpp, *op.cit.,* p. 463.

Magahar.[68] Those verses have been quoted as proof that Kabīr did in fact die at Magahar: he would have pronounced these words at the point of death. More probably, if Kabīr did not spend his last years in Magahar, he at least foresaw the possibility of his dying and being buried there - what he ironically describes as 'Making his dwelling in Magahar'. But the general meaning of this *pad* (and of the similar *pad* found in the *Bījak*) is clear: Kabīr ridicules the Hindu superstitious fear of Magahar while proclaiming his staunch faith in Rām, who is the same everywhere and who alone can save. This poem is not a statement of fact about Kabīr's actual moving to Magahar at the time of his imminent death, but a proud challenge especially directed at the bigoted Brahmins of 'Holy Kashi':

He who dies in Magahar becomes an ass -
so, have you lost all faith in Rām?
Dying in Magahar, you will not know death,
dying elsewhere, you'll put Rām to shame!
What is Kashi? What is the barren land of Magahar,
If Rām dwells in my heart?
If Kabīr dies at Kashi,
what homage will he render Rām?[69]

The legendary life of Kabīr follows well-known patterns of Indian hagiography. A saint's prediction and blessing - which cannot be-gainsaid - account for his parthogenous birth: he is found exposed on a lake, which is reminiscent of Viṣṇuite leg-

(68) Macauliffe, *SR*, vi. 138.

(69) *Bījak, śabda* 103, vv. 2-3.

ends.[70] Kabīr's denunciation by the Brahmins to the Muslim authorities as a fomenter of sedition finds a parallel in the story of the famous Bengali saint Chaitanya, whom the Brahmins of Nadia, exasperated by his *kīrtan-yātrā,* denounced to the Muhammedan governor. But whereas, according to the Gauḍīya tradition, the Muhammedan governor of Nadia, overwhelmed by Chaitanya's fervour, ended in joining the *såkīrtan* himself,[71] Kabīr is said to have been confronted by the formidable Sultan of Delhi, to whom he proudly refused to bow.

This noble and defiant attitude attributed to Kabīr seems in accordance with the proverbial strength of his character - besides, such an attitude conforms with what is expected of a great Hindu saint, as shown by the legend of Surdas contemptuously refusing Akbar's favours:[72] an attitude which seems to have been precisely opposed to the actual practice of the Vaishnav sectarians - especially the Vallabhites - who did thrive under the Mughal emperors' protection and benefited from their gifts. Yet, from the seventeenth century onwards, Vaishnav hagiography takes on a strongly anti-Muslim flavour, which is usually explained by Aurangzeb's fierce persecution of Hinduism.

The legend of the miraculous survival of Kabīr in spite of various attempts on his life is meant to demonstrate his magical powers as a great saint and Yogi: his floating on the Ganga on a deerskin (*mṛgachālā*) being a typical Yogic feat. And the attempt to bring to naught the saint's spiritual

---

(70) Cf. the legend of god Vishnu lying in the form of a child on a leaf upon the waters of *pralay:* the story is vaguely reminiscent of the biblical episode of Moses rescued from the waters by the Pharaoh's daughter.

(71) Cf. M.Y. Kennedy, *The Chaitanya Movement,* Calcutta, 1925, p. 27.

(72) Cf. Vaudeville, *Pastorales,* Paris, 1971, Introd., pp. 36-37.

achievement through temptations of the flesh - including the crucial test of his heroic continence by celestial damsels (*apsarās*) - is a common motif in Indian hagiography from Buddhist times. Kabīr's legendary life, therefore, bears a definitely Hindu stamp - though a faint glimpse of the Muslim ideal of the *shahīd,* the martyr of the monotheistic faith, may be perceived now and then, especially in the episode in which the saint refuses to prostrate himself before a king who is a mere man.

The hinduization of Kabīr's legend and the tendency to make him conform to the ideals of Vaishnav holiness, as depicted in sectarian writings from the seventeenth century onwards, probably account for a great deal of late interpolations as found in the present compilations of his verses.

The most ancient and reliable testimonies, as we have seen, do not throw much light on Kabīr's own life: they rather stress his extraordinary personality and express a great amount of perplexity about his teachings. The famous episode of Kabīr's mysterious death and his double funeral - though a Hindu story - does not conform to any known pattern. Yet it expresses, in a vivid and striking manner, the fundamental ambiguity of Kabīr's teaching which distinguished him from all the other Hindu or Muslim saints in India. Who, after all, was he, that Julāhā of Kashi? What was it that he taught so forcefully and how are his strange utterances to be interpreted? Here, the legendary account is not based on well-defined patterns of Indian hagiography - it is rather the expression of genuine puzzlement and wonder on the part of the Indian masses: the question-mark placed by posterity after Kabīr's illustrious name.

3

Kabīr and his times

1. JULĀHĀS, BUDDHISTS AND NĀTHS

Kabīr is the first great Indian poet to appear in Northern India after two centuries of Hindu-Muslim symbiosis. Qutb-ud-Dīn Aibak, who took over Muhammad Ghūrī's possessions after the latter's assassination in 1206, may be reckoned the first independent Muslim ruler of Northern India and the founder of the Delhi Sultanate. But it was Iltutmish who consolidated the Indian possessions into an independent kingdom. When the Khaljī Turks from Afghanistan displaced the Slave Kings at the end of the thirteenth century, the process of indianization of the invaders was already well on the way. For the first time, historians and chroniclers refer to the local Muslims as 'Hindustānīs'. Some converts, such as Mālik Kafūr, were occupying the highest positions in the state. The efforts of Muslim missionaries and propagandists, especially Sufis, had begun to bear fruit and a sizeable number of educated Muslim converts were available for the service of the state. The Khaljī period saw the conquest of Central and Southern India by 'Alā'ud-Dīn, the enforcement of Muslim rule and administration over a number of far-away provinces and the emergence of Delhi as a great centre of Muslim culture. It may be said that Muslim India attained cultural maturity in the days of ᶜAlā'ud-Dīn Khaljī.[1]

In the field of music and literature, the cross-breeding of the two cultures brought remarkable developments. The most brilliant representative of that period is Amīr Khusrau (c. 1254-1324), the greatest Indo-Islamic poet in the Persian language and a distinguished musician, who was associated with the royal court of Delhi. Khusrau belonged to a noble Turkish family, but he was born in India of an Indian mother, and his poetry is full of pride in his native land. Though his verses were composed in Persian, he was familiar with 'Hinduī', the idiom spoken by the common people in and around Delhi, and he experimented with it in some of his poems, so that he came to be considered later as 'the first Hindī poet'. His example was followed by a number of Hindu musician-poets, who flourished at the court of the Muslim rulers from the time of ᶜAla'ud-Dīn', such as Gopāl Nāyak and Baiju Bāvrā.[2]

The breaking up of the Delhi Sultanate, which began in the reign of Muhammad Tughlaq, ended in the tragedy of Timur's invasion and in the sack of Delhi in 1398. The end of the Delhi Sultanate ushered in a period of turmoil and confusion which saw the rise of the Sayyid and later of the Lodī dynasties at Delhi. But the disintegration of the Delhi Sultanate was concomitant with the rise of independent Muslim kingdoms, especially in the east - that is in Oudh, Bihar and Bengal, and in a part of the Deccan.

---

(1) Cf. the *Cambridge History of India,* Delhi, 1958, vol. iii; also S.M. Ikram, *Muslim Civilization in India,* New York, London, 1964; M. Mujeeb, *The Indian Muslims,* London, 1967.

(2) Gopāl Nāyak and perhaps Baiju Bāvrā were contemporaries of Amīr Khusrau; some of their songs were published by Narmadeshvar Chaturvedi, *Sangītajña kaviyô kī racnāê,* Allahabad, 1955.

The Eastern and Southern Muslim kingdoms of the fourteenth and fifteenth century played a great part both in the diffusion of Islam and in the elaboration of a new Hindu-Muslim culture. Among the Eastern kingdoms, that of Jaunpur, in the central Gangetic plain (then including Oudh and Eastern Uttar Pradesh) was independent from Delhi under the Sharqī ('Eastern') dynasty from 1393 to 1479, when Husain Shah, the last Sharqī monarch, was defeated by Bahlol Lodī. The kingdom of Jaunpur included Kanauj on the west, Ayodhya on the north and Kashi (Benares) on the east, south of the city of Jaunpur, built on the Gomti river. After Timur's invasion of Delhi, Jaunpur became the main centre of Muslim culture in Northern India, so that it was sometimes called 'the Shiraz of India'.[3]

In *The People of India,* a work based on the 1901 census, Risley distinguishes three main groups among Indian Muslims: 'Sayyeds', 'Paṭhāns' and 'Julāhās'. While the two first groups claim a foreign, noble origin, the third, by far the most numerous, is purely autochthonous. The Julāhās ('weavers' in Persian) are estimated by Risley as about three millions in number and are widespread from Rajputana to East Bengal and from the Kashmir frontier to Madhya Pradesh and Gujarat. They are specially numerous in the districts of Basti, Gorakhpur, Benares and Jodhpur, in Eastern Uttar Pradesh. They are either weavers (*korīs*) or cultivators and rank low in social estimation: they evidently represent one of the large Śūdra castes which passed *en masse* to Islam some time between the twelfth and the fourteenth centuries.[4]

There are many castes of weavers in India: with some local variations, their social status is very low; they appear affiliated

(3) Cf. H.P. Nevill, *Jaunpur Gazetteer,* Allahabad, 1908, pp. 88 ff.

(4) H.H. Risley, *The People of India,* 2nd ed. 1969.

with ḍefinitely non-Aryan groups, such as 'Ḍoms', 'Kols' and 'Dravidas'. The Indian word corresponding to the Persian *Julāhā* is *Korī,* 'a Hindu Julāhā'. In Uttar Pradesh there are no Hindu Julāhās, but Kabīr not infrequently calls himself a Korī, especially when referring to his trade.[5] So it appears that, even after embracing Islam, the Julāhās were still referred to as Korīs. The *Dhuniās,* cottoncarders, a caste closely related to the Julāhās, also passed to Islam without changing their caste name.

As is often the case in India, the changing of *dharma* or 'religion' leaves practically intact one's 'caste' (*jāti,* lit. 'birth') and it hardly raises one's status in the social hierarchy. Islamized or not, the Julāhās of Uttar Pradesh and the *'Jugīs',* the weaving castes of Bengal, retain their low status in Indian society, though their occupation does not make them into 'polluting' castes. The Julāhās, nevertheless, are the proverbial fools of many Indian stories, so that the word itself has come to mean 'a blockhead'.[6] This is alluded to by Kabīr himself, in a *dohā* found in the *Granth* about his own *jāti*:

---

(5) According to Titus (*Indian Islam,* Milford, 1930, p.3), "the Koris together with the Kanbis and Kharwas, all low-caste folks, were converted to Islam in Gujarat in the 12th century through Nur ud-Din or Nur Satagar, who came to Gujarat in the reign of Siddha Raj (1094-1143)". It is not known when the Korīs of Uttar Pradesh passed to Islam.

(6) Cf. Risley, *op.cit.,* pp.136-7 and 319; S.W. Fallon, in his *A New Hindustani-English Dictionary,* London, 1878, quotes a number of stories and proverbs turning the Julāhās into ridicule. R.K. Varma (*Kabīr kā rahasyavād,* 9th ed., 1961, p. 178, fn.) suggests that the legends spread by the Kabīr-panthīs about Kabīr's miraculous birth were principally motivated by their embarrassment at the fact that their supposed founder was held to be a 'vile' Julāhā.

Kabīr, that caste of mine
is a joke to every one:
Blessed indeed be such a birth,
that let me invoke the Creator! *sal.* 2.

It is significant that mass conversions to Islam in Northern India took place in a few artisan castes, such as the Korīs and allied groups which, though low in the Hindu social hierarchy, did not belong to the menial and so-called 'polluting' castes, such as the 'Chamārs', the 'Ḍheḍhs' and the 'Bhangīs'.[7] Ravidās, who was a Chamār, clearly distinguishes himself - an outcast - from Kabīr, a Muhammedan weaver. Whereas the outcasts remained, at least nominally, Hindus, the low artisan castes tended to become Muslims, which probably indicates a greater measure of independence on their part: they were poor and despised without being menials and serfs bound to the upper castes. It is also likely that the low artisan castes had already been influenced by the unorthodox Buddhist and Jaina *dharma,* a background which had fostered in them a spirit of rebellion against Brahmanical haughtiness and the rigidity of the Hindu social system.

It appears that weavers and allied castes had early adhered to the Buddhist creed in large numbers, especially in North-eastern India. Though Jainism attracted more converts in western India and in the Deccan, its deepest influence was on the Vaishyas, essentially merchant castes. In Eastern India, Buddhism remained alive till a comparatively late date. The *Pāla* Kings who reigned over Bihar and Bengal till the beginning of the twelfth century, were devout Buddhists. After the

(7) Mohan Singh *KB,* p. 7, fn.) remarks that, "both at Gorakhpur and Magahar, the Julāhās are accounted as Muslims and the Chamārs and Ḍheḍhs as Hindus".

conquest of Bengal by king Vijayasena of Orissa, the Pāla dynasty continued to rule in Bihar right up to the conquest of this province by Ikhtiyār-ud-Dīn Muhammad Khaljī, an officer of Aibak, who had established himself in Bihar at the end of the twelfth century.

Muslim missionaries, generally accounted as 'Sufis', were active in Oudh, Bihar and Bengal during the twelfth and thirteenth centuries. But their propaganda must have been facilitated by the anti-Brahmanical disposition of a good part of the common folk who had been deeply influenced by a somewhat degraded form of Buddhism. As noted by Titus:

> In this part of India (Bihar and Bengal), Hinduism was not nearly so well organized and consolidated as in the Northern, Western and Southern parts of the country. The inhabitants were under the influence of a crude form of Buddhism; and despised as they were by their proud Aryan rulers, who held them in disdain, they apparently welcomed the Muslim missionaries gladly".[8]

Low-caste Hindu and Buddhist converts to Islam seem to have been particularly numerous in the Northern part of Eastern Uttar Pradesh, the Gorakhpur-Basti area, near the Nepalese border: most of them were Julāhās, the very community in which Kabīr was born. Their islamization could not but have been superficial, and they probably retained their own customs and traditions. As noted by Mohan Singh:

> Upon their conversion, the high class Hindus and Muslims continued to look contemptuously on them, while the converts themselves never wholly gave up their own kind of Hinduism and went on cherishing several of the Buddhistic Tantric practices and much of the Hindu spiritual and mythical vocabulary. In fact, their contact with Hinduism and Buddhism continued

(8) Titus, *op.cit.*, pp. 44-5.

to be close and personal, whereas their knowledge of Islam did not exceed a bare acquaintance with orthodox Muslim terms and practices.[9]

It is difficult to say whether the Julāhās in those areas were converted to Islam from Hinduism or from Buddhism, since at that time and at their social level, both religions were amalgamated. The 'crude form of Buddhism' mentioned by Titus was a mixture of local Hindu cults and superstitions with some doctrines and practices borrowed from Tantric Buddhism. It appears that it had been popularized in Northern India from the earlier medieval ages, first under its Buddhistic and later under its Shaivite form, by the preaching of the *Sahajiyā Siddhas* and the *Nāth Yogīs*.

Both the Siddhas and the Nāths were the exponents and propagators of some form of Tantric Yoga or *Haṭha-yoga* which, through the more ancient *Vajrayāna* sect, found its origin in Mahāyāna Buddhism.[10] The Buddhist Sahajiyā teachings are recorded in the so-called *Dohā-koṣ*as and *Caryā-pad*s mentioned above.[11] Their 'eighty-four Siddhas' were held as great wonder-workers and the common folk regarded them as having attained immortality in the flesh. So were the Nāth-yogis, their

(9) Mohan Singh, *KB,* pp. 7-8.

(10) On the growth of the Buddhist Sahajiyā cult as a popular development of Mahāyāna Buddhism, cf. S.B. Dasgupta, *ORC,* pp. 14 ff. On their particular *sādhanā* or 'practices', cf. E. Dimock, *The Lord of the Lotus Moon,* Chicago, 1966.

(11) The oldest *pad*s known are the *Caryā-pada*s composed by the Sahajiya Siddhas, together with the Jaina Munis. On the use by the Jain Munis of some popular forms such as the *phāgu* and *bārahmāsā* to propagate the tenets of Jainism, cf. C. Vaudeville, *Bārahmāsā, les Chansons des douze mois dans les littératures indo-aryennes,* Pondichery, 1965, pp. xx ff.

Shaiva counterparts, who are the ubiquitous 'Jogīs' of medieval India.

The Nāth-Yogīs, a type of Shaiva ascetics who bear a resemblance to the ancient *Kāpālikas,* are known as *'Gorakhnāthī Yogīs'* after the name of their foremost guru, Gorakhnāth; they are also called 'Kānphaṭa Yogīs on account of their slit ears. The 'Nāths' or 'Masters' (of yogic powers) are generally reckoned to have been nine in all, though some of their names also appear on the list of the 'Eighty-four Siddhas'. Judging from the mass of legends current in the whole of Northern and Central India concerning the occult powers of the Nāths and their prowess as wonder-workers, their prestige with the Indian masses must have been considerable.

The great god Shiva himself is the first Nāth, the Ādi-nāth; the second is supposed to be *Matsyendra* or *Macchendra,* identified in the Bengali tradition with *Mīnanāth:* the latter is the ancient protector of Nepal, considered by Buddhists as identical with Avalokiteśvara. Macchendra, said to have somehow got hold of god Shiva's secrets, is supposed to have initiated Gorakh (*gorakṣa*). According to the Tibetan tradition, at the time of the Muslim conquest of Bengal, end of the twelfth century, Gorakh or Gorakhnāth, originally a Tantric Buddhist like his master Macchendra, had turned Śaiva in order to please the new rulers. Gorakhnāthī traditions agree in making Macchendra the guru of Gorakhnāth, but they recognize the latter as the foremost guru of their own sect, which bears his name and in which he is deified like Macchendra in Nepal.

Gorakhnāth's place of origin is uncertain: according to the western Indian tradition - and also the tradition of the Gorakhnāthī *maṭh* at Gorakhpur - Gorakh hailed from Northern Panjab; but the Tibetan, Nepalese and Bengali traditions make him come from the East. His dates are uncertain, but scholars agree that he may have lived between the ninth and the twelfth centuries. The literature of the sect, composed partly in Sanskrit and partly in some form of Old western Hindī, shows that the teaching of the Nāth-Yogīs - or at least their esoteric jargon - was very similar to that of the *Sahajiyā Siddhas* of old, though the language of the vernacular *bānīs*, lit. 'sayings', attributed to Gorakh and other Nāths is definitely later than the language of the *Dohā-koṣas* and the *Caryā-padas*. Like the compositions of the Sahajiyās, the Nāth writings evidently aim at teaching the illiterate mass the rudiments of their particular *sādhanā*: such compositions are purely didactic in character and extremely prosaic in style. It is apparently through the ubiquitous Nāth-Yogīs that Tantric beliefs and some Tantric jargon spread among the masses of Northern and Central India between the twelfth and the fifteenth century.[12]

The Gorakhnāthī Yogīs are often referred to simply as 'Jogīs'. They may also be called by various titles of respect, such as *Avadhūt, Gosain, Atīt, Sādh* - even *Faqīr* and *Pīr,* though such titles usually apply to Muslim holy men. All the Jogīs venerate Gorakhnāth, though they do not claim direct descent from him, but usually from some other Nāth. All Jogīs are not ascetics: there are actually some castes of so-

(12) Though Gorakhnāth and the 'nine Nāths' hailed from Northern India, their influence had already reached the Deccan by the end of the thirteenth century, since the great Maharashtrian poet Jñāneśvar, the composer of the famous commentary on the *Bhagavad-gītā* in Marathi verses known as *Jñāneśvarī* (1298), himself claims to be the spiritual descendant of Gorakhnāth through his own guru, Nivrittidev and Gahinīnāth: both the latter are unknown to the Northern Gorakhnāthī tradition, but Jñāneśvar's claim is a tribute to the prestige and fame of Gorakhnāth, whose disciples had, by that time, reached the Deccan.

called *gṛhasthī,* i.e. married, Jogīs. As we have seen, in Bengal, the so-called *Jugīs* constitute a caste of weavers. According to Dvivedi, the Jogī castes are composed of and originally descended from 'fallen' (married) ascetics.[13] It is more likely that 'Nāthism' itself, as a kind of anti-Brahmanical, half-Buddhistic creed, was already widespread among weavers and some other artisan castes at the time of the Muslim conquest. K.M. Sen claims that the Jugīs of Bengal were already outside the pale of Hinduism before most of them turned Muslim - as was the case with the Julāhās.

Kabīr himself seems to consider the 'Jogīs' (i.e. The Nāth-Yogīs) as a group distinct from both Hindus and Muslims when he says:

> The Jogi cries: 'Gorakh, Gorakh!'
> The Hindu invokes the Name of Rām,
> The Mussalman cries: 'Khudā is One!' -
> But the Lord of Kabīr pervades all. (*pad* 128, 7-8).

The very non-conformism of the Nāth-Yogīs, their strong opposition to caste distinctions and their contempt for the rules of ritual purity must have made social contacts with Muslims particularly easy for them. Besides, the Nāths were basically monotheist and their conception of the all-pervading Godhead as Parama-Śiva or the invisible Satguru made them more acceptable to Muslims than to the average *smārta* (orthodox) Hindus.

In *Casteism in India,* K.M. Sen claims that the 'Jugīs' of Bengal and allied castes were not Brahmanical Hindus at all, since "Nāthism is an independent and ancient religion".

---

(13) *Kabīr,* pp. 10-11. The *Jugīs* are popularly believed to be the offspring of Brahmin widows and (fallen) ascetics. This very supposition affords a measure of the contempt in which they were held.

Dvivedi considers that the Nāth-Yogīs were nearer to Islam than to Hinduism in belief. For Mohan Singh[14] "The religion of Gorakhnāth and Pūran Bhagat (another famous Yogī) represents what is left of Buddhism in the Panjab". It seems that the Jogīs did manage fairly well in their dealings with the Muslim establishment down to a late period and that the Mughal emperors themselves - even the fiercely bigoted Aurangzeb - had confidence in the Jogīs' magic powers and in their science of alchemy.[15]

H.P. Dvivedi remarks that Kabīr calls himself a *Julāhā* but never a *musalmān;* the Muslims in general, he refers to as 'Turks'. There cannot be any doubt, however, that the Julāhās as a group were regarded as Muslims. Circumcised or not, Kabīr was officially a *musalmān,* though it is very likely that his own ancestral tradition was a form of 'Nāthism'.[16] This alone can explain his relative ignorance of Islamic tenets, in contrast to his acquaintance with Tantric Yoga practices and his lavish use of esoteric jargon. Though Kabīr does not adhere

(14) *KB,* p. 67.

(15) It is well known that the Jogīs were experts in alchemy. A curious document, printed in *The Mughals and the Jogīs of Jakhbar* by R.N. Gosvamy and J.S. Greval (Simla, 1967), is a letter from the emperor Aurangzeb, sending an offering to the Mahant of the Jogī shrine and asking for a second dose of magically treated quicksilver.

(16) Such ancestry could explain a line found in the *Gurū Granth* (rāg *āsā* 3. 3), in which Kabīr speaks of his own father as *barā gosāin,* 'a great Gosāin'. 'Gosain' is originally a yogic title, which was later assumed by some Vaishnav Āchāryas (such as Vallabhāchārya's son and successors). Some priests from Assam also call themselves 'Gosains'. In Maharashtra, the 'Gosāvīs' are Shaiva mendicants. G.S. Ghurye (in *Indian Sadhus,* Bombay, 1964, p. 71) notes that the word is commonly used in a derogatory sense and applied to Nāthpanthī Jogīs and some low-caste sannyasis.

to Nāth-panthī beliefs, though he ridicules the Gorakhnāthī paraphernalia and even more their pretensions to immortality, he appears far more conversant with the Nāth-panthī tradition than with the Islamic orthodox tradition.

2. SUFIS IN NORTHERN INDIA IN KABĪR'S TIME

The history of Indian Sufism is dominated by that of the Chishtī order, introduced in India by Khwājah Muʿīn-ud-Dīn Chishtī, some time before the invasions of Muhammad Ghurī. Coming from Samarqand to Lahore, Muʿīn-ud-Dīn was in spiritual communion with Al Hujwīrī, the author of the *Kashf al-Maḥjūb,* upon whose tomb he remained during his stay at Lahore. From Lahore, he came to Delhi and Ajmer, then in the hands of the 'infidels'; though he was persecuted by the Brahmans of the town, his personal holiness was sufficient to impress and convert the Hindu Rājā of the place, Rām Deo.

To counteract the holy man's 'magic', the Brahmins had recourse to a famous Jogī, known as Jaipāl. But Jaipāl himself was defeated by the Khwājah and was converted to Islam. Muʿīn-ud-Dīn married a Hindu woman, who, in her turn, became an ardent propagator of the faith. Muʿīn-ud-Dīn and his disciples spread the Chishtī doctrines all over Northern India.

One of Muʿīn-ud-Dīn's disciples, was the Shaykh Farīd-ud-Dīn Ganj i-shakar, who died in 1265 at Pakpattan in the Panjab. Shaykh Farīd was a celebrated Sufi, whose tomb still attracts many pilgrims, both Muslim and Hindus. He was the head of a famous lineage of Sufis, who were, like himself, particularly liberal in theological matters. But his identity is now controversed.[17]

---

(17) Cf. Khaliq Ahmad Nizami, *The Life and Times of Shaikh Farīd-U'd-Din Ganj-i Shakar,* Delhi (first published in 1955). Also known

The most famous of Shaykh Farīd's disciples, Shaykh Nizām-ud-Dīn Awliyā,[18] who was a contemporary of the poet Amīr Khusrau and his spiritual guide, showed remarkably liberal and even pro-Hindu tendencies, holding that, in practice, each people was entitled to follow his own way to God. Shaykh Nizām-ud-Dīn is supposed to have said that God Himself had spoken to him in the *purbī* ('Eastern', i.e. Avadhī) language! The story is all the more surprising as Shaykh Nizām-ud-Dīn never left Delhi, where he died in 1325.

The Shaykh's disciples were to spread his renown far and wide, especially in Eastern India, in Jaunpur, in Bengal and in the Gulbarga area of the Deccan, where the famous Mīr Sayyid Muhammad, better known under the surname of Gesūdarāz, 'the man with the long locks', first introduced the Chishtī doctrines.[19] The story about Allah talking in the *purbī* language with Shaykh Nizām-ud-Dīn must have come from Jaunpur, whose provincial language was Avadhī. In their writings and especially in the *premākhyān,* or 'love stories' in Avadhi modelled on the Persian *mathnavī,* the Eastern Sufis preferred purely Indian themes to the old Arabic and Persian legends.[20] It was not in Delhi, but in the Eastern provinces, es-

---

as "Baba Farid. He was a great mystic and the Master of Khwāja Muʿīn-ud-Dīn Chishti, who introduced the *silsilāh* in India". Cf *infra,* Part II, The Ślokas of Shaikh Farīd; *Gurū Granth,* pp. 1377-1384.

(18) Nizām-ud-Dīn was fond of hearing 'Hindui' poetry and it was under his influence that Amīr Khusrau began to compose verses in that language; cf. Yusuf Husain, IM, p. 147.

(19) Gesūdarāz, who died in Gulbarga in 1422, was probably Kabīr's contemporary. His tomb, like that of Shaykh Nizām-ud-Dīn, is still a place of pilgrimage both for Hindus and Muslims.

(20) The first *premākhyān* in the Avadhi language was the *Candāyan,* composed by Mullā Da'ud ca. 1375. The theme is a folk legend originating

pecially in the kingdom of Jaunpur, in the fifteenth century, under the Sharqi dynasty and in Bengal, that the indianization of the Muslim rulers and establishment progressed at the fastest pace, a process in which the Chishtī Sufis played an important part.[21]

In Kabīr's time, not only Jaunpur,[22] the Muhammedan capital, but other provincial towns as well, such as Manikpur, on the Northern bank of the Ganges between Fatehpur and Allahabad, and Jhusi, a few miles from Prayag (renamed Ilāhābād, modern Allahabad), were the residence of a number of Muslim holy men. Among them, a special importance attaches to the name of 'Shaykh Taqqī'. According to Ghulām Sarvar in the *Khazinat-ul-Asafiyā,*[23] Kabīr himself, whom the author calls 'Shaykh Kabīr Julāhā', was a disciple and succes-

---

from the Bhojpuri area and current in Eastern Uttar Pradesh. The *Candāyan* tells about the illicit loves and adventures of the Ahīr (cowherd) hero Lorik and his beloved Candā. The same legend has inspired another versified romance, *Lor Chandrānī,* composed in Bengali by another Muslim poet, Daulat Qāzī.

(21) In Bengal, the Chishtī doctrines were propagated by Shaykh ᶜAlā' ul Haqq, who died in 1422. The Muslims of Bengal seem to have been more hinduized than in any other part of India. They wrote poems and ballads in Bengali mainly inspired by Hindu and 'Jogī' popular legends.

(22) The most probable etymology for Jaunpur is 'the city of Javanas'; the term *javan* (Skt *yavana*), originally applied to the Greek invaders, was subsequently applied to Muslims.

(23) 'The Treasure of Saints' published at Lahore c. 1858. In this work, Shaykh Taqqī is said to be a weaver, who lived in Mānikpur and died in 1574. He is said to have been the first to write about God and his attributes in the Hindui language. On account of his religious toleration, he was accepted by the Hindus who knew him as 'Pīr Kabīr', as well as by Muhammedans for whom he was 'Bhagat Kabīr' (Saint Kabīr).

sor of Shaykh Taqqī. Actually two 'Shaykh Taqqī' are known to have lived in the kingdom of Jaunpur in the fifteenth and sixteenth centuries: Shaykh Taqqī of Mānikpur Kaṛa, a Chishtī, and a cotton-cleaner by profession, who died in 1545; and another Shaykh Taqqī who lived at Jhusi and died in 1429. The latter belonged to the Suhrawardī order of Sufis and his tomb at Jhusi is still a place of pilgrimage. Westcott takes Shaykh Taqqī of Jhusi as Kabīr's *pīr*[24] - but he gives no evidence about it. Kabīr himself, in the *Bījak,* mentions Shaykh Taqqī of Manikur - whose religion he rejects:

Through Mānikpur, Kabīr had passed,
There he heard of the fame of Shaykh Taqqī.
At the place which they call Jaunpur,
And at Jhusi he heard the names of many pīrs:
There are written the names of the twenty-one pīrs,
People read the *khatmā* and sing the Prophet's praise.[25]

Hearing that talk, I could not restrain myself,
Seeing those graves, I was bewildered:
The works prescribed by that Friend of God and that Prophet,
And all their commands - all that is unlawful!

O Shaykh Aqardī, O Shaykh Saqardī,
  listen to my words:
With open eyes, consider
  the beginning and the end
  and the succession of ages. (*ram.* 48)

The whole poem is composed in a sarcastic tone and there is no suggestion that Kabīr himself was Shaykh Taqqī's

(24) *KPP,* pp. 23-27.

(25) *Khatmā* (Ar. *khatm*): the practice of reciting the Koran from beginning to end.

disciple. Two more poems in the *Bījak,* include another attack on the division of society into castes and into rival religions and races, Hindus and Turks. In the *sākhī* which ends *ramainī* 63, Kabīr concludes with a stern warning to Shaykh Taqqī:

He (God) is eternally (present) in all bodies:
listen, O Taqqī, you Shaykh! (*ram.* 62; 63)[26]

Though Yusuf Husain suggests that "Kabīr remained in spiritual communion with Shaykh Taqqī of Jhusi",[27] there is nothing in Kabīr's verses to suggest more than a casual acquaintance with the Shaykhs and Pīrs of his time. In one *pad* found in the *Gurū Granth,* however, Kabīr alludes ironically to his going on *haj,* i.e. pilgrimage, to a mysterious Pīr, dwelling on the bank of the Gomtī river:

My *haj* is to the bank of the Gomtī river,
Where dwells the *pītambar Pir:*[28]
Wah, Wah! How well he sings!
The name of Hari is pleasant to my soul.

Nārad and Śārad wait on him
And Bībī Kamlā sits by his side as his maid -
With a garland on my neck and the Name of Rām on my tongue,
Repeating the Name a thousand times, I offer my *salām.*
Says Kabīr, I sing the praise of Rām,
Holding both Hindu and Turk as one. (*āsā* 13)

Nothing is known of the 'Pītambar Pīr', if ever there was a Pīr of that name. But the simultaneous use of Hindī and Muslim references in this *pad* is evidently deliberate, with a challenging irreverence to Islamic and Hindu beliefs. The goddess Kamalā

---

(26) *ghaṭa ghaṭa avināśī ahai, sunahu takī tuma sekha.*

(27) Y. Hussain, *IM,* p.55.

(28) The yellow-clad Pīr.

(Lakshmī), Vishnu's consort, unceremoniously called 'Bībī Kamlā', is shown piously serving the 'Pīr' as her divine consort Himself! The general meaning of the *pad* is clear: whoever sings the Name of Rām with sincere devotion is Kabīr's true 'Pīr' - and the company of a true saint is more sanctifying than any pilgrimage. The conclusion of the *pad* stresses Kabīr's refusal to take into account the vain distinction between Hindu and Turk.

Though free from caste prejudice and nearer to the common folk than the haughty Brahmins, Indian Sufis in general, however tolerant and eclectic they may have been, were nevertheless faithful Musalmans. The Shaykhs did not go so far as to contest the injunctions of the Koran and they still perceived a difference between 'Hindu and Turk'; in Kabīr's eyes, therefore, they too were affected with spiritual blindness:

> Hindu and Turk have but one Master (*sāhibu*):
> What is the Mullā doing? And what Shaykh? (*Gu. Bhairau* 4.3)

Yet, as the Sufi preaching had spread all over Northern India in Kabīr's time, Sufi mysticism had impregnated the whole composite culture of that time. Kabīr's own religious ideas and representations could not but be somewhat influenced by Sufi thought and imagery, as suggested by many of his sayings. Such thoughts and imagery were already part of the warp and woof of the religious consciousness of the Indian masses, and *a fortiori* of the islamized weavers known as Julāhās living in the Muslim kingdom of Jaunpur.

The points of resemblance between Jogī and Sufi beliefs in medieval India have been stressed by several authors. In a very instructive paper, Simon Digby has shown the close contacts established between Sufis and Jogīs in Northern India at that time.[29] It is precisely among the Jogīs that the Sufis claim to have made their first converts. One of the first was a well-known Jogī called Ajipāl, Rāī Pithaurā's (i.e. Prithvīrāj) preceptor, who was won over to Islam by the famous Sufi Khwājah Muᶜīn-ud-Dīn Chishtī.[30] The Jogīs, however, do not seem to have suffered from any feelings of inferiority in their encounters with the Sufis and they too claim to have won over some distinguished Sufis to their own creed: even the prophet Muhammad became, according to them, a disciple of Gorakhnāth.[31] The Jogīs were also inclined to identify the series of Prophets who preceded Mohammad with their own famous Nāths.

Though the impudent claims of the Jogīs and their great prestige with the masses, Muslim and Hindu alike, did provoke some resentment in Sufi circles, on the whole, during the period of the Delhi Sultanate, Sufis and Jogīs seem to have coexisted in relative peace, each group regarding the other as a somewhat misguided variety of its own kind and both enjoying the veneration and confidence of simple folk. The fact that the Mahants of the Jogī *maṭh*s or *akhāḍās*, and famous Jogīs in general, are also called *pīrs*, reflects the confusion at work in the mind of the illiterate masses between the two main varieties of holy men and wonder-workers.

---

(29) S. Digby, *Encounters with Jogīs and Śūfīs in medieval India*, in: *A Symposium on Aspects of Religion in South India*, S.O.A.S. London (n.d.).

(30) Cf. M. Titus, *Indian Islam*, p. 44; also T.W. Arnold, *The Preaching of Islam*, London, 1896, p. 281.

(31) Mohan Singh (*KB*, p. 91). According to the *Dabistān*, Gorakh had vanquished Madar, a contemporary of Muᶜīn-ud-Dīn Chishtī and made a Jogī of him; the *Dabistān* says that, according to the Jogīs, the Prophet Muhammad was a disciple of Gorakhnāth!

Typical of the Hindu-Muslim hybrid cult of the Pīrs, are such very popular deities as *Guggā Pīr* or *Zahīr Pīr, Khwājah Khidr* or *Zindā Pīr,* and *Ghāzī Miyān or Satya Pīr.*[32] The cult of the Pīrs in Northern and Central India often developed by taking over an old Buddhistic site, or the shrine of some primitive Hindu deity. Another half-yogic cult is that of Shāh Madār, who is said to have come from Aleppo to India in the first part of the eleventh century. Shāh Madār is thought to have mastered the Yogic control of the breath. Shāh Madār's followers, known as Madārīs, appear to be a variety of Jogīs, whom they resemble in dress and behaviour. They are much addicted to the intoxicating drug known as *bhāṅg.*[33] They claim

---

(32) Guggā Pīr is supposed to have been converted to Islam by Khwājah Muʿīn-ud-Dīn Chishtī: he is honoured mostly in Eastern Panjab as a protector against snake-bite. Khwājah Khidr or Zindā Pīr (the 'Living Pīr') seems to have been originally a divinity of the Indus river; he is honoured as a god of rain in Sind and Panjab, and also in Eastern Bengal, especially by fishermen and boatmen. Satya Pīr enjoys great popularity in Eastern Uttar Pradesh and in Bengal. He is represented as a Muslim Faqīr and is also called *Satya Nārāyaṇ,* a popular form of the god Vishnu. He is supposed to be eternally alive, a distinction which he holds in common with the other divine Pīrs as well as with the celebrated Siddhas and Nāth-Yogīs. Like Krishna-Gopāl, *Satya-Pīr* holds a flute in his left hand; cf. Y Husain, *IM,* pp. 18 ff.; also: *A Shorter Encyclopaedia of Islam,* ed. H.A.R. Gibb and J.H. Kramers; London, repr. 1961, p. 235.

(33) According to a legend recorded in the *Dabistān,* the Prophet himself, as he was strolling in Paradise, lent his own turban to a party of *bhāṅg*-makers in order to strain the liquor. The turban turned green in the process, which explains why the descendants of the Prophet adopted green as their special colour! This irreverent story appears as a gibe directed at the descendants of the Prophet of Islam by *bhāṅg*-addicted Jogīs.

to be true believers and followers of the Prophet, which orthodox Muslims emphatically deny.

The tendency to replace benevolent local deities by kinds of immortal human beings endowed with magical powers is characteristic of the Tantric tradition inherited from Mahāyāna Buddhism. The Siddhas as well as the Nāths were conceived of as human beings who had acquired physical immortality and magical powers through esoteric Tantric practices: they were in fact self-made gods. As Islamic orthodoxy left no place for the minor deities who were the guardians of the people against evil spirits, those cults tended to take on a Muslim garb and to merge with the cult of the Pīrs, a cult disapproved of, yet somehow tolerated by orthodox Islam. The Muslim legends of the Pīrs were reinterpreted in familiar Jogī terms. In this process of interpenetration of Hinduism and Islam at the popular level, the 'Jogī' element played a preponderant part.

The process of integration of popular beliefs and superstitions belonging to Hinduism, to yogic cults and popular Islam must have been fairly well advanced in Kabīr's time. It is clear that, to his lofty mind, the cult of the Pīrs was no more acceptable than Hindu idol-worship or the claim of immortality of wonder-worker Jogīs. Whereas Kabīr rejects such beliefs and superstitions *en bloc,* he keeps exalting the perfect Guru and the Saint as the true conquerors of immortality within the human body. In Kabīr's verses, the yogic ideal of saintliness and its concept of salvation generally prevail over Hindu and Muslim views: gods and deities are of no avail. The true Saint alone approaches the supreme Reality, let him be called 'guru' or 'pīr'.

3. KABĪR AND RĀMĀNAND

Modern Hindu opinion tends to make Kabīr a disciple of the Vaishnav reformer 'Rāmānand': Kabīr is supposed to have received 'the Name of Rām' from him, by way of initiation. Having secured the *nām-dīkṣā* from Rāmānand, the Julāhā Kabīr should be considered as a Vaishnav convert. Yet, it seems that Kabīr was never a Rāmānandī, not even a 'Bairāgī', as Vaishnav ascetics in general were called. It is certain that Kabīr never received the *dīkṣā* from any Rāmānandī Bairāgī, and he was never known to be an ascetic.

The personality of Rāmānand, his time and origins have been much debated. According to sectarian records, Rāmānand was born a high caste Kānyakubja Brahmin. He studied in Kashi and became the disciple of Rāghavānand, the fourth Āchārya in the lineage of Rāmānuja. But, as he did not observe the strict rules of purity enjoined to the members of the *Śrī-saṃpradāy* sect, he fell out with his guru, and he initiated a sect of his own: the *Rāmāvat* or Rāmānandī *saṃpradāy,* with Rām and Sītā as its double divinity.

Uncertainties remain about Rāmānand's personality and about his actual teaching. Several works in Sanskrit and in Hindī are attributed to him, but their authenticity appears doubtful. Two Hindī *pads* attributed to Rāmānand are found in the *Sarbāṅgī,* compiled by the Dādū-panthī Rajab. One of those *padas* finds a correspondence in the *Gurū Granth* and can be translated as follow:

Wither shall I go? I am happy at home.
My heart will not go; my mind is crippled.
Once upon a day, I was inclined to go:
I ground sandal, I took aloes paste and perfumes
And I was proceeding to worship God in the temple,

When my Guru showed me God in my heart.
Wherever I go, I find but water and stones,
But Thou art contained in full in everything.
All Vedas and Puranas, I have searched:
Go ye thither, if God be not here!
O Satguru, I am a sacrifice unto Thee,
Who hast cut away my perplexities and errors:
Rāmānand's Lord is the all-pervading Brahman,
The Guru's word cuts away a million of bad deeds! (*basant* 1, p. 1195)

If this *pad* was really composed by Rāmānand, the latter should indeed be considered as a true follower of *Sant-mat:* idol worship is clearly rejected, the supreme Lord is conceived of as invisible and all-pervading, solely revealed through the *śabda* uttered by the Satguru, whereas Veda and Puranas avail nothing. The Rāmānand who is the author of this hymn does not mention the name of his guru, he only refers to the 'Satguru'. According to the Rāmānandī tradition, however, Rāmānand's guru was Rāghavānand, who is mentioned in the *Bhaktamāl*[34] as "a great Bhakta". He seems also to have been addicted to Yogic practices and well versed in *yogavidyā,* i.e. in magic. In the *Guru-prakārī* (end of 17th century), the Vaishnav author Mihīmlāl wrote that Rāghavānand was himself wearing the apparel of an *avadhūt* and he is represented as an addict to Haṭhayoga. Rāmānandī traditions therefore show a distinctive yogic strand, which explains why the Rāmānandī Bairāgīs also assume the yogic title of 'Avadhūt'.

Modern Rāmānandīs, however, claim their orthodoxy in matter of worship and caste: they worship god Rām (the *Rāmāyaṇ* hero) as the visible form of the supreme Being, together with his wife, Sītā, as the divine Māyā and his brother

(34) *chappay* 35.

Lakshman as the great Serpent Sheshnāg. They also worship the monkey-god, Hanumān, as a powerful magician. Though liberal in matter of caste, the modern Rāmānandīs are nevertheless very far in spirit from the older Sants who are said to have been Rāmānand's own disciples. They appear keen on asserting their link with ancient orthodox traditions and on claiming a respectable establishment within Hindu society. Though stressing the liberal-mindedness of their respective founders in matter of caste, the Rāmānandīs uniformly tended to exclude Shūdras from their places of worship.[35]

There is probably some truth in the traditional view according to which the so-called Rāmānand was a liberal saint - and it is undoubtedly due to that well established reputation that a number of very low-caste people, such as Ravidās the Chamār, Sain the barber, and Dhannā, the butcher, have been said to be his disciples, in spite of chronological impossibilities. That liberal saint may have been another Rāmānand but, of that other Rāmānand, we know nothing: he may have been influenced by Nāth-panthī beliefs and, at the same time, cultivated a preference for the Vaishnav name of Rām. It may well be that the second Rāmānand stands at the junction of Shaiva and Vaishnav mysticism in Northern India, as does the mysterious Nivritti or Nivrittināth, Jñāneshvar's famous guru, in the Deccan.[36]

According to a legend prevailing among Rāmānandīs, Kabīr became a Vaishnav by receiving the *Rām-mantra* from

---

(35) The same attempts at discouraging low caste people from visiting their shrines are manifested in the case of the Vallabhite shrines in the Braj area and in the Viṭṭhal temple of Pandharpur.

(36) Cf. Vaudeville, *Haripāṭh,* pp. 74-6: 'Nivritti et la Religion du Ńom'. In the Maharashtrian tradition Rāmānand is supposed to have been the guru of Viṭṭhalpanth, the poet Jñāneshvar's father, in Kashi.

Rāmānand's lips when the latter, by mistake, fumbling in the dark, uttered: 'Rām, Rām!'. Yet, nothing in Kabīr's own sayings suggests that he may have received the 'Name of Rām' from any one. On the other hand, there is evidence of the name 'Rām' being used in Yogic sects to designate the supreme Being or the supreme Reality - even though the yogīs as a whole consider themselves as Shaiva. In the Gopīchand legend, studied by Grierson, there is a curious scene of initiation of the hero into the Gorakhnāthī order of Jogīs: when the barber slits the ears of the novice, the latter cries: 'Rām - Rām!'.[37] In a *sākhī* found in Rajasthan, Kabīr says:

> They all repeat: 'Rām-Rām' -
> but each with a different intention:
> The way the Satī calls on Rām
> is not that of the wonder-worker![38]

This statement implies that magician Jogīs used to call on 'Rām' too. Yet, in another passage, already quoted, Kabīr says that whereas the Turks (i.e. Muslims) call God 'Khudā', the Hindus call Him 'Rām': this implies that, in Kabīr's time, 'Rām' was already the most common way for Hindus to refer to the supreme Divinity - as it is even today - without any reference to the hero Rāmachandra as an *avatār* of god Vishnu-Hari.[39]

---

(37) Cf. Grierson, in: *'The versions of the song of Gopīchand', JASBE,* 1885. It is a fact that the words *Rām-Rām* are often written or painted on the walls of popular deities, Devī or Shiva shrines.

(38) *KG, sā.* 28. 1. The *Satī* is the heroic woman who burns herself on her husband's pyre.

(39) Up to this day, the word 'Rām' is endlessly repeated by the pall-bearers and the people following a corpse to the burning *ghāṭ*: *'Rām-nam*

The legend according to which the Julāhā Kabīr somehow managed to snatch the *Rām-mantra* from Rāmānand appears to have been concocted with a view to 'hinduize' him. But it also reveals the embarrassment of Indian hagiographers about a saint - Kabīr - who had no known guru: to be *nirguru,* 'One without a Guru', is not respectable in Indian tradition.[40] Even if he constantly refers to the supreme Being as 'the Perfect Guru', Kabīr must have had one - or several? - human gurus, as some of his verses suggest. But it may well be, as believed by Chaturvedi, that he considered all true 'saints' to be his gurus.[41] The fact remains that he never named a human guru.

Kabīr's silence on this matter was not fully appreciated: for a Hindu religious teacher - and also for a Turk - to give the name of one's guru or pīr is to recognize a sectarian affiliation or at least a spiritual allegiance to a recognized religious teacher, belonging to a particular *paraṁparā* or, for a Sufi, a *silsilāh.* But we find that neither Nāmdev, nor Kabīr, nor any of the older Sants have revealed the name of their respective spiritual masters: in each case, however, the Indian hagiographers have filled the gap by attributing a guru or pīr to each one of them.

Such reticence on the part of the Sants appears all the more significant compared with the similar reticence shown by the Siddhas and Nāth-Yogīs of old. Except for the odd link be-

---

satya hai', which can be translated as 'God's Name alone is Truth'. *Rām-rām* is also used as a somewhat rustic way of salutation.

(40) Some hagiographers actually believe that Kabīr went to Rāmānand in order to be relieved of his own shame at being Guru-less!

(41) P. Chaturvedi (*UBSP,* pp. 161-3) gives examples of the use Kabīr made of the word *guru* and concludes that he probably held all true 'saints' to be his human gurus.

tween Gorakhnāth and Matsyendranāth,[42] the 'nine Nāths' appear as independent teachers relying, like the Siddhas, on their own *anubhav* or *paricay,* i.e. on their mystical experience. They appear in different areas, each having his own legend and his own human disciples, who are represented as powerful magicians, but not as infallible teachers themselves.

Kabīr and the other Sants undoubtedly inherited from Nāthism their claim to derive spiritual awareness not from a particular guru, but from direct experience, an experience which Kabīr calls *paracā* (Skt *paricaya*). *Paracā,* is conceived as the hearing of a mysterious Word or Sound (*śabda*), spoken in the depth of the soul by the *Satguru.* The silence Kabīr and the other Sant poets maintained about their human gurus was certainly for them not only a matter of tradition but also of conviction. Yet, it was not understood by later Vaishnav writers, who interpreted their silence as some accident due to forgetfulness. By the time of Nābhājī, the older Sants' narrow connection with the Yogic tradition was somewhat obliterated, so that a number of apparently guru-less saints, beginning with Kabīr, had to be fitted with a suitable guru, in the person of Rāmānand, a high-caste, very respectable and dignified saint.[43]

---

(42) On the curious Gorakh-Matsyendra relationship, cf. Briggs, *GKY,* pp.179 ff. Though Matsyendra is given as Gorakhnāth's guru, Gorakh rose so high over his spiritual master that he undertook to rescue Matsyendra when the latter had fallen a prey to the women of Kadalī!

(43) The Rāmānandī tradition is probably not ancient. The story according to which Kabīr turned a Vaishnav by receiving the *Rām-mantra* from Rāmānand is evidently a fairly recent concoction. Kabīr extols the 'Name' (of God) without ever referring to the divinized god Rām of the Rāmāyaṇ epic.

From this short survey of Kabīr's time, we may obtain a glimpse of the richness and extreme complexity of his cultural and spiritual background. Kabīr stood in the midst of several powerful currents which were in a constant process of conflict and interaction. The fifteenth century in Northern India, it has been observed,

"was marked by an extraordinary outburst of devotional poetry inspired by religious movements and this stands as one of the great formative periods in the history of Northern India, a period in which, on the one hand, the modern languages were firmly established as vehicles of literary expression and on the other the faith of the people was permeated by new ideas".[44]

We are inclined to think that this 'formative period' actually started earlier, around the twelfth or thirteenth century, both in Northern India and the Deccan, and that it was concomitant with the permanent establishment of Muslim domination in India. Shaiva Bhakti and the theories and practices of Tantric yoga, especially under their late form, Nāthism, played an important part in this process, which was strengthened by the influence of Islamic monotheism and the eclectic mysticism of the Chishtī Sufis.

Even when the influence of Islam does not appear to have been direct, it certainly acted as a catalyst, helping to release and bring to the fore deep undercurrents which were already present in the lower strata of Indian society, as they reflected the culture of the masses and their religious aspirations. Those popular movements, generally anti-brahmanical in character, found their natural expression in the emerging vernaculars of

(44) W. Moreland and A.C. Chatterji, *A Short History of India,* London, 1945, p. 193.

Northern and Central India, which they powerfully contributed to develop.

Being a man of the people, a poor artisan, Kabīr could hardly have had any formal religious training: what he knew, he knew from experience or from 'hearing' alone. There is no doubt that he was, as P. Chaturvedi put it, a *bahuśrut*, 'one who had heard much'. Living in and around sacred Kashi, he must have been in constant contact with the holy men of his times: Pandits, Yogīs, Shaiva Sannyāsīs and Vaishnav Bairāgīs, Vīrashaiva Jangamas, Munis and Tapīs - ascetics of every robe and denomination: the motley crowd of saints and sādhus which filled - even as today - the narrow lanes of the holy city, Vārāṇasī.

Jaunpur and Jhusi, sacred to Eastern Muslims and the residence of many Shaykhs and Pīrs, were not far away, and we know that Kabīr met them. This is the confused and somewhat discordant clamour that we perceive in his predication. Yet, though his sayings in many ways echo the turmoil and the conflicts of the time, Kabīr appears to stand alone - as if the loftiness of his mind and the depth of his spiritual awareness had made him impervious to the theological arguments and squabbling he so cordially despised. He could hear all those 'holy men' had to say, yet keep his own counsel, as vividly expressed in a popular couplet attributed to him:

Mix with all, meet all, take the Name from all,
To all and everyone say: 'Yes, Yes' - but dwell in your own village!"[45]

Reflecting in a striking way the deepest religious aspirations of his time, yet contemptuously rejecting most of their doctrines and practices, Kabīr's *sādhanā*, though not exempt from

(45) *saba se hiliye saba se miliye, saba se lijiye nāva*
hājī saba se kahiye, basiye apane gāva.

inner contradictions, is very much his own. It can be said that he never consciously followed any other guidance than that of the interior Master, the divine *Satguru* - so that his 'faith' or 'confidence' remained apparently supportless, like that of the mythological 'Fire-bird' to which he has been compared:

The Fire-bird has made his nest in the air,
  for ever He dwells in-between
From earth and sky he remains aloof:
  his confidence needs no support.[46]

4. TANTRIC CONCEPTS AND LANGUAGES IN KABĪR'S TIME

Some aspects of Tantric Yoga, and particularly the teaching and practices of the *Nāth-panthī* (or Gorakhnāthi Yogīs), constitute an important element of Indian medieval culture. Though Kabīr and the Sants after him generally did not adhere to Gorakhnāthī doctrines and though Kabīr himself emphatically rejected Tantric practices, the traditions that nourished his thought and provided him with his esoteric vocabulary are largely those of Tantric yoga. It is, therefore, necessary to take the Tantric tradition into account in order to evaluate the words in which Kabīr tried to express his own spiritual experience. Though Kabīr draws on several traditions and makes use of a variety of similes, the imagery and vocabulary peculiar to Tantric yoga provides him with a system of references, an elaborate complex of symbols which, however esoteric they may appear to the western reader, were certainly charged with much prestige and a real power of suggestion for the mass of

(46) *anala akāsā ghara kiyā, madhi nirantara bāsa|*
basudhā byauma bigatā rahai, bina ṭhāhara bisavāsa || KG. sal. 20. 8.

his listeners, who themselves had drunk deep of that ancient tradition.

Tantric yoga developed from the seventh century onward as a kind of offshoot of Mahāyāna Buddhism. It slowly impregnated most schools of popular devotion from the Middle Ages to modern times. As a result, Tantric beliefs and practices are found alive from Northern to Southern India. Tantricism is linked with the cult of the Shakti, the female energy of the supreme divinity, Shiva, and a legion of autochthonous goddesses, *devīs*, whose cult is linked with fertility, material prosperity and protection against evil forces of nature, especially with diseases. Those *devīs* have to be propitiated with blood offerings (*bali*) - their cult is known to have often entailed human sacrifices. The Devīs remain extremely popular to this day, though their cults are deemed impure and have been deprecated and vehemently opposed wherever Buddhistic and Jaina influences prevailed. Opposition to the Devī cults is rooted on the principle of ahimsa, or non-violence - as a prerequiste for the attainment of moksa, or liberation. Kabīr's radical condemnation of blood rites and animal killing, even for the purpose of food, stands on the same ahimsa principle.

Far from being addicted to such *vāmamārgī* practices, the Nāth-panthīs are staunch *Haṭha-yogi*s, addicted to strenuous bodily practices which, they claim, lead them to immortality. Renouncing all worldly ties and pleasures is a pre-requisite for the success of their *sādhanā*. In spite of the proverbial opinion, the didactic literature of the Nāth-panthīs adopts a very puritanical stance, especially in the matter of continence. They vehemently oppose association with women, who are depicted in the worst possible light. This ascetic ideal is emphasized by wandering Jogī minstrels, singing legends in which the link between indulgence of the senses and death is constantly emphasized.

This puritanical attitude also concerns the consuming of meat, liquor and drugs. The *Gorakh-bānī*s show Gorakhnāth as firmly opposed to all these:

> Consuming alcoholic drink, flesh and *bhāng,*
> one goes to hell, says Gorakh. (*GB* 164).

There are frequent allusions to liquor and alchemy, to *ras* and *rasāyan:* the true Yogi is supposed to be constantly drinking the Liquor:

> That Yogi is a hero (*sūra*) who drinks the Liquor (*vāruṇī*) day and night. (*GB* 137).

But that Liquor is the liquor of spiritual intoxication and deathlessness. It is not different from the *ras* or *amṛt* (ambrosia) which oozes from the moon of the *sahasrār*.

Certain terms associated with sexual practices seem to have been taken by the Nāth-panthīs with a notable different meaning. A particularly interesting example is the verb *ram,* which means 'to enjoy' (sexually), but also 'to stop, to stay, set at rest'. In Nāth-panthī literature it is frequently used to describe the condition of a Yogi in the supreme *sahaj* state, 'immobilized' in perfect bliss; the description of *śabda-yoga* or *suratị-śabda-yoga* is deliberately obscure.

In Tantric yoga, mythological deities hold an inferior position. Even for the more hinduized Nāth-panthīs, *Īśvara,* the personal form of Paramashiva, is of little consequence, whereas the human Guru remains the indispensable guide. The whole of Tantric literature, and especially the Buddhist Sahajiyā and the Nāth-panthī literature, abound in hymns of superlative praise to the Satguru, the perfect Guru, who is equated with the supreme Reality itself.

Like the Vajrayāna and Sahajiyā of old, the Nāth-panthīs are fervent adepts of *guruvād* (the Religion of the guru). But, in the popular form of Nāthism prevalent in Northern and Central India from the Middle Ages to the modern times, guru-worship tends to take the coarser form of Guru Gorakhnāth cult. The stone image of guru Gorakhnāth is worshipped in Nāth-panthī shrines like that of Macchendra (Matsyendranāth) in Nepal and that of Guru Dattātreya in Maharashtra.

The exaltation of the guru as a manifestation of the supreme Reality probably explains the remarkable silence maintained by the Siddhas and the Nāth-panthīs, as well as by Kabīr and the old Sant poets, on their human gurus, if indeed they had any. The role of the human guru as an external teacher and guide tends to be obliterated as he only makes manifest the true nature of Guruhood, which is expressed in the divine *Śabda,* participating of the transcendent nature of the Satguru.

The Śabda imparted by the Satguru is a mystical illumination which renders all other revelations - and, therefore, all scriptural evidence - totally useless, as expressed in the *Gorakh-bānīs*:

> Neither Veda nor Koran, nor abundance of words: all fell to the bottom,
> At the summit of the sky (*gagan*), the *śabda* is shining:
> there the knower (*vijñānī*) discovers the Invisible One (*alakh*). *GB* 4

The Nāth-panthī concept of Śabda as inner Revelation is closely linked with the notion of *paracā,* the experience of the supreme Reality:

> Get hold of the *śabda,* O Avadhūt! Get hold of the *śabda,*
> The stages (*sthān*) are useless obstacles,
> The supreme Soul (*paramātma*) becomes manifest within the
> soul as the moon is reflected in water. *GB* 124.

One may really wonder if such form of late tantric Yoga exposed in the vernacular writings of the Nāth-Yogīs can still be viewed as authentic Haṭha-Yoga. As a religion, Nāthism hardly comes within the pale of Hinduism and there appears to be some truth in the opinion held by some that it is a distinct religion. Mohan Singh has called it 'Shabadism' since the Śabda itself is held as the key to liberation.[47]

A unique hymn is found attributed to saint Rāmānand in the *Gurū Granth*:

Pilgrimage to the temple is pilgrimage to nothingness,
Pilgrimage to the *tīrth*as is nothing but water!
Pilgrimage to the *Atīts*[48] is the sole fruitful pilgrimage,
as they have words of ambrosia. *GB* 97.

According to popular belief, the two syllables which compose the Name of Rām (*rā-ma*) constitute the perfect *jap* (prayer) as those syllables are constantly repeated by the great Yogic god Shiva himself; the *rām-mantra,* they say, is Shiva's sole *jap*.

With Kabīr and the Sants, *rām-sumiraṇ* is an equivalent of *nām-sumiraṇ,* as a means of merging with God. It is emphasized by Kabīr himself and by all the Sant poets as well as the whole Sikh tradition, beginning with Guru Nānak.

The close parallelism between the Sant notion of *sumiraṇ* and the Sufi notion of *dhikr* has often been emphasized. Just as the Sufi *dhikr,* the Vaishnav *kīrtan* or *saṁkīrtan* is a musical performance which should be executed in a circle of Saints - i.e. devotees of god Vishnu-Hari, which is also a name of God. Just as the Sufi *dhikr,* the Vaishnav *kīrtan* should be always voiced, sung 'with mouth', since the mere voicing of the holy Name is

---

(47) On 'Shabadism' being the religion of saint Rāmānand and others, cf. Mohan Singh, *KB,* p. 68 and *passim.*

(48) *Atīt* is one 'gone beyond'.

believed to purify the mouth and soul of the singers and to bring countless blessings on the hearers, who themselves are purified by the contact of the 'Saints', the *satsang*. Sikhism and Islam, the two monotheistic religions in India, are close to each other, in spite of their endless feud. In his *Mathnavī,* the Muslim poet Rumi says: "Praise of God is pure (*pāk*); when purity comes, defilement goes out; when the holy (*pāk*) Name comes out of the mouth, neither impurity remains nor sorrow".

The common Vaishnav belief in the quasi-magical power of the utterance of the divine Name is demonstrated in the Vaishnav Puranas, especially in the *Bhāgavata Purāṇa.* In a number of legends, such as the legend of Ajāmīla, the name of god Vishnu (or *Nārāyaṇ*) is shown to possess salvific power *per se,* quite apart of the speaker's intention: it is really a kind of magic spell - so that god Vishnu himself, owing to his merciful nature, cannot but rush to save him who has uttered his Name. The same belief is clearly expressed in the *Haripāṭh* in old Marathi, a Vaishnav poem attributed to the poet Jñāneshvar, (the author of the famous *Jñāneśvarī*), with the refrain:

> Utter the Name of Rām with mouth (*bis*):
> Who could ever count the merits (so acquired)?[49]

Denial of the value of the Sound as such is in keeping with Kabīr's strong emphasis on an 'interior' and more specifically spiritual *sādhanā* as a way to salvation. On the other hand, Kabīr's exaltation of the Saints (whom he indifferently calls Sants, Sādhus, Bhagats, Harijans or 'Vaishnavas', and his insistence on *satsang* 'the company of the Saints', appear very much in keeping with Vaishnav popular belief in the extraordinary benefits to be acquired in this way. Yet, he frequently

---

(49) *hari mukhẽ mhaṇa, hari mukhẽ mhaṇa/*
punyācī gaṇana, kauna karī//

expresses his opinion on the scarcity of genuine saints in this world. If such a saint may be found, says Kabīr, "He is my Guru and my Pīr".

In several well established Sākhīs, Kabīr expresses his sorrow about the paucity of true saints:

Kabīr, that Path is strenuous,
no one can follow it:
Those who went never came back
none ever came to tell.

Kabīr's house is on the top,
where the path is slippery:
Even an ant can't hold its footing
and they go with loaded bullocks!"

If there is such a saint, says Kabīr, "He is my Guru and my Pīr" (*Bī. sā.* 57; 33).

It seems that, for Kabīr, Rām or Nām on the one hand and the Satguru on the other constitute, for the human *jīv,* the only possible means of apprehending the Divine - and ultimately of merging into It. The interior religion leads the human soul to the mystical experience he calls *paracā*: through *paracā,* the Jīva is reabsorbed into the oneness of Rām, 'as water merges into water'. Such is the mysterious state of Sahaj which can only be accomplished *within* - but the stakes are too high:

Such a one cannot be found
who burns down his own house,
Who knocks down the five Fellows
and remain absorbed in Rām. (Rāj, *Gu, sal.* 42, 83).

Such a one cannot be found
in whom we can take refuge,

For I have seen the whole world burning
each one in its own flames. (Raj, *Bī, sā.* 332).

5. THE TANTRIC TRADITION AND KABĪR'S WAY TO SALVATION

If some uncertainty and even confusion in the use of technical terms pertaining to Tantric Yoga are to be found in Nāth-panthī literature, we should not be surprised to find that the use of such technical terms by Kabīr and the Sants is even more erratic, since the latter explicitly reject the value of the tantric *sādhanā* as a means of salvation.

Several attempts have been made to interpret literally the Tantric terms and symbols used by Kabīr, especially the paradoxical poems known as *ulṭabāmsī*s, 'upside-down Words', patterned on the *sandhā-bhāṣā* of the Sahajiyā and Nāth-panthī masters:[50] the result obtained are at most approximative, since the author makes use of Tantric lingo with supreme independence, caring little for consistency. Often the context alone can give a clue to the intended meaning.

Even when Kabīr appears to speak as a Yogi, addressing another Yogi as Avadhūt, he speaks as one who has already fathomed the vanity of all tantric *sādhanā*: the trappings donned by the Nāth-panthīs he considers as vain contortions and sheer disguises, just as useless as Brahmanical ritual,

---

(50) See e.g. Barthwal, *NSHP*, 'The Experience Expressed', pp. 218 ff.; 'The Mystery Code', pp. 270-2; H.P. Dvivedi, *Kabīr*, pp. 82-4; also R.K. Varma, *Kabīr kā rahashyavād*, Allahabad, 1966, *et alii*.
The edition of the *Bījak*, in Hindī, by H. Shastri and M. Prasad, give, in an Appendix, the interpretation of Yogic terms.

pilgrimages and idol-worship to achieve salvation. In a similar vein, Kabīr mockingly affects to speak the language of a devout Mussalman, addressing Qāzī and Mullah in their own language interspersed with Arabic and Persian words and with Koranic allusions.

When Kabīr attempts to convey his own mystical experience, however, it is mostly the paradoxical style, inherited from Tantric yoga, which comes naturally to him. Unable to describe what remains forever as inexpressible as 'the sugar of the mute' (i.e. enjoyed by the mute), Kabīr takes refuge in the language of absurdity or upside-downness. Similarly, he makes use of the *sandhyābhāṣā*, or 'twilight language'. As remarked by Barthwal:

> The *ulṭabāmsī* is necessarily a paradox, while the *sandhyābhāṣā* is not. In the *ulṭabāmsī*, the apparent meaning, is usually an opposite representation of the actual behaviour or order of things: simply a means of startling the hearer and render him receptive to the real and hidden meaning hinted at.

Kabīr's cryptic language is really more allusive than properly esoteric: the real value of his paradoxes lie in the paradoxes themselves, in their mysterious flavour and strong power of suggestion for the Indian ear: 'the lotus which blooms without flower', 'the fire raging in the Ocean', the narrow passage where 'an ant cannot enter' and which people want to climb 'with loaded bullocks'... Sometimes Kabīr is a Bhakta talking the language of Yoga, sometimes he is a Yogi speaking the language of the heart.

Apart from Tantric language and symbols, Kabīr makes use of a great many comparisons, mostly of a realistic, trivial character. In order to suggest the misery of human condition, the soul's bondage and its spiritual quest, he largely draws images from the common realities of life. He frequently alludes to humble trades and crafts, especially his own, weaving, and to those associated to it, such as spinning yarn and dying cloth. His verses also contain numerous allusions to trading and hawking, to money-lending and to the frightful punishment meted out to the miserable debtor unable to redeem his pledge, who stands as a striking image of the plight of man in his mortal condition.

Highway robbery and house-breaking, petty larceny and pocket-picking, all kinds of knavery, roguery and cheating for which the ancient city of Kashi is particularly known (the famous *Banārasī ṭhagī*), dice-playing and gambling, the time-honoured business of prostitution carried out in the open bazaar, with Māyā herself as the most avid and shameless prostitute setting out to bring about the downfall of men - all this is pictured by Kabīr in an uniquely racy, sarcastic style, a bitterness lined with deep sorrow.

Though, as a resident of Benares, Kabīr was evidently more familiar with city life, he often mentions rural activities, such as tilling and watering the fields, drawing water through the well-known device called *arhat* or *rahat,* (the Indian *noria,* also called 'Persian wheel'), warding off the birds all day when the crop is ready and keeping watch over it all night - the endless toil of the Indian farmer. The typical activities of the cowherd folks, pasturing cows and buffaloes, milking, churning, and butter-making, all provide him with ready similes. Bird-catching and hunting in the wilderness are sometimes mentioned, with *jīv,* 'the soul' as the helpless deer, vainly trying to escape its Hunter, Death. All the everyday, commonplace realities of life, especially the life of the lower castes, are evoked by Kabīr to wake up and quicken the dumb sleepy mass of people going blindly to their doom, in 'the way of the world and the Veda', as they allow themselves to be led astray by the meretricious tales and mendacious promises of hypocritical

Pandits and fake Sādhus, only anxious to gratify their vanity and fill their belly.

For Kabīr, the way that leads to salvation is not the easy way. It is an abrupt, rugged path which few men find and even fewer can follow. Real Bhakti is conceived as a heroic path, open only to those men who have renounced all comforts and pleasures, who have left behind all desire or hope for bodily salvation and strive for the spiritual Meeting at the risk of their life.

That heroic path is that of the Lover: as the Sufi, he has a pact with death. The soul striving for salvation is compared to the *Satī,* the heroic Hindu wife, fearlessly leaving her home to climb the pyre and be reunited in death with her beloved spouse - or to the Rajput hero, the *Sūr,* going down to the battlefield in order to fulfil his pledge of fighting unto death.

Kabīr's imagination seems haunted with those two heroic figures, the *Satī* and the *Sūr,* who, for the Indian world, embody the highest ideal of perfect love and loyalty. For Kabīr, Rām, or the mysterious Sahaj state, which the Tantrikas conceive as perfect Bliss (*mahāsukh*), is only to be bought at the cost of one's life: he who wishes to be a *jīvanmukta,* 'one liberated whilst living', must, of necessity, be a *jīvanmṛta,* 'one dead while alive'.

The notion of *virah,* central in Kabīr's poetry, bears a close resemblance to the Sufi notion of ʿishq. In the profane realm, *virah* is a favourite theme of Indian poetry in folk ballads and folk songs. The pathetic *Virahiṇī* of the folk-songs becomes the symbol of the human soul wounded by 'the arrow of the Śabda', pining for the vision of her divine Spouse, Rām. The situation of the young girl married in infancy, who reaches adolescence without having ever met her Lord - a tragic situation, typically Hindu, which has inspired the famous

Rajasthani tale, the *Ḍholā-Mārū,* - is Kabīr's favourite symbol to suggest the situation of the human soul who, though already belonging to God and totally pervaded by His presence has not yet been able to 'meet' Him. But, here, it is no longer the distance or the Husband's forgetfulness that is the real obstacle - as in the *virah-gīt* - since the divine spouse is ever present *within:* the fault lies with the wife-soul itself, it is the impurity of her love which makes her spiritually blind. Only through the tormenting but purifying 'fire of Virah' can the wife-soul obtain union, a total merging into her true Lord, Rām. The theme is present in all the three recensions of Kabīr's sayings, but it appears more developed in the Rajasthani tradition, so much so that some of the Kabīr *sākhī*s in the *Kabīr-granthāvalī* could easily be interpreted as mere echoes of some popular love lyrics of Rajasthan. A large number of popular sayings current in Northern and Central India have taken the form of *sākhī*s attributed to Kabīr.

Death, its inescapable, frightful, tragic character, appears to be at the core of Kabīr's thought. He speaks about it in the most vivid and blunt manner, using a variety of images and symbols mostly borrowed from popular tradition. For him, as for the Tantrikas, Death - whether it be called *Mīc mṛtyu* (Yama-rāj or Kāl) - remains as the ultimate enemy, the insatiable Monster who knows no defeat:

Myriads of living beings are rocking,
whilst Death keeps meditating -
Millions of aeons have passed,
but to this day she has not known defeat! *Bi, Hiṇḍol* 3.

No other poet in India - perhaps no other poet in the world - has spoken about 'Kāl', Death, as Kabīr has done, with such tragic intensity:

All beings are parched grains for Kāl:
some in his mouth, the rest in his lap. *KG, sā.* 16.16.

True to the tradition he had inherited, Kabīr is not concerned with life after Death, but with the conquest of immortality, *hic et nunc,* within this fragile body which he himself calls 'a clay-pot' or just 'bones in a bag of skin'. And it is with that monstrous fiend Kāl, that Kabīr, following the Siddhas and great Yogīs of old, has engaged the battle. Yet, he believes that he has already vanquished since he has fathomed the mystery of life and death. For Kabīr, the secret of victory lies hidden within man, at that unknown depth where Kāl himself finds no place: he fades like a ghost at daylight when the ineffable Experience rises 'like a million of suns':

If God should die, then we shall die too,
But if God cannot die, how could we die?
Says Kabīr, our soul has merged into his Soul:
We have become immortal, we have found infinite Joy.
KG, pad 106, 2-3.

4

Kabīr's language and languages

There is no evidence that Kabīr ever composed a single work or even wrote a single verse - though a large number of works has been attributed to him by the *Kabīr-panthīs,* Kabīr's followers. The list of works attributed to Kabīr varies from forty to eighty or more. Though Kabīr's followers believe that *Sat Kabīr* was omniscient from the age of five, they do not assert that the Prophet himself wrote down the numerous compositions ascribed to him. They hold that he composed them orally and that they were subsequently written by his immediate disciples, among whom they name Surat-Gopāl, Dharmadās and Bhaggojī.

Moreover, Kabīr's social background as a low-caste weaver makes it likely that he was more or less illiterate, or at least that he had no formal teaching in reading and writing. In a couplet found in the *Bījak,* Kabīr says that he never touched a pen:

Ink or paper, I never touched, nor did I take a pen in hand -

The greatness of the four ages, I have described by word of mouth.

Bī. sā. 187.

The written word, holy scriptures in general, be they Veda or Qur'ān, he cordially despises:

Reading book after book the whole world died

and none ever became learned:

He who can decipher just a syllable of Love,
he is the true Pandit! *KG, Sā.* 33.3.

Kabīr's contempt for scriptural authority and contempt for the written word is rooted in the medieval Tantric tradition, especially the Sahajiyā Buddhists and the Nāth-Yogīs, disciples of the famous Master Gorakhnāth.[1] From the early Middle Ages, perhaps as early as the eighth or ninth century, Siddhas and Yogīs, mostly low-caste people, had been preaching their Gospel in the common tongue, *bhāṣā,* in some form of Western Apabhramsha or old Bengali. Kabīr shared the Siddhas' contempt for the sacred Brahmanical language, Sanskrit, as expressed in a couplet traditionally ascribed to him:

Kabīr, Sanskrit is like well-water
and the *Bhāṣā* like the live water of the brook!

Like the *bāṇī*s (*vāṇī*s) 'utterances' of the Siddhas and Nāth-yogīs, Kabīr's *bāṇī*s are mostly short, pithy utterances, whose terseness is often not exempt from obscurity. The metrical forms in which they are couched are the same as those used by the Siddhas and Nāth-Yogīs of old: essentially distichs called *dohā*s and short rhymed poems known as *pad*s or *ramainī*s.

The *dohā* (Skt *dogdhaka* or *dodhaka*) appears as the most typical form of Apabhramsha literature. It differs from the Prakrit *gāthā,* which it has replaced, as the last syllable or each line (*ardhalī*) is short, whilst it is long in the *gāthā,* and also

---

(1) The Sahajiyā Master Kāṇha says in one of the *Caryā-pads*: *jo mana-goara ālājālā, āgama pothi iṣṭamālā.*
"What the mind perceives is mere humbug and so are the *āgamas* (scriptures), the books and the bead-telling".
Shahidullah, *Les Chants mystiques de Kāṇha et Saraha: le Dohā-koṣa et les Caryā,* Paris, 1928, p. 115, 10.

because it introduces the rhyme.[2] This type of rhymed couplet is the principal metre used in the *dohā-koṣas* composed by the Sahajiyā Buddhists.[3] It was equally popular with the Jain Munis in the Middle Ages, as shown by the *Pāhuḍa-dohā* of the Jain ascetic Rāmasimha Muni.[4] In ascetic literature, the *dohā* appears exclusively in a didactic form - but it has also been used in lyrical compositions in *grāmya* popular Apabhramsha and in Old Western Rajasthani. The most ancient version of the famous Old Western Rajasthani folk ballad *Ḍholā-mārū-rā dūhā* includes a number of popular lyrics entirely composed in such *dūhās*.[5] Kabīr himself must have memorized an indefinite number of such *dūhās* or *dohās* in the vulgar tongue, which were freely sung and quoted by the common folk. In the *Gurū Granth* collection of Kabīr's sayings, the *dohās* attributed to Kabīr and the other Bhagats are called *saloku* (Skt *sloka*) i.e. witnesses: one should understand that the couplet is a pithy utterance, 'witnessing' to the ultimate Truth. At the same time, the *sākhī* itself is conceived as the

---

(2) According to the scholar H.P. Dvidevi, *Hindī sāhitya kā ādikāl,* Patna, 1952, p. 93, the *dohā* is the first *chand,* i.e. prosodical form, in which the rhyme was introduced.

(3) The Buddhist Saraha himself praises the *dohāchanda* in these terms:

ṇaü ṇaü dohā-saddena ṇa kahabi kimpi goppia.

"Through ever new *dohās*, nothing remains hidden" (i.e. all spiritual truth can be expressed in *dohās*); cf. Shahidullah, op.cit., p. 160, *dohā* 94.

(4) *The Pāhuḍa Dohā of Rāmasimha Muni, An Apabhramśa work on Jaina mysticism,* ed. Hiralal Jain, Karanja, 1933.

(5) On lyrical *dohās* in late Apabhramsha and in Old Western Rajasthani literature, cf. Ch. Vaudeville, *Les Dūhā de Ḍholā-Mārū,* Pondichery, 1962, pp.46-7 and 116-18.

Word (*śabda*) fallen from the guru's mouth - Himself the true and only Witness to the supreme Reality.[6]

The custom of invoking the witness of a great saint of yore in the last line of a stanza is well-established. It is already found in the *Dohā-koṣa*s and the *Caryā-pada*s composed by the Sahajiyā Siddhas and in the *Bāṇī*s of the Nāth-panthīs. In the *Caryā-pada*s, Kāṇha or Kāṇhupa, who calls himself 'naked Kāṇhilā', invokes the famous Siddha Jālandhari as his witness. The Siddha invoked as witness may or may not be the poet's own guru, but he is conceived as endowed with perfect knowledge: he embodies the 'Perfect Guru' (*satguru*) who is identical with the supreme divinity or essential Reality. Every *sākhī*, therefore, implicitly refers to the witness of the *Satguru*. The last couplet in the *Bījak* collection says:

> The *sākhī*s are the eyes of Wisdom: understand it in your mind:
> Without the *sākhī*s, there is no end of strife in this world.
>
> *Bī. sā.* 353.

Being the true fountain of wisdom, the 'witness' of the Satguru abolishes the need for all the other *pramāṇa*s or proofs: it puts an end to vain disputes and arguments, as it substitutes direct evidence transmitted by word of mouth for scriptural evidence. Though *sākhī*s may be written, a *sākhī*, by its very nature, is meant to be memorized: it lives in the heart of those whom it has struck and who have been penetrated by its message. Even when couched in the well-defined metrical form of a *dohā*, the *sākhī* is not merely a literary genre, but a privileged form of expression - or rather the evocation of the highest truth.

---

(6) Barthwal (*NSHP*, pp. 223-4) remarks that the terms *sākhī* and *sabad* (*śabda*) meaning 'witness' or 'authoritative word' (of the Guru) seem to have been originally used as synonyms.

Kabīr is known all over India essentially as a composer of *sākhī*s and all the main compilations of his verses contain a large number: the Sikh *Gurū Granth* has 243 *sākhī*s, the *Kabīr-granthāvalī* has 811; various editions of the *Bījak* have from 353 to 445 *sākhī*s. The smallest collection is that of the *Sarbāṅgī,* which includes 181 *sākhī*s out of a total 337 verses attributed to Kabīr.[7] But the number of *sākhī*s attributed to him is much greater. Their number is said to be infinite, as suggested by a verse found in the *Bījak* itself:

> Like the leaves of a great tree, like the grains of sand of the Ganges
> Are the words which have come from Kabīr's mouth...
>
> *Bī. sā.* 261.

1. KABĪR'S CRYPTIC LANGUAGE

Besides Old Avadhi, the ubiquitous *Nāth-panthī*s, who considered themselves as the disciples of the ancient Yogī Gorakhnāth, made use of various dialects: especially the Ḍingal (old Rajasthani) and the Pingal impregnated with old Braj-Bhāṣā. It seems that, in Kabīr's time, Dingal was dominant, as the language of the Buddhist Siddhas. On the other hand, before Kabīr, many Sufis had made use of the old Hindui dialect, mixed with Panjabi and Arabo-Persian vocabulary. It is certain that Kabīr used more than one of those languages, according to his audience and to his own fancy. We must also account for Kabīr's polemicist talent - an extraordinary virtuosity in adapting himself to his audience and in

(7) According to Tiwārī (*KG,* Preface, pp. ii-iii), there are no less than 1.579 *pad*s, 5.395 *sākhī*s and 134 *ramainī*s attributed to Kabīr in various compilations - and research could probably uncover more!

borrowing his adversaries' jargon. We give here a specimen of such blasting, for which he was famous:

O *Miyān!*[8] Your order is not just:
We are the poor servants of God - and You just seek glory!
Allah is the Master of Religion, He did not order to oppress the poor:
Your *Murshīd* and your *Pīr,*[9] tell me, where did they come from?
You observe the *Ramzān*[10] and you keep spelling prayers -
but that Kalimā[11] won't earn you heaven:
He who knows Him through the Experience,
his soul possesses seventy Kaabas[12]

In Kabīr's words, the technical terms of Tantric Haṭh-yoga are already detached from ancient traditional meaning. Tantric Yoga practices, while passing from the ancient Buddhist Siddhas to the Shaivite Nāth-panthīs, have been considerably modified. The mythical founder of the sect, Matsyendra (or Macchendra), followed by the ancient Master Gorakhnāth, appear as reformers. In the writings attributed to him, Gorakhnāth himself does away with exterior practices. He rejects the cult of fancy deities as well as the distinction of castes, and he preaches detachment, chastity and sobriety.

The Goal is to accede to a state of 'non-conditionment', 'pure spontaneity', leading to Immortality. That mysterious

(8) 'Sir', addressed to a Muhammedan.

(9) 'Murshid': a leader, an eminent person. 'Pir': a Muhammedan Saint, a holy man.

(10) Ramzān: the ninth month of the Muhammedan year, in which fast should be observed from early dawn, to sunset.

(11) Kalimā: the sacred formula of the Muslim faith: Allah is God and Muhammad is his Prophet.

(12) Kaaba: the sacred square building at Mecca, visited by all Muslim pilgrims.

state, or 'Country' described in paradoxical terms, is the *sahaj* state itself. The word has been variously translated by scholars. Shahidullah chooses 'l'Inné', Snellgrove 'The Innate'; Kwaerne adopts Guenter's translation, 'The Co-emergent', based on the literal sense of *sahaj.*[13] Essentially, it refers to 'Transcendence and Immanence, Subject and Object, indivisibly blend'. The Co-emergent is an ontological category: it is the true nature of 'the World'- all that which can be experienced. It is also that infinite Bliss which the Yogī finally obtains as a permanent condition.

The mysterious Reality which is at the centre of Kabīr's practice or *sādhanā* is expressed in a rich variety of terms. Some are Islamic terms, such as Allah, Khudā, Hazrat, Pīr and so on. A few come from the Vedantic tradition, negative epithets such as Alakh, Nirākār, Anant, Guṇātīt; a few are philosophical notions, such as Brahman, Ātman, Āp, Sār. Other terms are directly borrowed from the Haṭhayoga language and practice, such as Śabda, Anāhad, Sahaj and Śūnya, the last two being key-words:

O *Avadhūt!* The true Yogī is detached from the world,
He has his dwelling in the sky, He does not see the world,
seated on the seat of Conscience:-
Outwardly, He wears the frock,
but His soul contemplates the Mirror.
His body, he has burnt in the Fire of Brahman
and He remains awake in the triple Confluent:
Says Kabīr, such is the King of Yogīs,
who has immerged Himself in the *Sahaj-śūnya.*

Sahaj is realized when duality is abolished and the Yogī accedes to transcendental Oneness, in the *sahaj-samādhi.*

---

(13) 'Co-emergent' may also be interpreted as 'Essential'.

The term *Śūnya,* the Void, also belongs to the Buddhistic tradition. Without going back as far as the philosopher Nāgārjuna, *Śūnya* is often mentioned by the *Vajrayānī* Siddhas. In the Haṭha-Yoga, *Śūnya* becomes an equivalent of Keval, Brahman, Sahaj, Nirañjan to call the supreme Reality: as in the *Gorakh-bānīs*:

> *Śūnya* is my Mother, *Śūnya* is my Father,
> *Śūnya* is Nirañjan, the own of my Own!

For Kabīr and the Nāth-Yogīs, *Śūnya* is an equivalent of *Sahaj* - and the two terms are often associated. *Śūnya* means both the supreme Reality and the 'Place' where the human being (*jīvātmā*) operates its junction with that Reality:

> *Kabīr,* the Pearl germs in the Fortress whose summit is the Void.

Potions of Immortality play a great part in Tantric theories. *Amṛt* (ambrosia) is conceived as a Liquor flowing from the Moon, i.e. the *sahasradal* formed by 'a thousand petals'. The Nāth-yogīs believe that, from the *sahasradal,* flows a wonderful Liquor: by the blockade of the breath, the Yogī forces the liquor along the *suṣumnā-nādī* into the *sahasradal,* where it is drunk by the *jīvātmā,* the living Soul which then obtains Immortality. Kabīr apparently makes use of that language - but he gives another meaning to words such as *rasa, amṛta, sahajaras*: those terms are now taken in the sense of Rām's Love, or of Rām Himself. The Tantric interpretation is rejected: for the true Saint, Rām himself, is the only Drink of Immortality:

> The Shāktas die, and the Saints live
> as their tongue drinks Rām's Liquor!

and:

> He got absorbed in Sahaj-rām.

Though the alcoholic practices of the Shāktas are negated, Kabīr enhances the spiritual intoxication produced by that Liquor:

He who has drunk of Rām's Liquor,
is intoxicated for ever...

The word *khumār,* or intoxication is borrowed by Kabīr from the language of the Sufis, who have often described that 'Intoxication of Love'. But the Sufis themselves had borrowed from the Tantrikas such terms as *ras* and *varuṇī,* which they interpret as *prem-ras,* mystical Love:

He is the true Yogī, who wears his ring in Spirit:
Night and day, He keeps watch:
In spirit is his posture, in spirit his practice,
in spirit his litanies, his asceticism, in spirit his words;
In spirit his skull, in spirit his whistle -
blithely he plays on the flute the silent Music.
He who has reduced his five senses to ashes,
That One will conquer Lanka, says Kabīr.

Surati is a difficult word to interpret - probably derived from *śruti,* 'audition' (of the unspoken Word). In the *Kabīr-granthāvalī,* the *surati* is compared to the Well from which the Water of Love springs up:

Surati is the balancing pole, Absorption is the rope,
and the Spirit rocks the pulley -
In the Well of the Lotus,
the Yogī keeps drinking the Liquor of Love.
The Ganga and Yamuna are within the heart,
and the Yogī has merged in the *Sahaj Śūnya* -
There Kabīr has built his hideout,
while holy men look for a Path!

2. KABĪR'S OWN LANGUAGE

Kabir's own language and the languages in which his 'Sayings' were originally composed have long been a matter of controversy. According to Ahmed Shah, who translated the *Bījak* into English, Kabīr composed his poetry in the language spoken in his own area, i.e. in Benares and its neighbourhood, in Mirzapur and Gorakhpur.[14] In Gorakhpur, the regional language is Bhojpuri, an Eastern dialect of Hindi, spoken from the Easternmost part of present Uttar Pradesh to the Westernmost part of Bihar and spreading to the North up to the Himalayan border. Grierson argues, however, that there is hardly any trace of the Bhojpuri language in the *Bījak.*[15] For Grierson, the basic language of the *Bījak* is old Avadhi, which seems to fit in with an often-quoted *sākhī* of Kabīr:

bolī hamārī pūraba kī, hami lakhai nahī koī
hama to to soi lakhai, dhura pūraba kā hoy

My language is of the East—none understands me:
He alone understands me who is from the farthest East.

---

(14) Ahmed Shah, *op. cit.*, p. 29.

(15) G. Grierson, *The Bijak of Kabir*, JRAS, 1918, p. 152.

Grierson however remarks that any dialect spoken east of the Braj Bhāṣā area is called 'Eastern' in Northern India, and that Avadhi itself is often referred to as *pūrbī*.[16] Yet the meaning of the above-quoted *dohā* which both Grierson and Ahmed Shah have taken literally, is far from obvious. A literal interpretation appears hardly plausible: the idea that no one (in the West?) understands Eastern Hindi is a rather flat statement. P. Chaturvedi argues that *pūrab dīsā*, 'the Eastern region', symbolizes the ultimate spiritual stage which is the aim of the Yogis.[17] Kabīr's 'Eastern' languages, therefore, means a cryptic language, understandable only to the Yogis and Siddhas who are the dwellers of that mysterious country. Actually, in the *Bījak* itself, another mention of that far-away land confirms Chaturvedi's interpretation: *pūraba dīsā hamsa gati hoī*, 'The Eastern region is the resort of the Hamsa.'(Bi. ra 5.5).

Following R.C. Shukla, most Indian scholars have stressed the heterogeneous character of Kabīr's language, which seems to borrow freely from a variety of dialects. Shukla, however, draws the conclusion that Kabīr's nondescript idiom is essentially based on the idiom used before him by the Nāth-panthī Yogis and other itinerant preachers, and he proposed to call it *sādhukkarī bhāṣā*, lit. Sādhus' jargon.

---

(16) B.R. Saksena's opinion in the matter is cautiously stated: '*Pūrbī* means "Eastern" and is sometimes used for Avadhi and at others for Bhojpuri. It may well be a suitable name of Eastern Hindi to distinguish it from Western Hindi.' *Evolution of Avadhi*, Allahabad, 1937, p. 2.

(17) P. Chaturvedi, *KSP*, pp. 209–10; see also D.V. Bharati, *Siddha-sāhitya*, Allahabad, 1965, pp. 447–8.

The first editor of the *Kabīr-granthāvalī*, S.S. Das, also stresses the composite character of Kabīr's language, giving examples, in his Introduction, of *vāṇīs* composed in Khari Bolī, i.e. old Hindī, and also in Rajasthani and Panjabi, besides Avadhi. For S.S. Das Kabīr's language is *panchmel kichrī*, 'a hotch-potch.'[18] Other Indian authors do not give up so easily. The editor of the old Rajasthani ballad, *Dholā-Mārū-rā Dūhā*, thinks that Kabīr's language is mostly Rajasthani.[19] S.K. Chatterji's opinion is that 'Kabīr's poems are composed in mixed Hindi (so-called Hindustani) and *Braj-bhākhā*, with occasional Eastern Hindi (Kosali) and even Bhojpuri forms'.[20] The difficulty of the problem is largely due to the uncertainties of the textual tradition: the various recensions of a single verse often exhibit dialectical variations. P. Chaturvedi has shown that the same *pad* may be found with characteristic Avadhi forms in the *Bījak*, with more Kharī Bolī in the *Gurū Granth* and with a few Braj forms in the *Kabīr-granthāvali*, the latter representing the *Dādū-panthī* tradition. None of the three main recensions, however, is wholly consistent: all show dialectical variations.

Given the complex linguistic pattern which prevailed in Northern India at the time, it cannot be taken for granted that

(18) *KG I*, Intr., pp. 71–75.

(19) *Dholā-mārū-rā-dūhā*, eds. Ram Simha, S.K. Parik and N.D. Svami, Benares V.S. 1991 (1934), pp. 167–8.

(20) A review of conflicting opinions about Kabīr's language is found in P. Chaturvedi, *KSP*, pp. 208ff.

Kabīr preached only in his own dialect. What could have been Kabīr's dialects? As a resident of Benares and a Muslim, he must have been familiar with at least two idioms besides Hindui: the two regional languages, Avadhi and Bhojpuri. Bhojpuri probably was his home language - but he must also have been familiar with Avadhi or *Pūrbī,* the language of the Muslim kingdom of Jaunpur, which included Benares. Houlston notes that "in the Eastern Patna and Gaya districts, where the regional language is Magahi, the dialect of South Bihar, Avadhi is used by many Muslims and Kayasthas, who were scribes in the service of the Moslem rulers; also that, in part of Eastern Uttar-Pradesh, where the regional language is Bhojpuri, the Muslims and Kayasthas do speak Avadhi". But there are good reasons to believe that, in Kabīr's time, the illiterate crowds already used, as a *lingua franca,* the ancient composite idiom known as Hindui: the language of the bazaar.

The language of the *dohā*s differs from that of the *pad*s and *ramainī*s. As noted by Barthwal, "the style is more archaic in the *dohā,* a metre natural to Apabhramsha". Western dialectal forms (Kharī Bolī, Rajasthani, and some Panjabi forms) are more numerous in the *sākhī*s, whereas Braj tends to dominate in the *pad*s. The latter can be explained by the very nature of the genre: the *pad*s are lyrics and, already by Kabīr's time, Braj (or *piṅgal*) had become the lyrical language *par excellence*. As to the Rajasthani and Panjabi forms in the *sākhī*s, Barthwal, like Shukla, is of the opinion that they reflect "the language of renunciates" discourse (*sādhukkaṛī bhāṣā*), prevalent at the time. Actually the language of Kabīr's *sākhī*s resembles the language of the *Gorakh-bānī*s, the sayings attributed to Gorakhnāth by the Nāth-panthīs.[21] This nondescript Western

(21) Cf. *Nāth siddhȯ kī bāniyȧ,* ed. H.P. Dvivedi, Benares, Vi.S. 2014, 1957 A.D.

idiom is probably inherited from the *dohā-kos*as described by Chatterji as popular (*grāmya*) Apabhramsha. An interesting point is that the dialectical difference between the *dohā*s and *pad*s attributed to Kabīr corresponds to the difference noted between the language of the *Dohā-koṣ*as and *Caryā-pada*s composed by the Sahajiyā Siddhas.[22]

Though agreeing with Shukla and Barthwal about the influence of the Nāth-panthī language and style on the language of Kabīr's *sākhī*s, Chaturvedi remarks that many such *sākhī*s appear directly influenced by folk-songs and ballads in dohās.[23]

As a matter of fact, the language used by Sant poets, whose works are preserved in the *Granth,* such as Senā, Pīpā and Ravidās, who may have been Kabīr's younger contemporaries, are composed in a very similar language. Even Nāmdev, who lived in the fourteenth century and hailed from Maharashtra, used this mixed Western dialect in his Hindi hymns recorded in the *Granth.*[24] During the course of the fourteenth to the fif-

---

(22) S.K. Chatterji (*ODBL,* vol. 1, Calcutta, 1926, pp. 112-13) characterizes the language of the *Dohā-koṣ*as as a king of Western (Sauraseni) Apabhramsha and the language of the *Caryā-pad* s "a form of old Bengali".

(23) Among those Southern Indian Sufis, Shah Burhanuddin, who flourished at Bijapur and who might have been Kabīr's contemporary, wrote a short work called *Sukh-sahelā* which had the vocabulary and metres of 'Hindu Hindi'. S.K. Chatterji (*Indo-Aryan and Hindi,* p. 206) writes that the Hindi found in the *Sukh-sahelā* "is very like the Hindi we find in Kabīr's poems and in the works of the Saints".

(24) The dates of Nāmdev, who in the North is given as Rāmānand's disciple and in Maharashtra as a contemporary of Jñāneshvar, remain uncertain. Besides, the Maharashtrian tradition knows more than one 'Namdev'; cf. P. Machve, *Hindī aur marāṭhī kā nirguṇ sant-kāvya,* Benares, 1962; see also Bhandarkar, VS, pp. 124 ff. The Hindi hymns of Nāmdev have

teenth centuries, old Hindui or Kharī Bolī had become to be recognized as a *lingua franca* fit for the propagation of popular religious teaching - mostly unorthodox and anti-Brahmanical: one may say that Hindui was the language of the Indian 'Reformation'.[25]

Kabīr himself being an Easterner, would naturally have mixed some forms of his native dialect into his verses. With Benares situated in the Bhojpuri linguistic area, one would expect to find an admixture of Bhojpuri forms in his *sākhī*s; actually such forms are rare, whilst there is general evidence of the Avadhi influence. The reason seems to be that the Bhojpuri language was then, and had remained since, merely a spoken dialect without any written literature, a rural idiom to which the dominant Muslims do not seem to have paid attention. It was not so with Avadhi or *Pūrbī*, which had become, after Persian, the language of the Muslim kingdom of Jaunpur under the Sharqī, (Eastern) dynasty. Like Hindui in the West and in the Deccan, Avadhi, which was already a written language before the time of the Muslim conquest, had begun to be cultivated by the Eastern Sufis, as a means to propagate their own doctrines. Born as a Muslim Julāhā and living about Benares, Kabīr certainly was conversant with the dominant provincial language, Avadhi, and he was probably more familiar with it than with rural Bhojpuri. But there is no reason to suppose that he composed his *sākhī*s in *ṭheṭh* (pure) Avadhi: he more probably used a composite language, Hindawi or Hindui.

---

been edited, in Hindi, with a substantial Introduction by Bhagirath Mishra and R.N. Maurya: *Sant Nāmdev kī hindī padāvalī,* Poona, 1964. A critical edition and English translation has been prepared by Winand M. Callewaert & Mukund Lath, *The Hindī Songs of Nāmdev,* Leuven, 1989, 432 p.

(25) Vaudeville, *Kabīr's language and languages: Hindui as the Language of Non-conformity,* Madison University, 1987.

Amīr Khusrau, in his *Masnavī,* defines the language of the time:

> Now in India, every province has a peculiar dialect of its own: There is, for instance, Sindhi, Lahori, Kashmiri, Canarese, (...) and Oudhi (Avadhi). But in Delhi and all around it, the current language is the same Hindawi that has been used in India from ancient times and has been used for all forms of speech.

The language of the aristocratic Khusrau, like that of the poor Julāhā Kabīr, must have been basically the same: good old Hindui, the language of the bazaar, though the language of the heart may still have been Avadhi.

3. THE CONCLUSION OR 'SIGNATURE'

The *dohā*s and *pad*s being, by their very nature, *muktak,* i.e. detached, independent verses, their authors often claim ownership by the simple device of introducing their own name in the verses themselves in the last line. This practice, which constitutes a kind of signature, is ancient. It appears already established in the *Dohā-koṣ* and *Caryāpad* of old, composed by the 'Sahajiyā Siddhas' and the 'Nāth-panthīs'. In the *Dohā-koṣ,* we find formulas such as *sarahapa bhaṇanti* or '[the Master] Saraha says'. The formula is called *bhaṇitā* or 'what is said'. In the Tantric Sahajiya and Nath-panthī literature, the *bhaṇitā* is not regularly found. In the *Caryā-padas,* it is found in a more developed form such as 'Kanha says', 'Sarahpā says'. Often, the name of the poet, who is a Siddha, is directly introduced in the line as the subject in a clause, such as: *kāṇha vilasiā āsava-mātā,* '[The Master] Kāṇha sports, drunk with liquor'.[26]

The use of the *bhaṇitā,* also called *mudrikā,* 'stamp', seems to have become generalized in Northern and central India from the fifteenth century onwards, before Kabīr. It is found in the so-called *abhaṅgas* in archaic Marathi, as well as in the *pads* of the Northern saint-poets. In the *sākhīs,* however, the full *bhaṇitā* is rarely found: either there is no signature at all, or else the single word *kabīr* is used at the beginning of the first line of the *dohā,* rarely of the second.[27] It is then used as a 'stamp' without having any syntactic function in the clause, which then becomes susceptible of a double interpretation.

4. THE LITERARY LANGUAGES OF THE MUSLIM MEDIEVAL PERIOD

Between the 14th and the 16th centuries A.D., under the influence of the Sufis, especially the Chishtiyas, two Indian vernaculars had emerged as literary languages in Northern and Central India: the highly persianized Dakhani in the Bijapur-Golconde area of the Deccan and the 'pure' (*ṭheṭh*) Avadhi in Eastern Uttar Pradesh - an idiom practically free from Arabo-Persian vocabulary. The former reflected the language of the literate Muslims, the latter was attuned to the ear of educated Hindus. The works composed in those literary dialects had an ecumenical ring, as their Sufi authors were eager to build a bridge between 'the Two Religions', Hinduism and Islam, to

(26) Quoted in R. Sankrityayan, *Hindī kāvya dhārā,* Allahabad, 1945, p. 151.

(27) In the *Gurū Granth,* the word *kabira* is regularly added at the beginning of each *saloku* (śloka) without consideration for the rhythm. We have omitted it in translation.

unite rather than divide. All those works were written in the Persian script, with which literate Hindus, especially the Kayastha caste, had long been familiar.

Meanwhile the uneducated masses of Northern India went on with their own provincial languages and dialects, to which a *lingua franca* was superposed out of the necessities of common intercourse, especially between low-caste Hindus and equally low-caste Muslim converts: as we have seen, that *lingua franca* was *Hindui,* whose origin was probably anterior to the Muslim conquest and the Muslim predication: a mixed language of Northwestern origin, used by itinerant holy men of various denominations, mostly by the ubiquitous *Gorakhnāthi* or *Nāth-panthī* Yogīs. A hybrid language from the start, Hindui easily absorbed the Arabo-Persian vocabulary, with any amount of phonetic variations and deformations. Persianized Hindui, later called 'Hindustani' seems to have been spoken - or at least understood - all over Northwestern India and the Ganges valley, including Bihar and Central India, and also in part of Maharashtra - all regions where the Nāth-panthī propaganda had been active from the tenth century onwards. The very plasticity of old medieval Hindui made it the perfect medium for the spreading of new ideas and new religious values among the down-trodden masses of India: it was the privileged idiom of the anti-Brahmanical propaganda carried on by the Nāth-panthīs and the Sufis with equal fervour. In the Deccan, the Hindui language appears to have been familiar to the unorthodox, bitterly anti-Brahmanical Manbhau (*mahānubhāv*) sectarians, themselves indebted to the Nāth-panthī predication, though antagonistic to their cult. This is confirmed by the *Caupaḍī*s (i.e. *caupāī*) verses of Dāmodar Paṇḍit, a Manbhau author belonging to the 13-14th century (1237-1316) whose verses were composed as a retort to the philosophy of the Nāth cult.[28] According to V.D. Kulkarni, out of 60 verses (*caupadī*) in that work, 35 are composed in a language which is predominantly the regional language, *Marāṭhī* - whereas the other 25 represent the language of the Nāth-Siddhas - a language that the author describes as "a harmonic blending of Hindi and Marathi words, without any Arabic or Persian element".[29]

The Caupaḍīs of Dāmodar Paṇḍit testify to the extraordinary plasticity of 'Hindui', as used by unorthodox preachers. V.D. Kulkarni notes that the language of the Caupaḍīs is close to the language of the Gorakh Bānīs. Apparently, as a Sādhus' jargon, Hindui could include and assimilate any amount of words borrowed from other Indo-Aryan dialects. The fact that the Caupaḍīs of Dāmodar Paṇḍit contain no Arabo-Persian vocabulary, suggests that their origin goes back to the pre-Muslim period. Later Manbhau literature is entirely and exclusively composed in Marathi. In spite of its strongly monotheistic trend, the literature of the Marathi *abhaṅgas* appears more akin to Krishnaite Bhakti than to the religion of the Northern Sants, including the old saint-poet Nāmdev from Maharashtra. Nāmdev, who probably belongs to the fourteenth century, is the author of a large number of *abhaṅgas*, short devotional poems in medieval Marathi. Though Nāmdev is not a northerner, the Sant tradition invariably names him as Kabīr's predecessor - and the *Dādū-panthī* themselves name him as the first (i.e. the earliest) of the Northern Sants. He is known to have expressed himself in the *lingua franca* of the time: old 'Hindui'. The inclusion of the old saint Nāmdev among the Sant poets of Northern India is based on the sixty-

(28) V.D. Kulkarni, 'The *Caupaḍīs* of Dāmodar Paṇḍit'.

(29) A few Arabo-Persian words, however, are found in the Hindi *pads* and also in the Marathi *abhaṅgas*, attributed to saint Nāmdev.

one Hindi hymns attributed to him in the *Gurū Granth* of the Sikhs. Some poems attributed to Nāmdev are composed in a queer mixture of Hindi and Marathi;[30] moreover, a number of *pad*s attributed to Nāmdev in other collections also include Marathi grammatical forms. Nāmdev is the oldest poet in the Sant *paraṁparā*: after him, the tradition diverges. The Maharashtrian Sants become more devotional and more vaishnavized, while the old Nāth-panthī, anti-brahmanical trend of thought and Tantric vocabulary is on the wane. The case of Dāmodar Paṇḍit as well as that of Nāmdev suggests a strong link between the old Hindui language and the rejection of Brahmanical orthodoxy and social establishment. First used as a *lingua franca* by the Nāth-panthīs to spread their gospel of religious and social rebellion, Hindui remains in use in vast areas in which more developed literary languages already existed, as in Eastern India and in Maharashtra: old Hindui emerges as essentially the language of non- conformity and the Indian medieval Reformation. The Arabo-Persian script becomes the only script available to all, Hindus as well as Muslims, for mundane affairs as well as religious expression - as seen in the *premākhyān* love tales, in old Avadhi. The ancient *devanāgarī* script remains the privilege of the Pandits, and the *Kaiṭhī* script that of the Kayastha scribes, who use it concurrently with the Arabo-Persian script. If the poor Julāhā Kabīr was somewhat acquainted with any script, it could only have been with that Arabo-Persian script.

---

(30) The Hindi hymns of Nāmdev have been edited with a substantial Introduction by Bhagirath Mishra and R.N. Maurya: *Sant Nāmdev kī hindī padāvalī,* Poona, 1964; for the mixed language, see *pads* 15, 20, 31, 34. See also Callewaert-Lath:1989.

5. KABĪR'S STYLE

Much has been said and written about Kabīr's style. All critics, especially modern ones, have emphasized its extraordinary vigour - a quality in which his verses stand supreme in the Hindi language and perhaps in the whole Indian tradition - as well as its abrasive roughness. Indifferent to 'literature', unskilled in the delicate art of ornate poetry, Kabīr cannot be called a *kavi,* 'poet', in the traditional Indian sense. Some Indian scholars would rather consider him as a social reformer and a mystic than as a poet. Not only are Kabīr's verses devoid of all literary ornaments (*alaṁkāra*) and figures of speech, but the very bluntness of his expressions, the triviality of his comparisons and his scoffing, are likely to shock the reader or listener whose ears are attuned to the refinements and intricacies of *kāvya* poetry.

H.P. Dvivedi is not wrong when he argues that "Kabīr found the Hindi language still in infancy, yet put it to severe trial and somewhat attempted to bend it to his needs". The same scholar calls Kabīr "a dictator of language"; "Language trembles before him, unable to serve him and to comply to his will..." Actually, no scholar who ever read Kabīr in the original could fail to be struck by the unique forcefulness of his style. As noted by W.G. Orr, "for sheer vigour of thought and rugged terseness, no later bhakti writer can be brought into comparison with him".

More so with Kabīr than with any other Indian author, the peculiar quality of the style seems to reflect an outstanding and somewhat mysterious personality. Indifferent or opposed to traditional beliefs and values, apparently unconcerned with the pleasure or displeasure of his audience, Kabīr fearlessly voices his inner conviction. His blunt language, his bitter irony bespeak ardent indignation - but also a desperate effort to awaken his dumb, sleepy fellow men, unaware of their impending doom.

The heroic striving of the soul awakened by the 'Satguru's arrow' to reach the unseen, inaccessible Beloved, the dangers and torments of the spiritual Path, inspire him with stirring words, revealing the depth of his own suffering and despair. On the other hand, the ineffable bliss of Union in that faraway 'land', beyond the 'impassable Pass' - yet hidden in the depth of man's own soul - the ecstasy of the secret, silent merging into the One, in which all duality is abolished, are evoked in strange, often obscure words, yet endowed - at least for the Indian ear - with an extraordinary power of suggestion.

Even when chaotic and somewhat obscure, Kabīr's style, at least in his well-established sayings, is never dull, never lacking in naturalness and spontaneity, which gives it its inimitable charm. Dvivedi has found suggestive words to evoke Kabīr's style: 'Tender as a flower, hard as a diamond'. And it is true that Kabīr's best utterances are endowed with a diamond-like quality, the transparency, multi-faceted brilliancy and mysterious glow of pure diamond. If not a learned poet, a *kavi* in the traditional sense, the little weaver of Benares was indeed a great poet, one of the greatest known in India and elsewhere.

Part Two

Selected Verses

KABĪR AND THE KABĪR VĀṆĪS

The measure of authenticity to be attributed to the various recensions of the *Kabīr-vāṇī*s or 'the Sayings of Kabīr', is a particularly vexing one. Scholars agree that Kabīr, born towards the middle of the fifteenth century in Benares or in near-by Magahar, as a Muslim weaver, must have been illiterate - or at most half-literate. It is unlikely that he himself wrote down any of his compositions and even more unlikely that he composed any literary work. His famous utterances, couched in a form of old 'Hindui' must, therefore, have been transmitted orally at least one century before they were first written down.[1]

This oral mode of transmission naturally let the door wide open to all kinds of alterations, interpolations and additions - so that the number of verses attributed to Kabīr today may well run into the thousands:

> Like the leaves of a great tree, like the grains of sand in the Ganga
> are the words which came out of Kabīr's mouth.[2]

Besides the numberless oral or written additions to the cherished treasure of Kabīr's Sayings, a number of composed

(1) Cf. P.N. Tiwārī, *Kabīr-vāṇī-saṅgraha,* Allahabad, 1970, p. 120.

(2) *Bī. sā.* 261.

works were attributed to him, especially by the sectarian *Kabīr-panthīs*, 'Kabīr's Followers' - a later sect - who claim to have been founded by Kabīr himself, their now divinized Guru.

The Eastern tradition of Kabīr's Words: *Bījak*

The Kabīr-panthīs' treasure is the *Khās Granth,* whose original manuscript is said to be preserved in the 'Kabīr Chaurā Maṭh' (temple) at Benares, the main center of the Kabīr-panthī sect or 'those who follow the way of Kabīr'. The last book in that compilation, and by far the most revered by the Kabīr-panthīs, is a collection of Kabīr's verses called *Bījak,* literally 'seed' or 'chart' of sacred treasures. Several other manuscripts of that famed compilation are still in the possession of the 'Kabīr Chaurā Maṭh' and some other *maṭh*s belonging to other sections of the same sect elsewhere. However, the Mahants or 'authorities' of such *maṭh*s are reluctant to have them published. The 'original copy' of the *Bījak* in daily use and daily worship at the Kabīr-Chaurā *maṭh* appears to be an old lithographed copy of one of those manuscripts.

Supposed to represent the authentic Kabīr-panthī tradition of Kabīr's verses as prevalent in Eastern Uttar Pradesh and in Central India, the *Bījak* may be taken as representative of the 'Eastern' recension of the Kabīr-*vāṇīs* - as opposed to fairly ancient recensions of the same, current in Western India. The *Bījak* itself has come down to us in two main forms: a longer and a shorter form. Yet, even in its shorter form, the text cannot be accepted as totally genuine, as shown by Parashuram Chaturvedi and other Kabirian scholars: the *Bījak* not only includes a number of meaningless and obviously corrupt verses, but it also contains numerous references to the elaborate cosmogony and religious beliefs peculiar to the sectarian Kabīr-panthīs themselves.

The 'Bārābānkī' edition of Kabīr's Words includes 84 *rāmainī*s[3] and 115 *śabda*s, followed by an acrostic composition called *Bipramacautīsī.* Then follow 12 poems called *Kahāra, Basant, Cancarī, Belī, Birahulī* and *Hindolā,* evidently modelled on popular types of folk-songs. After the *pad*s or 'songs' comes a list of 353 *sākhī*s or *dohā*s.[4] The edition also includes a glossary and lists of interpretations relating to symbolical numbers, similies and allegorical allusions, which are found in the *Bījak* text as it has come down to this day. The 'Bārābānkī edition' has been reprinted many times with a modern Hindī paraphrase (*ṭikā*): that *ṭikā* was the work of a Kabīrpanthī scholar, who called himself Sadhu Abhilashdas.

The collection of satirical verses and paradoxical utterances called *ulṭabāmsī* in the *Bījak* are particularly striking. In spirit and style, they match rather well with similar utterances found in the other two main recensions of Kabīr's verses compiled in Northwestern India. But the *Bījak* verses have been largely interpolated: it has become a separate tradition, which we call the 'Eastern tradition' of Kabīr's verses.

As the major authoritative collection of Kabīr's verses in the hands of the Kabīr-panthīs, the *Bījak* early attracted the attention of Western missionaries and scholars, from the nineteenth century onwards. A first attempt at editing and translating some of it in English was made by the Reverend Prem Chand, as early as 1890; another English translation of the *Bījak* by the Reverend Ahmed Shah, a local clergyman who happened to be a Christian convert, appeared in 1917.

(3) 84 is a sacred number in Indian tradition.

(4) *Sākhī* means 'testimony': it is an equivalent of *śIok* or *saloku,* a two-lines utterance; *dohā,* or *duhā,* an equivalent of *sākhī,* means 'a couplet'.

None of the first translators were very successful, and the result of their efforts is hardly understandable to the Western reader today. Yet, those early attempts at deciphering and translating Kabīr's purported 'Sayings' were a witness to the newly-awakened interest for his teachings among the first generation of Christian missionaries in India.[5]

Ahmed Shah and the *Bījak*

Ahmed Shah's own appreciation of Kabīr's religious and philosophical thought in his 'Introduction' is fairly balanced. Like other Christian writers before him, he believes that 'religious toleration and the brotherhood of mankind' were among the chief lessons that Kabīr had set himself to inculcate - but he does not commit himself on the question of a possible Christian influence. Yet, he underlines Kabīr's originality: "Though thoughts resembling his are to be found in the writings of Hindu philosophers, and also in the words of Muslim Sufis of all ages, yet the presentation of them is peculiarly his own".[6]

Ahmed Shah admits that Kabīr was brought up as a Muslim Julāhā, but he remarks upon the latter's considerable knowledge of Hindu concepts and practices, as well as of Puranic mythology, relying on a number of passages in the *Bījak,* which he evidently regards as representing the essence of Kabīr's authentic teachings. On the other hand, Ahmed

---

(5) K.F. Keay, as well as other Christian missionaries did not believe that Kabīr himself came into contact with Christians or knew anything of Christian teachings, but he considered as 'almost certain' that the Bhakti movement as a whole, to which (according to him) Kabīr belonged, was influenced by Christian ideas. His views were accepted by George Grierson. See F.E. Keay, *Kabīr and his Followers,* Calcutta, 1931, p. 172.

(6) Ahmad Shah, *The Bijak of Kabīr,* Hamirpur, 1917, p. 36.

Shah remarks on the scant knowledge of the doctrines of Islam revealed by Kabīr in the *Bījak*: for him, "the contrast between Kabīr's intimate acquaintance with Hindu thought, writings and ritual and his purely superficial knowledge of Moslem beliefs revealed in the *Bījak* are too striking to be ignored".[7]

The same author, therefore, seeks an explanation for Kabīr's expansive knowledge of Hindu tradition and beliefs in his contact with his purported Guru, Rāmānand, in whose company Kabīr is supposed to have spent a considerable time. In this, he agrees with the *Kabīrpanthī*s, or 'those who follow the path of Kabīr' and also with the Hindu tradition as a whole - in accordance with which he even admits that the weaver Kabīr was born a Hindu! Ahmed Shah suggests that it was because Indian Muslims welcomed Kabīr's efforts in combating idol-worship that they claimed him as a Muslim - and they went so far as acknowledging him as a *pīr,* a Muslim Sufi or saint, for his self-denying and pious life.[8]

Ahmed Shah's English translation of the *Bījak* was hailed by Grierson with enthusiasm, not so much for its literary achievement - which was rather poor - as for Kabīr's extraordinary personality:

> What a wonderful man Kabīr must have been! A lowly Muslim weaver who by a stratagem gained accession to a Vaishnav community - universally despised and hated by both Mussalman and Hindu, maltreated by the Muslim emperor and persecuted by the Brahmanhood of Benares - with unparalleled audacity he dared to set himself face to face against

(7) *Ibidem,* p. 40.

(8) The desperate efforts of Ahmed Shah, himself Muslim-born, and some others, to prove that Kabīr was indeed Hindu-born, appears puzzling. But the fact is that, as a convert, it is more difficult to be a Hindu convert than a Muslim convert, at least in India.

both Islam and Hinduism, the two religions of the 15th century India, and won through. Each he attacked in its tenderest point - its shibboleths and its rituals - and over both rode triumphant, teaching and converting thousands who became his devoted followers. Not only did he found an eclectic monotheism that survives in India till the present day, but he became the spiritual father of Nānak who founded Sikhism.

The *Gurū Granth* or *Ādi Granth* of the Sikhs

The two other ancient and important compilations of Kabīr's verses originated from Northwestern India: in Panjab and Rajasthan. It is apparently in those areas that the *Kabīr-vāṇīs* made the greatest impact on both the Hindu and the Muslim masses, and that his teachings were enthusiastically received, assimilated and later written down. Several religious sects were founded in those regions, at least from the sixteenth century onwards, which were directly or indirectly influenced by Kabīr's teachings: such were the *Dādūpanthī* and the *Naranjanī* sects of Rajasthan, and the *Sikh Panth* in the Panjab. The latter, founded by Guru Nānak in the early sixteenth century, evolved into a religion independent from Hinduism proper.

The teachings of Guru Nānak and the four Gurus who were his immediate successors were gathered into a large compilation which was known as the *Ādi Granth,* literally 'The Original Book'. The *Ādi Granth,* the sacred scripture of the Sikhs, was later called *Gurū Granth.* It includes a collection of 243 *saloku*s or *ślok*s attributed to Kabīr.[9] It is a very important document and the only one which can be dated with precision:

---

(9) The 243 *saloku*s attributed to Kabīr in the *Gurū Granth* (pp. 1364-1377) are immediately followed by the 130 *saloku*s attributed to the famous saint Shaykh Farīd (pp. 1377-1384).

1604. The *Gurū Granth* is free from the Kabīr-panthī sectarian element which imbues a part of the *Bījak,* and its authenticity is the best established of all. Yet, some *pad*s, especially those which recall Kabīr's miraculous escapes from various attempts on his life, or the legend of the Vaishnav saint and martyr Prahlād, have a hagiographical character. Allusions to the mythical great Bhaktas (devotees) of yore, such as the holy bird Shukdev, the Vaishnav saint and martyr Prahlād and the learned monkey Hanumān, do not fit in with Kabīr's radical rejection of Brahmanical scriptures and Hindu lore.

According to Sikh tradition, the compilation of the *Ādi Granth* was completed in 1604 and the sacred Book was installed in the Sikh temple at Amritsar by Guru Arjan Singh himself.[10] A second recension of the *Granth,* including a few additions by Guru Bhai Banno, did not meet with Guru Arjan Singh's approval and remained, therefore, confined to its author's descendants. The third and final recension, including the sayings of the ninth Guru, Tegh Bahādur Singh, was dictated to Mani Bhāi Singh by the tenth Guru of the sect, Govind Singh, who died in 1708 AD.

Before he died, Guru Govind Singh had passed the 'Guruship' of the Sikhs to the *Ādi Granth* itself, which then became known as the *Śrī Gurū Granth Sāhib* and was enshrined in the Golden temple at Amritsar. Govind Singh bode the Sikhs henceforth to obey the *Granth Sāhib,* held as identical with the 'visible body of the Guru'.[11] He is said to have refused to add his own compositions into the sacred Book - the only additions he tolerated being the verses composed by the

(10) Cf. Teja Singh and Ganda Singh, *A Short History of the Sikhs,* vol. 1, p. 33.

(11) Quoted in S.S. Kolhi, *A Critical Study of the Ādi Granth,* Delhi, repr. 1976, p. 19.

ninth Guru. The Sikhs consider their *Śrī Gurū Granth Sāhib* as identical with the original Granth, the *Ādi Granth,* once compiled in the *gurumukhī* script by Guru Arjan Singh.

Besides the *pad*s (songs) and the *saloku*s (*ślok*s), taken as an equivalent of *dohā,* and composed by the Sikh Gurus, the *Gurū Granth* includes a very large number of verses attributed to a number of ancient, (pre-Nānak), Hindu and Muslim saints: the latter are revered by the Sikhs, as some kind of spiritual precursors to the final revelation embodied in the compositions of Guru Nānak and the first Sikh Gurus. In the *Gurū Granth,* those saints are called *bhagat*s (*bhakta*s) or 'devotees'. The Bhagats are staunch monotheists: they uphold the right type of *bhakti* or 'Devotion to the supreme God', without any concession to idol worship.

The 'Bhagats' mentioned in the Gurū Granth belonged to various times, but, as a whole, they may be dated from the fourteenth to the early sixteenth centuries AD. The tradition gives Jaydev (or Jayadeva) as the earliest, but his time and location remain uncertain. Macauliffe believes that the 'Jaydev' who is held as the author of two hymns found in the Granth, is the same as the famed Sanskrit poet who composed the *Gīta Govinda,* in the second part of the twelfth century AD - but this appears very unlikely. As to *Rāmānand,* a high caste Brahman: according to the *Gurū Granth* tradition he was born around 1400 AD and lived in the early part of the fifteenth century, so that he may have been Kabīr's own guru, which however is very unlikely.

Farquhar believes that Rāmānand belonged to an ancient Ramaite sect in South India, and that he was the author of the *Adhyātma Rāmāyaṇ.* Neither Grierson nor Parashuram Chaturvedi, however, accept Farquhar's view about Rāmānand - the latter being sometimes represented as Kabīr's own guru, and sometimes as a dealer of magic spells. The present Rāmānandīs, as high caste Brahmans, composed books in Sanskrit.[12] Two Hindī *pads* compiled by the Dādū-panthī Rajab, are found in the *Sarvāṅgī* and one of them found its way in the *Gurū Granth.*[13]

Some particularities of the *Gurū Granth*

In the *Gurū Granth,* as written by the scribe Bhāī Gurdās under Guru Arjan's dictation, the words were not divided off, as is customary in Indian manuscripts. Modern editions are now printed under the supervision of the Gurudvārā at Amritsar, both in the Gurmukhī and the Nāgarī characters. In all those editions, the original disposition is rigorously kept - but for the division of the words: the *verse numbering* and even the *page numbering* always remain the same. The cutting of the words, however, appears sometimes doubtful. Another difficulty stems out of the composition of the *Gurū Granth* itself, whose intricacies make it difficult for the non-initiate to discover and pick out the verses of the Bhagats - or, for that matter, of any particular Guru. Indication of the page number is, therefore, necessary when referring to a particular verse.

In the *Gurū Granth,* the distichs (*dohās*), called *salokus (ślok)* are found listed together in a continuous series, without any classification according to the theme - and the *saloku*-list occurs after the *pads* of the last *rāg.*[14] In the treatment of the *dohās*, the *Gurū Granth* recension agrees with the *Bījak* (in

---

(12) Cf. Vaudeville, *Haripāṭh,* pp. 74-76, 'Nivṛtti et la Religion du Nom'. In the Maharashtrian tradition, Rāmānand is supposed to have been the Guru of Viṭṭhalpanth, (Jñāneshvar's father) in Kashi.

(13) *Basant,* 1, p. 1195.

(14) *Rāg* or *rāgu* refers to a specific mode of singing.

which the *dohās* are called *sākhīs*, lit. 'witnesses'), but it contrasts with the *Kabīr-granthāvalī* recension, in which the *sākhīs* are classified into *aṅgas* or chapters, according to the subject-matter.

As to the poems (*pads*) *Gurū Granth,* they are found classified under thirty-one different *rāgs*, or musical modes, beginning with *sirī rāgu* (*Śrī rāg*) and ending with *jaijāvantī rāgu.* At the end of each *rāg,* the poems to be sung by the Bhagats in that particular *rāg* are listed immediately after the last of the poems composed by the Sikh Gurus.

The near totality of the *salokus* attributed to Kabīr in the *Gurū Granth* begin with the name of the presumed author, Kabīr, accompanied by the so-called *bhaṇitā* 'Says Kabīr'.

It is apparently to alleviate the difficulties encountered by non-specialists, and to make the *Gurū Granth* collection of Kabīr's verses available to Indian students that R.K. Varma published a collection of his verses, entitled *Sant Kabīr* (Allahabad, 1947), together with an Introduction in Hindī.[15]

Within the collection of poems attributed to the *Bhagats* in the *Gurū Granth,* the 'Words of the Bhagat Kabīr' are invariably listed first, Kabīr taking precedence even over the older saint Nāmdev.

As we have seen, poems attributed to Kabīr in the *Gurū Granth* are found classified in seventeen different *rāgs*. As to the longer compositions attributed to him, they are found at the end of *gaurī rāgu,* the second and the longest section in the whole of the *Gurū Granth.* A composition in the form of an

(15) Unfortunately, the comparison of R.K. Varma with the text shows a fantastic amount of copying - or printing - mistakes. As to the added *ṭīkā,* it is only a popular one, and the author made no attempt to elucidate the obscure passages in the text. Moreover, references to the relevant page numbers in the *Gurū Granth* (1364-1377) are missing.

acrostic poem called *Bāvan akharī*, literally 'The fifty-two letters', also includes *tithi* (list of lunar dates) and *vār*, or 'Weekdays'. What makes the use of the *Gurū Granth* even more puzzling to the non-initiate is the confusion in terms. Short poems known as *pad*s in Hindī poetical tradition are also referred to as either *śabda* or *pāürī*, the latter literally meaning the 'rung of a ladder'. But various compositions with a given *rāg* are classified according to the number of *pad*s they include, as *dupade* (two *pads*), *tipade* (three *pads*) and so on - the longest being the *aṣṭapadī* (eight *pad*s) and the *solhā* (sixteen *pad*s).

Most of the *pad*s attributed to Kabīr in the *Gurū Granth* are made of two to four stanzas, including a refrain. Each given stanza is made of either two long lines rhyming together or four short lines and two rhymes.

The refrain itself, *rahāü*, is usually made of two short lines, or one short and one long line rhyming together. The refrain is invariably included in the first stanza and is never numbered separately, so that it constitutes either the two first lines or the two last lines of the poem. All those peculiarities, plus a number of unwarranted variations within the general pattern, may well drive the non-specialist (and even the specialist) to despair, and drive him to resort to the Macauliffe translation! Yet those short, naive utterances have a charm of their own:

O Madhao! In water, I couldn t quench my thirst:
in that water, a huge fire has sprung up
You are the Water, and I, the little sea-fish,
in water I live, yet, for Water I pine!

The *Kabīr-granthāvalī* recension

The so-called *Kabīr-granthāvalī* recension essentially coincides with the *Dādū-panthī* tradition of Kabīr's sayings - a tradition which developed in Rajasthan, and may also be called the 'Rajasthani' recension of the *Kabīr-vāṇīs*. This tradition goes back to Dādū Dayāl, a low-caste Muslim like Kabīr. He was a *dhuniyā* or cotton-carder from Ahmedabad, who settled in Rajasthan and flourished in the second half of the sixteenth century. The recorded *vāṇīs* of Dādū Dayāl show a close dependence on Kabīr's thought and style. Besides Kabīr, their purported founder, the Dādū-panthīs hold Nāmdev, Ravidās and Haridās as their most revered saints.

The *Pañc-vāṇī* literature composed by the Dādū-panthīs of Rajasthan is based on the words of the 'Five Saints' among whom the most prominent (apart from the founder Dādū himself) is Kabīr. It was found that the two manuscripts on which Shyam Sundar Das based his edition of the *Kabīr-granthāvalī* closely followed the texts found in the *Pañc-vāṇīs* of Rajasthan. Both, therefore, are considered as belonging to the same tradition.[16]

The standard edition of the so-called *Kabīr-granthāvalī* is the above-mentioned S.S. Das edition (often referred to in India as 'the *Sabhā* edition'), which was reprinted a number of times. This edition, which we have referred to as 'KG1' includes 811 *sākhīs* (or *dohās*) classified into 59 *aṅgas*, 'parts' or 'chapters', whose length may vary from 2 to 62 *sākhīs*. The KG1 *pad* collection, placed after the *sākhīs*, includes 403 *pads*, classified under 16 *rāgs* - each of which may include any number of *pads*. The third and last section of KG1 also includes a very large number of *ramainīs*: a case of *inflation galopante*! It is not possible to ascertain the number of such

(16) The date ascribed by S.S. Das to his first manuscript (*ka*) has been disproved (Vaudeville:1974, pp. 19-20), but it is a valuable manuscript of the so-called Rajasthani tradition.

ramainīs and the so-called *pads* within the *ramainīs* are not numbered.

Clearly, the 'standard edition' of the *Kabīr-granthāvalī* (KG1) compiled by S.S. Das was of little value: the editor had done little more than reproducing his first manuscript (*ka*), adding in the footnotes the extra verses found in the second manuscript (*kha*). In the Appendix are listed the verses (*sākhīs*, *pads* and *ramainīs*) found in the *Gurū Granth* and nowhere else. But references to the text are not given.

Though the first of the two manuscripts on which S.S. Das based the 1928 edition is not as ancient as he himself thought, it is a valuable manuscript which, when compared with the *Pañc-vāṇī* manuscripts, gives a fair idea of the contents of the Dādū-panthī or Rajasthani tradition of the Kabīr-vāṇīs. The comparison, however, was not undertaken by S.S. Das himself and the title he gave to his edition: *Kabīr-granthāvalī,* was somewhat misleading, since it only gave the text of the first *Nāgarī Pracāriṇī Sabhā* manuscript, with variant readings found in the second manuscript in the foot-notes. This edition, which for a long time, remained the only printed text of the main tradition of Kabīr's verses, was reprinted a number of times. Later, different *ṭīkās* or paraphrases of the S.S. Das text appeared, published by various Indian scholars. None of such *ṭīkās*, unfortunately, is of much help.

Another important compilation of Kabīr's verses is that found in the *Sarbāṅgī* of the poet Rajab, from Sanganer in Rajasthan, who was the foremost disciple of Dādū Dayāḷ in the middle of the sixteenth century. The *Sarbāṅgī* compilation includes sayings of sixty-six Siddhas and saints, whose verses are divided, according to the subject, into 144 *aṅgas* (chapters). The collection of verses found in the *Sarbāṅgī* includes 337 verses: though it is much shorter than the Pañc-vāṇī manuscripts, it clearly belongs to the same tradition. The *Sarbāṅgī* seems to contain an epitome of what is generally called the Dādū-panthī or Rajasthani tradition of Kabīr's verses.[17]

The first, and so far the sole attempt at a critical edition of Kabīr's verses, was the work of a young scholar of the Allahabad University, Dr. Parasnath Tiwārī. His edition was first published in 1961, by the University of Allahabad under the same title: *Kabīr-granthāvalī.* It is the P.N. Tiwārī edition of the *Kabīr-granthāvalī* that we refer to as 'KG2'.[18] The method adopted by the author was to retain and include, in his own edition, *all the verses* he found in *two* or *more* independent *pāṭh*s, (i.e. readings), giving the references in the footnotes and classifying the numerous variants found in the texts. This enormously painstaking effort was only partly successful: some of the eleven *pāṭh*s obviously were not worth much (especially the older printed compilations) - and not to be treated on a par with the *Bījak,* the *Gurū Granth* and the best manuscripts in the Rajasthani tradition. This methodological error led to the acceptance, in 'KG2', of a large number of verses of doubtful authenticity.

The comparison of the three recensions of the Kabīr *vāṇī*s, namely the Eastern recension (represented by the *Bījak*) and the two Western recensions, (namely the Panjabi *Gurū Granth*) and the Rajasthani (called *Kabīr-granṭhāvalī*) recensions, clearly brings out the fact that, on the whole, the tradition of the *sākhī*s and *ślok*s of Kabīr, is better established and more coherent than that of his *pad*s. The comparison be-

(17) Four manuscripts have been critically studied and partially translated into English by Winand M. Callewaert:. *The Sarvāṅgī of the Dādūpanthī Rajab,* Leuven, 1978. The *Sarvāṅgī* means: 'all the *aṅgas*', brought together by Rajab.

(18) In opposition to the S.S. Das edition: 'KG1'.

tween the three recensions also brings out the fact that, the shorter the poem, the more likely it is to be found in two - or even in all the three recensions. This tends to confirm the presumption that the original verses composed by Kabīr were either in the form of distichs (*sākhī*s or *ślok*s), or in the form of short compositions (*pad*s), probably not exceeding four or five rhyming verses, in which the first or the last line was used as a refrain. It becomes clear that the longer poems found in one or the other of the three recensions are either spurious or heavily interpolated.

In the *Bījak* and the *Gurū Granth,* the *dohā*s (whether called *sākhī* or *saloku*) are found jumbled together without any apparent order. In the Dādū-panthī or Rajasthani recession, they are classified into *aṅgas,* i.e. 'chapters', according to the subject matter - such as *'Guru kau aṅg', 'Viraha kau aṅg'* etc. P. Chaturvedi is of the opinion that this division might have been an innovation introduced by Rajjab.[19] Yet precedents can be found in ancient Indian literatures: in the *Dhammapada,* a Pali text belonging to the Buddhist canon, the so-called *gāthā*s are classified into *vaggo*s (Skt *varga*) according to the subject. In Indian medieval poetry, the short lyrics known as *pad*s are traditionally classified according to the *rāg,* the type of melody in which they are to be sung. In the *Gurū Granth,* each *rāg* includes first the *pad*s composed by Guru Nanak - by far the longest list - then the words composed by the other Sikh Gurus, and finally those composed by holy men, the *Bhagats.* In the *Bījak,* the poems, called *sabads* (*śabda*s), meaning 'holy utterances', are also chanted, though the *rāg* is not indicated in the text. The 'Dādū-panthī' or Rajasthani tradition seems to hesitate: the *pad*s are sometimes classified under a particular *rāg,* as in the *Gurū Granth,* and sometimes treated as non-

(19) Chaturvedi, *KSP,* p. 78.

musical utterances. The *Bījak* includes a large number of so-called 'Ramainīs' and 'Shabads' (*śabda*) composed in the *caupāī* metre. Such *ramainī*s mostly appear in didactic compositions. Besides the *sākhī*s, *śabda*s and *ramainī*s, the *Bījak* includes a few long poems with particular rhythms, named after popular folksongs and dances, such as *Basant, Camcar* (or *Carcari*) and *Hindola:* those songs are meant to impart spiritual teachings in the form of simple village songs or short rhymed ballads. It is difficult to ascertain whether such compositions can be ascribed to Kabīr. They are only found in the *Bījak*.

Experience has shown us that the greatest hurdle to be confronted by Kabirian scholars is the lingering uncertainty about the relative value and degree of authenticity to be accorded to any given verse. Another hurdle consists in the non-existence of cross-references between the main recensions: for instance, a Hindī scholar trying to read the Kabīr *ślok*s in the *Gurū Granth* text has no way of knowing if a particular verse is found anywhere else attributed to Kabīr, and under which form. If he manages to lay his hand on the KG2 edition, he cannot ascertain whether a particular verse finds a correspondent in the *Gurū Granth* or in the *Bījak* recensions, since lists of the few verses common to all the three recensions are nowhere to be found.

In presenting in a single volume the three principal texts of the *Kabīr-vāṇīs,* our intention has been to make those treasures available to the scholars concerned and to all 'Friends of Kabīr'. But such a compilation would have been of limited value without fairly reliable Concordance-Tables. The author, therefore, endeavoured to establish such Concordances, which are printed at the end of the volume.

We sincerely hope that our endeavour will not be in vain and that it will encourage Indologists with an interest in Indo-Aryan literatures and/or medieval Hinduism to attempt a direct approach to the *Sayings of Kabīr,* the most quoted - and also the most misquoted - of all the great Indian poets and mystics.

RAMAINĪS AND ŚABDAS IN THE BĪJAK

THE RAMAINĪS

1

ram. 77

First of all, invoke Him in your soul:
  there is none that to Him may be equalled.
None can find His limits,
  none has ever found his beginning or end.
Formed or formless He cannot be said,
  light or heavy He cannot be weighed.
He knows neither hunger nor thirst,
    neither sunshine nor shadow:
  in all, He remains void of pleasure or pain.

  Unmanifested, boundless, the Brahman
    is pure knowledge,[1] all-pervading:
  With much pondering, I came to understand
    that there is none like Rām.

2

ram. 75

He[2] never took birth in King Dasharath's lineage
  nor did He punish the King of Lankā [Rāvaṇ].

---

(1) *gyānarūpa,* lit.: 'in the form of Knowledge'.

(2) The whole *pad* ridicules the Vaishnav belief in the many *avatārs* of the supreme Being.

He never was a *shaligrām* stone in the river Gaṇḍaka,
nor a wild Boar,
Nor did He play in water with Fish or Tortoise.
He never uprooted Mount Govardhan, holding it up high,
nor did he roam the forest in the milk-men's company,
He didn't leave his body at Dvarka,
nor was his mortal frame buried at Jagannath![3]

Says Kabīr,
all these are but vain tales:
Far beyond such fables
is He who pervades the universe.

3

ram. 35

Reading and pondering on the Veda, the Pandits went astray:
the mystery of their own self, they never pierced!
Evening rites and libations, the six prescribed acts:
to such practices they cling, and to their stages of life!
In all the four ages, they keep teaching their *Gāyatrī*.[4]
tell me, when did they reach salvation?
You pride yourself on your exalted virtues,

---

(3) According to popular belief, after Krishna was cremated at Dvarka, his ashes were committed to the sea. From the sea emerged a bright *pinda* (lit.: a 'ball', as an offering to the dead) or a 'bodily form', which eventually reached the shore of Puri-Jagannath, in Orissa, where the 'body' was cremated. This legend seems to allude to a double funeral for Krishna: both a Kshatriya's and a Yogi's funeral.

(4) Originally a simple invocation to the Sun, the *Gāyatrī* became regarded as a mystical formula of universal power, and the most sacred verse in Hindu scripture.

but such boasting won't do you any good:
He whose very Name is the Crusher of Pride
how will he bear your insolence?
Give up your caste pride,
seek the stage of Annihilation:[5]
Once both seed and sprout[6] are gone,
then only you'll enter the supreme Stage![7]

4

ram. 23

Fleeting instants of happiness - and then endless pain:
this Mind is crazy, like an elephant in heat!
As the moth gets burnt up by the flame of the lamp
just to gratify its eyes,
He who sought pleasure and comfort
never found any:
Through greed, he has ruined his life
and now the end draws near:
Death comes all of a sudden.
Having obtained a human birth,
Why did he squander it?

---

(5) *pad nirbān* or the Nirvan stage: for Kabīr, an equivalent of the 'Sahaj' state.

(6) The body is the sprout and the seed is the *karma,* which causes the Jīv to be born again and again.

(7) Lit.: 'the stage of being bodiless': this 'bodiless' stage is identical with the *sahaj* state.

5

ram. 19

They crave for the Experience of the Anāhad:[8]
  see the bizarre show they put up!
Watch that comedy, O my Brother:
  they've departed for a place they call 'Void'!
Longing for the Void, they went to emptiness,
  loòsing their grip, they remained empty-handed.
The whole world is a prey to Doubt.
  The Hunter, Kāl,[9] hunts from morning to night.
    Invoke the Name of Rām!
      Kāl holds you by the hair:
    Who knows where he will strike you,
      either at home or abroad?

6

ram. 7

When there was neither air nor water,
  when no creation has emerged,
Then there was neither body nor dwelling,[10]
  neither earth nor sky,
When there was neither embryo nor root,
  neither bud nor flower,
When there was neither Word nor flavour,[11]
  neither Science nor Veda,

---

(8) *Anāhat,* a mysterious sound, which preludes to *samādhi.*

(9) *Kāl* is Death.

(10) No dwelling for the body (*piṇḍa*).

(11) *sabada na svāda*: the association seems to be brought about by alliteration: both *śabda,* 'word' and *svād* 'flavour' are connected with the tongue.

Then there was neither Guru nor disciple,
  neither 'Accessible' nor 'Inaccessible':[12] but One Path!

7

ram. 40

Adam, the first Man, never found out
  where Mama Eva had come from!
Then there was neither Turk nor Hindu,
  neither Mother's womb nor Father's seed.
Then there was neither cow nor butcher:
  who was it, who ordered to kill 'in Allah's Name'?[13]
Then there was neither family nor caste:
  that Paradise and that Hell, where do they come from?

If you fancy a thing, it's good,
  If you dislike it, it's no good:
For the enjoyment of the tongue
  So many ways are found!

8

ram. 48

At Manikpur Kab̲īr had stayed:
  there he heard the praise of Shaykh Taqqi.
He heard it again in the town of Jaunpur

---

(12) *gam agam* refers to the two aspects of the supreme Reality, which are *saguṇ* and *nirguṇ*.

(13) *bisamilla,* Arabic 'Bismillah' (lit.: "In God's Name"). For Kabīr, the Koranic rule about the butchering of an animal has no other ground than man's own greediness: God has nothing to do with it.

and at Jhusi he heard the names of the Pīrs.[14]

The names of twenty-one Pīrs are written there,
people hear the *khatma*[15] and the Prophet's Name:
Listening to them, I couldn't bear,
looking at those tombs, I lost my head!
God's Friend, the Prophet and the Prophet's deeds:
All that's based on their authority is illegitimate![16]

9

ram. 61

The makers of pious tales,
everyday get up early to tell lies -
Morning lies, evening lies:
in their heart, nothing but lies!
Of the mystery of Rām they know nothing,
they've concocted a religion of Vedas and Puranas -
The injunction of the Veda, they don't even observe:
the fire burns for ever.
They go singing the praise of the Ineffable
while they bring about their own perdition:
This body of earth mixes with earth
and the breath of air with air.

---

(14) A saintly man, a spiritual guide, an equivalent of the Hindu Guru.

(15) Ar. *khatma*: the recitation of the Koran from beginning to end.

(16) *haram* forbidden by the Koranic law.

10

ram. 31

He who, in this Kali Age, taught the *Kalimā*[17]
could never understand God's Power.
Wonderful are the deeds of the All-merciful -
worthless the Veda and the Koran!
False is the Koranic Law and the sacred Thread[18]
neither Turk nor Hindu ever grasped that mystery.
The enigma of the Mind, they cannot unravel -
yet, in their folly, they keep talking of two Religions!
From a mixture of earth and water
was this universe born:
When the Śabda is re-absorbed into the Void,
what then will 'Caste' mean?

11

ram. 32

Vedas and Puranas are the Mirror of the blind -
Could the spoon taste the savour of food?
Like an ass loaded with sandal-wood,
the poor beast, could he enjoy the sweet perfume?

Says Kabīr, in vain did they search the depths of the sky:
never did they meet Him who could cure them of their pride!

---

(17) *Kalimā*: the Muhammedan profession of Faith.

(18) The sacred thread *janeu* (Skt *upavīta)*, worn by men belonging to the three higher *varṇs*, symbolizes Hinduism, as the Koranic Law, the *sunnat*, embodies the tenets of Islam.

12

KG2 ram. 10; Bī ram. 26

In the fire of the womb,
  He cooked them all,
All the while taking
  good çare of them -
And when they came out
  of His oven,
He called them
  either 'Shiva' or 'Shakti'.[19]

---

(19) Shiva and Shakti, of course, stand for Man and Woman.

Such a sarcastic, pessimistic *śabda* is found both in the *Bījak* (*ram.* 26) and in the *Kabīr-granthāvalī, ramainī* 10. God Himself, here called *'Kartā'*, literally 'the Creator', is compared to a Potter who makes only one kind of pots - though He takes care to paint them in different colours and He gives them different names.

THE ŚABDAS

1

śabda 103

As water mixes with water,
so will Kabīr mix with dust.

If Mithila be your true home,[20]
let your death be at Magahar.
He who dies at Magahar becomes an ass, they say:
so, have you lost faith in Rām?
Dying in Magahar, you won't know death,
Dying elsewhere, you'll put Rām to shame.
What is Kashi? What is the barren land of Magahar,
so long as Rām dwells in your heart?
If Kabīr leaves his body at Kashi,
what honour will he render Rām?

2

śabda 108

Now I have become like a fish out of water,
priding myself on the austerities of my former lives:
Then I had been a *Bairāgī* in soul,
renouncing both world and family, I stuck to Rām.

I had left Kashi - so foolish was I!
O Lord of my life, tell me, what will be my fate?
Am I a bad servant or are You ungrateful?

---

(20) The town of Mithila prides on its reputed scholars, and Magahar is known as a particularly wretched locality: hence the sarcasm.

which one of us is to blame, O Lord?

I have come to seek refuge in You -
but nowhere do I see Hari's feet!
I have come to seek your Presence:
your servant Kabīr is in despair!

3

śabda 47

O Pandit! Be careful about your water!
In this mud-house where you're sitting,
are the remains of all living beings:

Here fifty-six crores of Jadons[21] drowned in water,
together with eighty-eight thousand sages -
At every step there are prophets buried,
all of them rotted and mixed with earth.

From that very earth is your pot made, O Pañde:
Be careful about the water you drink!

Fishes, tortoises and crocodiles have given birth therein:
your water is full of their blood -
That river-water flows straight down to hell:
beasts and men, all have rotten in it!

Oozing from their bones, the marrow dissolved in it:
where could milk-like water be found?
Taking that water in your palm, you sit to your meal, O Pande,
and you pollute earth itself!

---

(21) The Jādons (*Yādav*) were known as a multitude of heroic fighters.

Put away that Veda and those holy books, O Pande:
  all that is but foolishness:
Says Kabīr, O Pande, listen!
  It's all the effect of your own *karma*.

4

śabda 44

Think it over, Pandit, and tell me:
  is she male or female?
In the Brāhman's house, she is a Brāhminī,
  in the Yogi's house, a disciple.
Reciting the *Kalimā*[22] she became a Turk
  and in this *Kali Age* she remains alone.
She stays in her own home,
  she doesn't sleep with her Lord:
Says Kabīr, she[23] lives for ever
  to destroy and ruin all families.

5

śabda 35

Hari is my Husband and I, his little wife -
  He is very big and I so small!
Hari is my spinning-wheel, and I, the little spinner:
  invoking Rām's Name, she's spun, the little wife.

By lengths of six months, she's spun the whole skein of life -

---

(22) The *Kalimā* is the Mohammedan profession of faith; the *Kali Age* is the sinful age in which we live.

(23) The mysterious woman is Greed.

and people say: "How well she's spun, that poor little one!"

Says Kabīr, for sure, she's spun a beautiful thread -
but it was not the Wheel, it was her Lord who saved her.

6

śabda 36

Hari, like a Brigand, has robbed the whole world,
yet, without Hari, how can I live, O Brother?
Who has a husband? Who has a wife?
Death encompassed all-untellable story!
Who has a son? Who has a father?
Who is dying, who is enduring pain?
The Thug has robbed them all -
yet none has guessed Rām's brigandage:
Says Kabīr, of that Brigand I am enamoured,
and the brigandage was over
when I recognized the Brigand.[24]

7

śabda 104

How shall I escape, O Lord? How shall I escape,
loaded as I am with sins!
How shall I serve You, how shall I meditate on You?
See, I am like the crane - white on top!
See, my nature is vicious like that of the snake,
my devotion is not sincere, I am treacherous as a cat!
See, my soul is full of hatred and folly,

(24) The 'Brigand' is God.

enclosed in the veil of the six systems.[25]
Says Kabīr, O you, Hari's servants, listen:
The whole world has fallen in the snares of the Witch![26]

8

śabda 103

People, you are fools!
As water mixes with water,
so will Kabīr mix with earth.

If you are a true scholar of Mithila,
why don't you go and die in Magahar?

Dying in Magahar, one becomes an ass, they say:
So, have you lost faith in Rām?
Dying in Magahar, you won't know death,
dying elsewhere, you'll put Rām to shame.

What is Kashi? What is the wasteland of Magahar
if Rām dwells in my heart?
If Kabīr dies in Kashi,
what honour will he bring Rām?

---

(25) The six *darśan* are the six principal systems of philosophy.

(26) The Witch is Māyā.

9

śabda 106

The blackbee[27] has taken flight,
the white[28] duck has come:
She trembles, she trembles, the little soul:
I don't know what will my Beloved[29] do?

In the unbaked pot,[30] water can't remain,
when the soul flies away, the body withers:
Putting crows to flight,[31] my arm is aching -
says Kabīr, that's the end of the story.

(27) 'Youth'.

(28) 'Old age'.

(29) 'God'.

(30) 'The human body'.

(31) 'Putting crows to flight' is a way of divination; the direction the crow takes is watched as an omen.

Part Three

Sākhīs

THE SĀKHĪS OF KABĪR[1]

1. S.S. Dās, *Kabīr-granthāvalī,* NPS, Granthamālā, 33, Publ. NPS, Kashi, 5th edition, 1928.
2. P.N. Tiwārī, *Kabīr-granthāvalī,* Hindī Parishad, Prayāg, 1st ed., 1961.

An analysis of the *Kabīr-granthāvalī* shows how the *sākhī*s of Kabīr have undergone an enormous inflation, first in Shyam Sundar Das' and second in Parasnath Tiwārī's *Granthāvalī*. The older work includes 809 *sākhī*s, divided in 59 'Chapters' -whereas the P.N. Tiwārī collection of the same has a little less: 37 chapters and 744 *sākhī*s in all.

Compared to the older S.S. Dās' work, the P.N. Tiwārī collection appears more valuable: the text is carefully printed and the correspondences and variations for each and every *sākhī* are given in the footnotes. Moreover, each of the 744 *sākhī*s in Tiwārī's collection find a correspondence in the Notes - so that any *sākhī* in the *Granthāvalī* can be easily located and compared with the other *sākhī*s.

The Tiwārī text is now accepted as 'standard'. Its peculiarity is that it includes first the 'good'- i.e. the well-established *sākhī*s - and then adds the less valuable and probably spurious ones - which, unfortunately, include by far the greatest num-

(1) Basically, all following *sākhī*s are found in the 'Rājasthānī' recension of Kabīr's Sayings, the *Kabīr-granthāvalī.* For the references in the *Gurū Granth* or in the *Bījak* see App. 1: Concordances.

ber. Apparently unwilling to reject the mass of spurious or less valuable material collected by his former Guru, Tiwārī's device consisted in separating the 'good', (i.e. the 'well-established') *sākhī*s found in each of the 34 chapters from the dubious ones, which were jumbled together at the end of each chapter.[2]

In each of the 34 chapters included in the *Kabīr-granthāvalī*, Tiwārī first introduced the 'good' *sākhī*s found in the *Bījak*, the *Gurū Granth* and, partially the Rajasthani tradition, marked as *Raj*, *Gu* and/or *Bī*, and then dumped all the rest as *Raj* alone: the 'Raj alone' *sākhī*s actually stand as spurious. Our analysis brings out the enormous inflation of Kabīr *sākhī*s in the *Kabīr-granthāvalī*.

(2) In 1974, the present author hesitated to scrape the dubious *sākhī*s because 'Tradition oblige' - which was certainly a mistake. This led to the present edition.

Analysis of the *sākhīs* of Kabīr in the *Kabīr-granthāvalī*[3]

1. The Guru's Greatness:	Raj-Gu-Bī: 5 to 11
	Raj alone: 12 to 55
2. Love in Separation:	Raj-Gu-Bī: 1 to 9
	Raj alone: 10 to 55
3. The Greatness of Prayer:	Raj-Gu: 1 to 5
	Raj alone: 27.
4. In Praise of the Saints:	Raj-Gu: 14
	Raj-Bī 4
	Raj alone: 19 to 43
5. The Search for the Guru's Teaching:	Raj-Gu: 1
	Raj-Bī: 1
	Raj alone: 11
6. Humble Prayer:	Raj-Gu: 1
	Raj alone: 11
7. The Recognition of the Spouse:	*Raj alone*: 12
8. God's Omnipresence:	Raj-Gu: 3
	Raj alone: 14
9. The Experience:	Raj-Gu: 3
	Raj alone: 38
10. The Subtle Path:	Raj-Bī: 6
	Raj-Gu: 1
	Raj alone: 9
11. The Faithful Wife:	Raj-Gu: 2
	Raj-Bī: 4
	Raj alone: 8
12. The Liquor:	*Raj alone*: 9

(3) The *Raj* alone *sākhīs* actually stand as spurious.

	Raj-Bī: 1 sākhī
13. The Creeper:	Raj-Bī: 2
	Raj alone: 1
14. Heroism:	Raj-Gu: 5
	Raj alone: 35
15. Warnings:	Raj-Gu-Bī: 35
	Raj alone: 54
16. Death:	Raj-Gu-Bī: 9
	Raj-Gu: 6
	Raj alone: 25
17. The Root Of Immortality:	Raj-Gu-Bī: 1
	Raj-Gu: 1
	Raj alone: 6
18. The Connoisseur:	Raj-Bī: 2
	Raj-Gu: 1
	Raj alone: 7
19. The Living Dead:	Raj-Gu-Bī: 1
	Raj-Gu: 9
	Raj alone: 7
20. The Middle Path:	Raj-Gu: 4
	Raj-Bī: 9
	Raj alone: 11 to 17
21. True Asceticism:	Raj-Gu-Bī: 1
	Raj-Gu: 3 to 13
	Raj-Bī: 14 to 16
22. Worthless Men:	Raj-Bī: 2 to 4
	Raj alone: 5 to 16
23. Slander:	Raj-Gu: 1
	Raj alone: 2 to 8

24. Companionship:	Raj-Gu: 1 to 6
	Raj-Bī: 7-8
	Raj-Gu-Bī: 9
	Raj-Bī: 10
	Raj alone: 11 to 18
25. Hypocrisy:	Raj-Gu: 1 to 3
	Raj alone: 4 to 7
	Raj-Bī: 8-9
	Raj alone: 10 to 24
26. Dispelling Error:	Raj-Gu: 1 to 3
	Raj-Bī: 4 to 5
	Raj alone: 6 to 11
27. Apprehending The Essence:	Raj-Gu: 3 (?)
28. The Right Intention:	Raj-Gu: 1
	Raj-Bī: 4
	Raj alone: 2 to 5; 7 to 8
29. The Mind:	Raj-Gu: 3
	Raj-Bī: 2
	Raj alone: 5 to 23
30. Sensual Desire:	Raj-Gu: 1
	Raj alone: 2 to 25
31. Māyā:	Raj-Bī: 1, 2
	Raj-Gu-Bī: 1
	Raj alone: 2 to 25
32. Confidence:	Raj-Gu: 1, 2
	Raj alone: 4 to 28
33. Saying and Doing:	Raj-Gu: 1-2
	Raj alone: 3 to 9
34. Sahaj:	*Raj alone*: 1-3

Total: 118 *sākhī*s in Raj-Gu; Raj-Bī; Raj-Gu-Bī against 626 *sākhī*s in '*Raj alone*'.

THE SĀKHĪS OF KABĪR

[A SELECTION]

1. OF THE GURU'S GREATNESS

1. To dispel the darkness of night
   there were eighty-four lakhs of moons:[4]
   Without the Guru, they rose
   and still one could not see.

2. What can the poor Guru do
   if the fault lies with the disciple?
   In vain He tries to waken him
   but He's blowing a bamboo pipe![5]

3. If the Guru be blind,
   the disciple is born blind:
   When the blind is leading the blind,
   both fall into the well.[6]

---

(4) A *lākh* is equal to 100.000; eighty-four is a sacred number. The eighty-four lakhs of moons allude to the traditional number of *yoni*s or bodily forms of existence through which the soul, the *jīv,* must wander before obtaining 'the boon of a human birth'.

(5) The unworthy disciple is compared to a hollow bamboo-pipe, which cannot retain breath.

(6) An old proverb; it is already found in the *Dohā-koṣ* of the Siddha Sarahpā.

4. Doubt has devoured the whole world
 but none has ever eaten Doubt -
Only those pierced by the Guru's Word
 have picked and eaten up Doubt.

5. Let the Guru be the Burnisher,[7]
 let Wisdom be his tool:
Scraping with the scraper of *śabda*
 let Him polish your soul as a mirror.[8]

6. The Satguru is the true Hero,
 who loosed up a single Arrow:
The moment it struck, I fell to the ground
 and a wound opened in my breast.

7. I was drowning but I was saved
 when the Guru's wave rose up:[9]
I saw the vessel fall to pieces
 and I jumped clear!

8. I found stability and salvation
 when the Satguru made me firm -
Kabīr, the Diamond is for sale[10]

---

(7) The mystical *śabda* is here compared to a *cholnā,* an instrument used to clean rust.

(8) The comparison of the human soul to a mirror is very ancient in India. It is already found in the *Śvetāśvatara Upaniṣad* II. 14. Here, rust symbolizes the passions which tarnish the soul.

(9) Literally: 'the Guru's wave flashed'. This sudden flashing of the Guru's 'wave' or whim suggests the sudden illumination of the disciple's soul.

(10) The Diamond, *hīrā,* symbolizes the supreme Reality as well as the Vision or the Experience (*paracā*) which gives access to the supreme stage

on the bank of Mānsarovar.

2. OF LOVE IN SEPARATION

1. Once the snake of Virah[11] has entered the body,
   no *mantra* can control it -
   He who is separated from Rām won't survive,
   or, if he does, he will go mad.

2. The snake of Virah has crept in my body,
   it has bitten the inmost heart,
   Yet the saint does not flinch:
   "Let it bite as it pleases", says he.

3. The Kunjha crane[12] cries plaintively in the sky,
   thunder roars and the ponds are filled -
   But she whom her Lord has deserted
   endures untold torment.

4. The Chakvī bird[13] is separated throughout the night,

---

of *sahaj*. The *mānsarovar* (*mānas-sarovar*) is a celebrated lake in the Himalaya.

(11) *Viraha,* lit.: 'separation', expresses the longing of a soul for an absent lover or husband.

(12) *Kunjha* (Skt *krauñca*): a kind of curlew whose pathetic cry is interpreted as a call to an absent Beloved.

(13) The Chakvī is the female of the Chakvā (Skt *cakravāka*), the 'Brahminy duck', another water-bird. The Chakvā pair are said to be separated from each other all through the night, in which resounds the cry of the Chakvī.

yet at daybreak, she meets her mate -
But those who are separated from Rām
find Him neither by day nor by night.

5. When the flames arose, the wallet was burnt up,[14]
the begging-bowl broke into pieces -
The Jogi who was there has vanished;
ashes alone keep the posture.

6. Parted from the Ocean,
O Conch, wait ! Do not lament:
In every shrine you'll have to cry
at the rising of the Sun![15]

7. Within the heart, a forest-fire is burning
yet no smoke is visible:
He whom it consumes knows that flame
and He who kindled it.[16]

8. The damp log in the flame of Virah
smoulders, spits and smokes:
It won't ever escape from Virah
until it is turned to ashes!

9. The Virahinī stands up and falls again and again,
longing for your Vision, O Rām!

---

(14) The begging-bowl of an ascetic is made of clay; its wallet is a large cloth-bag, which is part of the Kānphaṭ Jogī's paraphernalia.

(15) The conch is blown in every shrine in the early morning, to awaken the Deity.

(16) He who kindled the fire is the *Satguru,* God Himself; the torment of *virah* remains a secret between the soul, the *Virahinī,* and God.

If you grant her the Vision after death,
what use will that be to her?[17]

10. I found a raft made of a snake
in this Ocean of Existence:
If I let go, I'll drown,
if I hang on, it'll bite my arm![18]

11. He who is smitten will die,
even if the dart be blunted:
Moaning, he lies under a tree,
will he die today or tomorrow?[19]

12. That Fire which took to the water
burnt up all the slime
And the Pandits from North and South
died in deliberating.

13. O Physician, go home!
There is nothing you can do:
He who caused that painful disease
He alone can cure it.

14. Do not abuse that Virah,
for Virah is a King -
The body deprived of Virah

---

(17) For Kabīr, salvation can only be achieved *hic et nunc,* within the human body.

(18) The poisonous snake is *virah,* which brings both death and salvation.

(19) The dart of *virah* kills slowly and painfully, as does a blunted shaft.

is for ever a burning-ground![20]

3. OF THE GREATNESS OF PRAYER

1. *Kabīr,* what are you doing, sleeping?
   get up and lament your fate!
   He whose dwelling is in the tomb,[21]
   how can he sleep happily?

2. If you can plunder, then plunder,
   let the Name of Rām be your booty!
   Or else later you'll repent
   when you breathe your last.

3. Call and cry for Keshao,[22]
   do not endlessly sleep!
   If day and night you cry piteously,
   He will hear you in the end.

4. *Kabīr,* it is no easy task
   to invoke Hari's Name:
   As when playing above a stake -[23]

---

(20) This famous *sākhī* is also attributed to Shaykh Farīd in the *Gurū Granth* (*sal.* 36, p. 1379).

(21) *gora mai*: the Persian word *gūr* clearly alludes to burial, in a Muslim context.

(22) *Kesau,* (Skt *keśava*), is another name of Hari-Krishna. It is not used elsewhere in the *sākhīs*.

(23) Allusion to the acrobatics performed by a *naṭ,* a professional dancer and juggler.

he who falls is lost.

5. Repeating 'Thou, Thou', I became Thou,
In me, no 'I' remained:
Offering myself unto thy Name,[24]
wherever I look, Thou art!

4. IN PRAISE OF THE SAINTS

1. *Kabīr,* the Sandal-tree's fragrance
pervades the Dhak-Palāś shrub:[25]
It has made all that surrounded it
the likeness of itself[26].

2. A saint retains his holiness
in the midst of ungodly crowds,
As the Malaya tree retains its coolness
in the embrace of a poisonous snake[27].

---

(24) Doing the *vārī* or *balihārī*: 'self-offering'.

(25) The *Dhak-Palāś* is a useless 'jungle' tree, which, in spring, brings forth red bright flowers.

(26) Just as the Sandal tree's fragrance penetrates even a worthless tree like the Dhak-Palāś, so do the saints' virtues purify even the wicked people who approach them.

(27) This couplet, composed in Kharī Bolī with an admixture of Persian, could have been borrowed from the sayings of some Indian Sufi, who did not care for pilgrimage (Ar. *hajj*). For the Sufis, the ritual performance of the pilgrimage is useless since the Beloved is within: "The Kaaba is in the faithful worshipper's heart".

3. Horses, elephants in plenty,
   royal canopies and fluttering banners:
   Rather beggarliness than such abundance,
   if the beggar never ceases invoking Hari!

4. Beautifully built is that city,
   everywhere full of delights -
   Yet, if it harbours no lover of Rām,
   to me, it's a desert!

5. I have two companions with me,
   one is Rām, the other is the Vaishnav:
   One is the Bestower of salvation,
   the other makes me invoke the Name.

6. *Kabīr,* I was on the way [to the Kaaba]
   when Khudā stood before me,
   Mīrā [the Lord] then asked me:
   Who ordered you to go[28]?

7. *Kabīr,* he who has known Rām's Name
   get's frail of body[29]-
   Sleep does not come to his eyes
   nor do his limbs fill out.

8. He who pines for Rām[30] is already in pain -
   let no one distress him further:
   From a mere touch, he may die,

---

(28) 'Order': *farmāī.*

(29) Literally, 'his cage is worn out'; the cage which imprisons the soul is a symbol of the body.

(30) *Rāma biyogī,* 'He who endures *Viyog'* or [separation] from Rām.

so great is his torment[31]!

9. Though conscious, he remains unconscious,
feeble, devoid of strength:
Says Kabīr, let no one dare to clasp the hem
of such a saint's garment!

10. Rubies do not fill store-rooms,
Hamsa-birds do not fly in lines,
Lions are not found in flocks
and saints do not walk in troops[32].

5. OF THE SEARCH FOR THE GURU'S TEACHING

1. Such a one cannot be found
who burns down his own house[33],
Who knocks down the five Fellows[34]

---

(31) The first line is different in *Raj* and *Bī*; the Rajasthani text gives the line: "Like a betel leaf, he turns yellow from day-to-day", referring to the withering body of the *Viyogī*. The *Bījak* reading (given in the Tiwari edition) appears more appropriate:

"So great is his torment, he writhes in anguish".

(32) Kabīr's ideal of the Man of God, bound to suffering, evokes the experience of the ancient Saint and Sufi, Shaykh Farīd of Panjab: cf. *infra,* The Ślokas of Shaykh Farīd.

(33) The perfect Yogī is He who, by controlling his senses and his mind, 'burns down his own house', i.e. reduces his own body to naught.

(34) 'The five senses'; the 'five fellows' may also allude to the five 'faults': lust, anger, greed, ignorance, pride.

and remains absorbed in Rām[35].

2. Such a one cannot be found
   in whom we can take refuge -
For I have seen the whole world burning
   each one in his own flame.

3. I have burnt my own house,
   torch in hand,
Now I'll burn the house
   of him who follows my Path.

6. OF HUMBLE PRAYER

1. *Kabīr,* I am the dog of Rām,
   'Mutiya'[36] is my name:
On my neck I wear a chain,
   wherever He leads me, I go.

2. In myself, there is nothing of mine,
   all there is is Thine:
Whatever I offer Thee is Thine already,
   how can the gift be mine?

---

(35) *lau* means 'flame'; in Kabīr's language, it is also an equivalent of *lay,* 'merging ', 're-absorption' into the One Reality.

(36) *Mutiyā* is a diminutive of *motī* or 'pearl', which is a common dog's name. It is derived from *mukti* or 'salvation', and thus it could be interpreted as 'the liberated one'. 'He who wears the chain of Rām' is *ipso facto* 'free from the chains of this world'.

8. OF GOD'S OMNIPOTENCE

1. I have done nothing and nothing can I do,
   this body of mine is good for nothing:
   Whatever is done is Hari's work:
   it is He who made Kabīr 'great'[37]!

2. If I made the seven seas my ink,
   and all the trees of the forest my pen,
   And the whole expanse of the earth my paper,
   still I could not write the greatness of Rām[38]!

3. *Kabīr,* what good deed can you do,
   if Rām comes not to your aid?
   Since every branch you step upon

---

(37) *bhayā kabīra kabīra*; there is a pun on the name 'Kabīr', which means 'great' in Arabic and is also an epithet of Allah.

(38) A similar statement is found in the Introduction to the *Padmāvat,* a *premākhyān,* or a spiritual love-tale, composed in Avadhi by the Sufi poet Muhammed Jāyasī in the 17th century:

"Very immeasurable are the makings of the Maker;
no teller can tell them!
If all the writers of the universe took the seven heavens as paper
and filled the seas of the earth with ink,
And took as many branches as cover all the forests of the world
and turned them all into pens and wrote -
still they could not write the shoreless Ocean of His wondrous deeds".

Jāyasī's poetical utterance seems based on a Sanskrit verse in praise of God Shiva, quoted by Tiwārī, *KSS,* p.126. According to Schimmel, a similar statement is found in the Koran.

yields and gives away?

4. That One is my wholesaler
who deals only in the Sahaj -
Without rod, without scales,
He weighs the whole World.

9. OF THE EXPERIENCE

1. When I was, Hari was not,
now Hari is and I am no more:
All darkness vanishes
when I found the Lamp[39] within my heart.

2. The effulgence of the supreme Being
is beyond imagination[40]:
Ineffable is His beauty:
seeing is the only 'proof'[41].

3. It was a good thing, hail fell on the ground,
for it lost its selfhood:
Melting, it turned into water

---

(39) The Lamp symbolizes *paracā,* the mystical Experience, given by the *satguru.*

(40) *unamān* (Skt *anumān*): such splendor cannot be grasped by means of 'inference' or 'guess'.

(41) The only possible 'proof' (*pramāṇ*) is direct vision (*pratyakṣa*), as opposed to *anumān.*

and rolled down to the pond[42].

4. Him whom I went out to seek,
   I found just where I was:
He now has become myself
   whom before I called 'Another'!

10. OF THE SUBTLE PATH

1. *Kabīr,* that Path is difficult[43],
   no one can follow it:
Those who went never came back
   none ever came back to tell about it!

2. Kabīr's house is on the top[44],
   where the path is slippery:
An ant cannot hold its footing
   and they go with loaded bullocks!

3. From over there, no one came back,
   to whom I could run and ask -
Yet, on that path, they all set off,

(42) Hail, to which the *jīv,* the living being, is here compared, is really nothing but Water (the One Reality, God): once it has fallen on the ground, i.e. once the *jīv* is incarnated in a human body, through the Experience, it looses the consciousness of its own falsely assumed identity and is reabsorbed into the One.

(43) The path which leads to emancipation from worldly existence: *samsār*.

(44) Allusion to the 'Circle of the Void', where the *sahaj* state is attained.

loaded with heavy burdens!

4. In that Forest where no lion roars,
   where no bird takes to flight,
 Where there is neither day nor night,
   there dwells Kabīr, entranced[45].

5. They all repeat: "Let's go! Let's go!"
   but I have my doubts:
 They're not acquainted with the Lord -
   where will they find refuge?

6. We don't know the name of that Village
   without knowing, how can we go?
 A whole age has passed walking,
   walking to that Village near by[46]!

7. Between Gangā and Yamunā,
   on the *ghāṭ* of 'Absorption' [*Sahaj-śūnya*],
 There Kabīr has built his hermitage
   while the Sages search for a path!

---

(45) The 'Forest' is the mysterious stage of *sahaj*.

(46) The Gangā and Yamunā rivers suggest the *Triveṇī* at Prayag: the holiest of all *tīrth*s, where countless Sādhus make their dwelling.

11. OF THE FAITHFUL WIFE

1. She who longs for Rāṃ alone,
   loathing everything else[47],
   Is like the Ocean shell
   thirsting for the raindrop of Svāti[48]!

2. *Kabīr,* this world holds no happiness
   for him who has many friendships:
   Those whose hearts are bound to the One,
   they alone obtain constant joy.

3. That soul which clings to the One
   obtains release,
   But he who blows two trumpets at a time[49]
   deserves to be slapped!

4. *Kabīr,* dawn is long passed[50],
   evening has come:
   Setting her mind on man after man,
   the harlot remains barren.

---

(47) *dūjī āsā nirāsa.* Trumpp and Macauliffe translate: 'all other hope is hopeless'; for the faithful soul, all worldly desires are self-defeating and lead to despair.

(48) According to popular belief, the rain-drop of Svāti, when falling into an oyster-shell, produces a pearl.

(49) 'He who blows two trumpets at a time': a popular way of saying: 'He who indulges in double talk'.

(50) The dawn (youth) has gone; the night (death) draws near; yet the young woman (the wife-soul) has not met her divine Spouse.

5. If a wife, betrothed to her spouse[51],
   keeps company with another -
If she cherishes another in her heart,
   how can she find grace with her Lord?

6. I think only of You,
   but you think of something else -
Says Kabīr, how did that come about:
   one soul in two places?

13. OF THE CREEPER

1. First the forest is consumed by fire -
   and then it grows green again,
I render homage to that Tree
   which bears fruit when cut down[52]!

2. If I cut it down, it brings forth leaves,
   if I water it, it withers[53]:

---

(51) In this context, the *sākhī* should be interpreted as a reproach of the Husband (God) to the wife-soul.

(52) These three *sākhī*s are composed in the paradoxical style called *ulaṭabāmsī* (upside-down language). *Belī,* the Creeper, symbolizes the human body. Gupta remarks that, in the *Gorakhbāṇī, belī* symbolizes *ātma-tattva* (*Gorakh-bānī,* ed. p. 206).

(53) On the significance of these paradoxes, cf. Dasgupta, *Obscure Religious Cults,* pp. 41-2, quoting a song by the Tantric Sahajiya Master Bhusukapāda:

"... It is just like the son of a barren woman
sporting and playing all kinds of games,

For such a marvellous creeper,
no praise is adequate!

3. In the courtyard is the Creeper, the fruit hangs in the sky,
It's like the milk of a calfless cow,
The bow is made of a hare's horn,
the barren woman's son plays about.

14. OF HEROISM

1. Now the time has come,
when she obtained her heart's desire:
How could the Satī fear death,
when she has taken the *sindūr*-box in hand[54]?

2. That death which the world dreads
is joy for me:
When shall I die ? When shall I behold the One
who is Plenitude and Joy supreme?

3. Climbing the pyre, the Satī calls and cries:
'Listen, O my Friend Masān'[55]!

It is like oil coming out of the sand,
like the horns of a hare, like a flower in the sky..."

(54) Climbing the pyre, the *satī* holds the *sindūr*-box, the symbol of her status as a *suhāginī* or 'happily married wife'.

(55) The *masān,* or burning-ground, is conceived as a frightful place, haunted by ghosts and evil fiends. The expression 'my friend Masān' in the mouth of the saintly wife, the *Satī,* is striking: the holy Satī is beyond all fear

All the people, passers-by, have gone[56]
only you and I remain in the end!

4. He who threw the shaft gave a roar
and the wounded cries ever louder -
Yet, smitten by the Śabda,
Kabīr fell silent on the spot!

5. Joy-giving is the blow of that shaft
which, when it hits, just draws a sigh:
I am a slave to that Guru
who can withstand the Śabda's blow.

6. Stricken to death, he won't escape,
Listen, O foolish Mind!
Kabīr died on the open field,
fighting his five senses.

15. OF WARNINGS

1. Kāl[57] stands at the head of your bed:
wake up, O my dear Friend!
Away from kindly Rām,
how can you sleep in peace?

---

or any evil influence, she can even befriend the horrifying 'Masān' or burning-ground.

(56) All relatives have gone and left her. For her, they were just *baṭāū* or 'passers-by'. Secure in her love, the Satī confronts death alone.

(57) Death.

2. Even a flickering instant you cannot hold
   and you make plans for tomorrow!
 Kāl will pounce on you suddenly
   as the hawk upon the partridge.

3. *Kabīr,* that *naubat*[58] of yours,
   but for ten days make it resound:
 This town, this borough, this lane,
   you'll never see them again.

4. *Kabīr,* collecting a little dust,
   one has wrapped up a small packet[59]:
 It was but a four-day show:
   in the end, nothing but dust!

5. A human birth is hard to get
   and it comes but once:
 The ripe fruit fallen on the ground
   will never return to the branch.

6. Having obtained a human birth,
   if you miss your chance,
 You'll fall back into the whirlpool of Existence
   to receive blow after blow!

7. The bones burn like dry wood,
   the hair burns like straw -

(58) *naubat* is music played, usually five times a day, above the gate or palace of a grandee. 'To play the *naubat*' means 'to show off one's importance'.

(59) *puriya* is a small packet made of a folded leaf: this *puriyā* is the human body.

Seeing the whole world aflame,
Kabīr loathed it[60]!

8. As the fruit is born on the tree,
so it remains till the end:
Saving cowrie after cowrie,
man gathers millions [of sins]!

9. *Kabīr,* it's like dreaming in the night
and then opening one's eyes:
The soul has suffered a great loss -
yet, on waking up, nothing is changed.

10. Man knows not the name of that Village[61]
and he had strayed from the path:
Tomorrow you'll be enmeshed in thorns -
why don't you run in time?

11. Within the heart is the Mirror,
yet the Face cannot be seen:
The Face will appear only then
when Duality is banished from the heart[62].

12. Why roam around doling out water?
The Ocean is at everyone's door[63]:

---

(60) *bhayā kabīra udāsa,* lit.: 'Kabīr became indifferent' (disgusted).

(61) The blind seeker takes a whole aeon - and never reaches the 'village' of Salvation, which is the *sahaj* state, often referred to as a 'place'.

(62) *dubidhā* means 'perplexity', but its etymology is Skt *dvidhā*, 'divided': dividedness or duality between the living being (*jīv*) and the Ultimate Reality is an obstacle to enlightenment.

(63) All beings are immersed in the supreme Reality.

He who is really thirsty
will drink at any price[64]!

13. Allow the Musician to play[65],
don't tease the *kukuhī* of Kaliyug[66]!
What do you care for other people affairs?
Mind your own business!

14. People have not known the Name of Rām,
they have pursued evil ways:
This body is a wooden pot
which can't be put twice on the fire!

15. Man didn't know the Name of Rām,
he kept feeding a legion of cousins[67]-
Involved in this business, he died
and there was no hue and cry.

16. *Kabīr,* this body is passing away,
make it stay if you can!
Devote yourself to the Saints' service

---

(64) *jhakha māri*: a colloquial expression, meaning 'at any cost'. He who really seeks God will spare no efforts and will ultimately discover God within himself.

(65) *bājamtari,* the 'Musician', alludes either to God, or, more probably, to the human soul. There is an allusion to *anāhat nād* or 'the unsounded Sound'.

(66) *kukuhī* means 'a hen'; the *Bī* reading adopted by Tiwārī does not give a satisfactory meaning; the *Da* variant: *tu kali jamtanī mati cheri* or 'do not pluck the lute of Kaliyug', seems better. It may be interpreted as 'Don't engage in worldly affairs'. Kaliyug is the wicked Age in which we live.

(67) As the hard-pressed breadwinner of a Hindu 'joint family'.

or sing Hari's praise.

17. *Kabīr,* this body is passing away,
make it come back if you can!
Empty-handed they have gone
all those millionaires[68].

18. *Kabīr,* do not pride yourself
on the fairness of your body -
Today or tomorrow you'll leave it and go
as the snake sheds its skin.

19. *Kabīr,* do not pride yourself
on the height of your dwelling[69]-
Today or tomorrow, you'll lie in the grave
and grass will grow above you[70].

20. *Kabīr,* do not pride yourself -
you are bones in a bag of skin,
Those with a fine horse below and a canopy above,
they too will be thrown into the pit!

21. *Kabīr,* a chain binds the whole world,
don't let yourself to be bound -
It'll vanish like salt in the flour
that golden body of yours!

---

(68) Lit.: 'those owners of lākhs and crores. A *lākh* is 100,000 and a crore is 10,000,000. Both terms are used in the sense of 'myriads'.

(69) Or: on the tallness of your body.

(70) A clear allusion to burial, as in *sā.* 24, below. The target is a Muslim grandee.

22. They put on dazzling garments
    and they chew fragrant betel-leaves[71],
Yet without the Name of the one Hari
    they go in chains to the City of Death.

23. *Kabīr*, the boat is rickety[72],
    holed in a thousand places:
Those travelling light crossed over,
    those carrying burdens on their head were drowned.

24. Led astray by the world, man died,
    worrying over the honour of his family[73]!
Who will care about your family's honour
    when they take you and
        dump you on the burning-ground?

25. For the sake of this world you let go Religion[74],
    yet the world won't follow you -
You have chopped your own feet with the axe,
    recklessly, with your own hands!

26. *Kabīr*, I went wandering in the world

---

(71) *pān supārī*: the fragrant betel-leaf folded and filled with minced betel-nut and spices: a highly appreciated delicacy.

(72) The human body is often compared to a 'boat' made to cross the 'Ocean of Existence'.

(73) Lit.: 'while promoting the honour of his lineage'.

(74) *dīna gamvāyā dunī sau,* lit.: 'giving up Religion for the World'; the link includes an alliteration with two Persian words: *dīn,* 'religion' and *duniyā* 'world'.

a tabor over my shoulder[75]-
I have seen and inquired from all[76]:
nobody has anyone.

16. OF DEATH

1. *Kabīr,* the lute is silent
for all its strings are broken:
What can the poor instrument do
when the Player has departed[77]?

2. Scorched by the forest-fire[78],
standing, the tree cries aloud:
Let me not fall into the Blacksmith's hands,
lest he burns me a second time!

3. *Kabīr,* the deer is lean
despite the greenery round the pond:
For a single living being, many thousand hunters[79]:
how many times will he escape the arrows?

---

(75) *mādalu* (Skt *mardala*): a kind of small *ḍhol* (or *ḍholak*) also called *mandar* or *mandariyā* and played by wandering 'Jogīs'.

(76) *thomki bajāi,* lit.: 'beating a drum', is a colloquial expression meaning 'to conduct a thorough inquiry'. The result of Kabīr's thorough investigation is just that: 'Nobody has anyone'.

(77) The musical instrument is the human body, the Musician is the living soul, the *jīv*.

(78) *dhau* (Skt *davā*), 'a forest-fire', symbolizes the suffering of worldly existence. The Blacksmith is Kāl, Death.

(79) The deer is the *jīv;* the hunters are the lures of the world.

4. Poisonous is that forest[80] where I dwell,
 snakes are coiled around the trees.
 Fear grips my soul
 and I spend the night on the watch.

5. Seeing the mill revolving,
 Kabīr wept:
 Of those caught between the grinding-stones,
 none escaped unscathed[81]!

6. Gods, man and Munis,
 the seven continents and the nine regions,
 Says Kabīr, all have to suffer punishment
 for taking bodily form.

7. Like the fish, you won't escape,
 for Death is your Fisherman:
 In whichever swamp you wander[82],
 there He will cast his net.

8. I saw the fish offered for sale
 at the court of the Fisherman[83]-
 "O You with the red eyes[84],

(80) The forest is the human body.

(81) Human beings are compared to the grains ready to be ground in the stone-mill of Death. Whoever comes in-between, i.e. whoever is born in this world, will be crushed.

(82) I.e. in whichever body you are reborn, within the unending cycle of the *samsār*.

(83) The *darbār* of the Fisherman is the Court of the God of Death, Yam.

(84) The 'red eyes' suggests that the 'fish' has been shedding tears.

how did you get caught?"

9. "In water I had my dwelling,
on the bottom I had my couch -
Then the noose of *karma*[85] fell on me
and I was entangled in it."

10. O you dull-witted Fish,
the Fisherman has cast its net:
In a shallow-pond[86] there is no escape,
take refuge in the Ocean!

11. *Kabīr,* as a bird picks piece by piece,
instant after instant slip in vain:
The soul escapes not from the net
and lo! Yam has come, beating his drum[87]!

12. Why plaster that building
with its high walls and verandas?
Your real house is but three cubits and a half[88]-
at most three and three-quarters.

13. When did they ever invoke Rām?

---

(85) The *Bījak* reading: *karīm,* appears as a deformation of *karma,* or destiny.

(86) Tiwārī (*KSS,* p. 113) suggests that the 'shallow pond' alludes to idol-worship and the like; it may simply refer to finite existence, as opposed to merging with the Infinite, Rām.

(87) As the reckless 'fish' pursues worldly pleasures, he does not heed the approach of the Fowler, Death. King Yam beats the drum of victory.

(88) Three cubits and a half represents the average human size - and so it is the traditional length of a grave.

Now old age has come:
Once the fire has reached the front-door,
what can be taken away[89]?

14. Man is but a doll made of the five elements
to whom a human name was given -
We are but guests of four days,
taking up so much room!

15. Putting off the issue, the day has passed,
the interests kept mounting[90]-
Man didn't worship Hari nor cleared his debts[91]-
and lo! Kāl has arrived!

17. OF THE ROOT OF IMMORTALITY

1. *Kabīr,* my mind found peace,
when I found *Brahmagyān*[92]:
That fire which torments the whole world[93],
to me became cool as water!

2. Know that solace is to be found

(89) Lit.: 'what can be drawn out?'; it may refer to the invocation itself, which can no longer be uttered by the dying man.

(90) The payment of old debts (*karma*) is still pending.

(91) 'The deed was not torn up' and the debtor remained a prisoner of Kāl, the Hawk.

(92) The knowledge of the *Brahman,* here an equivalent of the *sahaj* state.

(93) Probably an allusion to the three types of suffering (*tapas*) which torment the creatures in this world.

by entering into Indifference[94]:
The man who rejects partiality, who takes no side,
no evil word can wound.

3. Take your repose under that Tree[95]
which bears fruit twelve months in the year:
Cool is its shade, abundant its fruit
birds play in its branches.

18. THE CONNOISSEUR

1. Hari is the Diamond[96], the devotee is the Jeweller
who displays his wares on his stall,
If a Connoisseur[97] be found
they will fetch a good price!

2. A strange thing indeed have I seen:
The Diamond is on sale in the market -
But for want of a Connoisseur
it's going for one cowrie[98]!

---

(94) *samatā*: the state in which all differences or opposites are abolished, as all appear 'equal' to the true Yogi; *samatā* pertains to the Hindu (especially to the Yogic) idea of saintliness.

(95) The Tree of Detachment and Impartiality.

(96) *hīrā*: cf. *supra sākhī* 1.8; *hīrā* or 'diamond' symbolizes the supreme Reality, or *paramārtha,* as well as the Vision or Experience (*paracā*) which gives access to the supreme stage of *sahaj*.

(97) *pārikhū,* 'he who has tested' and estimated a gem; the 'Connoisseur' of the Gem of Rām is the Saint; the cowrie is the smallest coin.

(98) *Ibidem.*

3. Pearls were scattered on the path
   but those who came by were blind:
Without the Light of the Lord[99]
   the world steps over them.

4. Having found that precious Gem of Rām,
   O Kabīr, don't loose your waist-knot[100]-
For that Jewel has neither market-town nor Connoisseur,
   no buyer and no price!

5. Where there is the true Buyer, there's no 'I'[101],
   where 'I' remains, there's no Buyer:
Without the Experience man goes puffed with pride,
   having grasped but the shadow of the *śabda.*

6. My language is of the East:
   none can understand me -
He alone will understand my language
   who really is an Easterner[102]!

7. Do not display the Diamond
   in the vegetable market[103]-

---

(99) *Jagadīs,* 'the Master of the world', usually refers to god Shiva; here, *jagadīs* clearly refers to the supreme Reality, Rām.

(100) *gāmthi na kholi,* lit.: 'do not undo the knot': the knot of one's garment, tied at the waist, which serves as a purse.

(101) No ego-consciousness or feeling of separateness from the supreme Reality.

(102) On this much discussed *dohā,* see Introduction.

(103) Do not throw pearls to the swine.

Easily, easily[104], tie up your waist-cloth
and go your way.

19. OF THE LIVING DEAD

1. Death after death, the world dies
but no one knows how to die -
The servant Kabīr died such a death[105]
as he won't have to die again.

2. Dead is the Physician, dead is the patient,
the whole world is dead,
Kabīr only won't die
who has his support in Rām.

3. When a saint dies, why do you cry?
He is going home -
Shed tears on the miserable Shākta,
who is sold from market to market[106]!

4. Infallible is the Touchstone of Rām[107],

---

(104) An allusion to the *sahaj* state. *Sahaji karai byaupāra* can be interpreted as 'He trades easily' or as 'He trades in the Sahaj'. This *double-entendre* is found repeatedly in Kabīr's verses.

(105) Kabīr has 'died' to the world and he has obtained the state of *jīvanmrit*: 'one who, alive, is dead', the aim of the perfect Yogi or Siddha.

(106) I.e. endlessly reborn.

(107) *kasauṭī,* or 'the touchstone' is a kind of black stone used by jewellers to test gold; rubbed on the *kasauṭī,* pure gold leaves a golden mark on it.

no falsity will stick to it:
He alone will stick to that Stone
who, though living, be dead.

5. I yearn for death, but if I die
may it be at Rām's door,
And may Hari not ask: 'Who is he
who has fallen at my door'[108]?

6. Be like pebbles on the path,
renouncing hypocrisy and pride -
If there be such a servant,
he will meet Bhagavān[109]!

20. OF THE MIDDLE PATH

1. From heaven and earth, I kept aloft
by the grace of the Satguru:
In the Joy of His lotus feet,
I remain for ever.

3. *Kabīr,* saffron is yellow,
and plaster is white by nature,
Yet, when the Lover meets Rām,
both lose their colour.

4. On the way the Pandits departed,
the whole world followed in a crowd -

---

(108) 'May God recognize me as His own'.

(109) A servant (*jan*) of such humility; Bhagavān: the Lord, God.

On the inaccessible *ghāṭ*,
Kabīr has climbed and there he stays.

5. Between sky and lower world,
two hollow gourds are bound:
The six *darśan*s tumbled down
with the eighty-four Siddhas!

7. Taking sides this way or that,
the whole world was led astray:
He who prays Hari without taking sides
he is a Saint and a Sage.

8. The Anal-bird[110] has made his nest in the air,
for ever, he stays in-between -
From earth and sky, he keeps aloof,
his confidence needs no support.

---

(110) The fabulous Anal bird (i.e. Fire-bird) is said to make his nest in the air, without ever touching earth. The Anal bird is probably identical to the Phoenix (Arabic *Quqnus,* Persian *Ātishzan*) who sets itself aflame with its own song and is later reborn from his own ashes. It is mentioned in the *Padmāvat* of Muhammad Jāyasī under the name *kakanū*: 'Like a kakanū bird, he [the King] prepares his own pyre' (*Padmāvat,* ed. V.S. Agarwal, p.205). The Anal bird's peculiarity is to dwell 'in the middle' (*madhi*) or 'in the space' (*ākāś*), which, in Tantric language, is equivalent to the 'Void' (*śūnya*). For Kabīr, the Fire-bird's achievement is not a trick of magic but a feat of Love: total reliance on faith (*viśvās*) makes up for all other support (*ṭhāhar*).

21. OF TRUE ASCETICISM

1. While they are preaching to others,
   dust falls into their mouth -
   They watch over people's crop
   whilst their own field is eaten[111]!

2. *Khichrī*[112] makes a good meal
   if seasoned with a little salt -
   To get game and baked bread
   who would put his head on the block?

3. The Brahman is the Guru of the world,
   but he is not the devotees' Guru:
   He got entangled in his four Vedas
   and there he died[113].

4. Violently they kill living beings
   and they call it 'lawful'[114]!
   When the Accountant asks for the accounts,
   what will be their plight?

(111) While pretending to guide others to salvation, they go to their-own doom; the 'crop' symbolizes *mukti,* or 'liberation'. The line is a proverb.

(112) *khichrī*: a dish of pulse and rice boiled together, which suggests plain food.

(113) For Kabīr, all rituals are so many strings preventing man to reach salvation.

(114) *halāl,* Ar. *halāl,* 'lawful' according to Koranic law.

5. That violence, it is a crime[115],
for which you'll have to answer God:
When the Accountant asks for your dues[116]
you'll get a blow on your face!

6. If the Shaykh be devoid of patience[117],
of what use is that Kaaba pilgrimage ?
How can he whose soul is not firm
ever hope to reach God ?

7. Though a man builds his house by the side of Kashi
and keeps drinking pure Ganges water,
Without Hari's Name, there is no salvation -
so says Kabīr, Rām's servant.

8. *Kabīr,* that wooden hut[118]
caught fire on the ten sides -
All the Pandits were burnt to death,
the ignorant escaped with their lives.

9. A pig is worth more than a Shākta[119],

---

(115) *juluma,* Ar. *zulm,* 'lawful' according to Qāzīs and Mullahs - but killing living beings is an act of oppression. Though a Muslim, Kabīr is strictly vegetarian.

(116) *daftari*: a 'clerk' or chief Accountant, who keeps record of the credits or deeds; in Hindu mythology, he is a glorified 'Kāyastha' (scribe), who is Yam, the God of Death.

(117) *ṣabūrī* or 'patience' (Ar. *sabir*: patient): a virtue which ought to shine in a holy man like the Shaykh.

(118) The human body.

(119) The Shāktas are men addicted to drink and women and suspected of abominable Tantric practices.

for it keeps the village clean -
When the Shākta, the wretch, has died,
nobody will take his name.

10. Man got bogged down in family cares
and he neglected Rām:
Then Dharmarāj's[120] myrmidons suddenly appeared,
fully attired, in the midst of all!

11. I weep over the world -
let none weep over me:
He alone'll weep over me
who, through the Śabda, has found Discernment.

12. You have betrayed the Lord,
plotting with thieves -
You will understand, O Living Being,
when you get the blow!

13. Going in endless pilgrimages, the world died
exhausted by so much bathing -
They never knew the Name of Rām
and they fell a prey to Kal!

22. OF WORTHLESS MEN

1. *Kabīr,* those dull-witted ritualists[121]
are stone from head to foot -

(120) Dharmarāj is the God of Death.

(121) *karamiyā*: the ritualists, who are followers of *karma-yoga*.

What can the Bowman do,
since his arrows don't pierce them[122]?

2. Trying to teach a fool,
you'll soon come to the end of your wits[123]:
Coal will never turn white
even with ten hundredweights of soap[124]!

3. The Bowman kept aiming and aiming,
but his shots never pierced:
All his arrows fell to the ground:
tossing away his quiver, he left.

4. *Kabīr,* a hundred maunds of milk
were wasted drop by drop:
The milk curdled and turned sour
and all the *ghī* was lost[125]!

24. OF COMPANIONSHIP

1. The pure raindrop from the sky
when it falls to earth gets sullied:
Without good company, human life is ruined,
reduced to ashes.

---

(122) The *Bowman* is the *Satguru,* whose arrow is the *śabda.*

(123) Lit.: "the wisdom in your pocket comes to an end".

(124) A proverb; *sābun* or 'soap', from Arabic *ṣābūn.*

(125) The *ghī,* melted and clarified butter, is said to be the 'Essence' of milk; here, it symbolizes the supreme Reality.

2. I die of the plague of Bad Company,
like a plantain by the side of a Jujube:
As the Jujube moves its branches, the Plantain is torn -
beware of contact with Shāktas!

3. *Kabīr,* the mind is like a bird
flying in all the ten directions:
depending on the company it keeps,
it will feed on this or that[126].

4. Let it be for a *gharī*[127]- or half of it,
or even a half of the half -
Kabīr, the company of Saints
abolishes sins by millions.

5. Like a hovel full of soot
such is this world -
I offer myself in sacrifice to that devotee
who entered it and got away!

6. It's a hovel full of soot[128],
it's a whole fortress of soot -
Blessed be that devotee
who sticks to Rām.

7. If you seek the oil of Love
then use only ripened seeds[129]:

---

(126) This seems to be a proverb.

(127) A *gharī* is worth 24 minutes.

(128) *kājara kerī obarī*: *kājara,* or 'lamp-black', 'soot', symbolizes the impurity of sensual desires; the 'hovel full of soot' is this world.

(129) The ripe seeds' are the true saints.

Crushing unripe mustard-seeds
yields neither oil nor oil-cake[130]!

8. Associate only with the holy,
shun others like plague:
Vile is the company of the wicked,
an unbearable torment.

25. OF HYPOCRISY

1. Be loyal to the Lord,
be fair to others,
Then either let your hair grow long
or shave your skull as you please!

2. You turned Sadhu? What of that?
You've put four rows of beads,
Outwardly you've donned a pinkish robe -
but inside you're full of filth!

3. It's that Beast Mind[131] you should shave -
what's the use of shaving your hair?
All that was done was the Mind's work,
your hair had done nothing.

4. By wearing so many garbs,

(130) A proverb.

(131) *maivāsi* might be a corruption of Arabic *mavāshī*, 'cattle', 'quadrupeds' - here it seems to be a term of abuse applied to *man* (*manas*), the Mind.

the soul's error is not dispelled -
Without the Experience imparted by the Satguru,
duality remains in the soul.

5. *Kabīr,* in the Shāktas' assembly
do not take your seat -
How could the same enclosure do
for *nīlgāy,* ass and cow[132]?

26. DISPELLING ERROR

1. It is but an image of stone
which they worship as 'Creator'!
Those who put their trust in it
were drowned in a black torrent.

2. *Kabīr,* they built a cell made of paper
with gates made out of ink[133]-
In the ground, they've sown stones[134]
and the Pandits loot them all[135].

3. Why does that Mullah climb the minaret?

---

(132) *nīlgāy,* 'blue cow', also called *rojhā,* is a big, fast-running antelope, known to damage farmers' crop- it won't be found in the same enclosure with an ass and a cow (proverb).

(133) The *Pandits* go to hell with their 'holy books'.

(134) The 'stones' are the idols which yield no other crop than income for the Pandits.

(135) *pārī bāt*: a colloquial expression which suggests an attack by a band of brigands.

Allah is not outside!
Him for whom you shout the call to prayer[136]
you should recognize in your heart.

4. Two fellows went on a pilgrimage,
the fickle Mind and the hypocrite Soul:
They could not get rid of a single sin,
and they loaded two hundredweights more.

5. Pilgrimages and rituals are a poisonous Creeper
which has spread all over the world -
Kabīr has pulled it up by the roots
lest people eat the poison[137].

29. OF THE MIND

1. The Door of Bhakti is narrow[138]
like the tenth of a mustard-seed -
Mind is an elephant gone mad:
how could it go through the Door?

(136) Persian *bānga*: a loud cry, especially referring to the cock-crow at dawn; here it alludes to the call of the *mu'azzīn*.

(137) *halāhạla* alludes to the poison drunk by god Shiva at the time of the Churning of the Milk Ocean.

(138) The door of Bhakti is as narrow as the *brahmarandhra* (lit.: 'hole of Brahman'), conceived as an infinitesimal hollow within the pericarp of the 'thousand-petalled lotus', which is the abode of 'Paramashiva'.

2. This body is a pitch-dark forest[139]
 and Mind is a mad elephant,
The Jewel of Wisdom is the goad -
 but few are the saints to apply it.

3. More tenuous than water,
 more subtle than smoke,
Swifter than wind,
 such is the Friend[140] Kabīr has made.

4. The three worlds were plundered,
 stripped of their all -
But Mind is a faceless Thief
 whom no one recognizes.

5. The Mind is aware of all,
 knowingly, it does wrong:
Will you fare any better,
 falling into the well, lamp in hand?

31. OF MĀYĀ

1. *Kabīr,* Māyā is a harlot,
 who sets her snare in the market place:
The whole world was trapped
 but Kabīr cut himself free.

---

(139) *kajarī bana,* lit.: 'a forest of soot'; *kājal,* 'soot' or 'collyrium', symbolizes worldly desires, cf. supra 24.5,6.

(140) The 'Friend' (Persian *dost*), both immaterial and invisible, cannot be distinct from the supreme Being.

2. In the flame of Māyā, the whole world is burning,
   lusting after women and gold -
 Tell me, how can one keep fire
   wrapped up in cotton?

3. What point is there, giving up Māyā,
   as long as pride remains?
 Through pride were the great Sages lost,
   pride devoured them all!

4. Māyā never died nor did the Mind,
   body after body kept dying -
 Desire and thirst never died,
   so said Kabīr.

5. I'll make Desire into my fuel,
   I'll burn my mind to ashes,
 I'll put a stop to that Yogī's wanderings:
   Nameless I'll be reborn.

Part Four

Pads of Kabīr[1]

1. AUTOBIOGRAPHICAL VERSES

1

KG2 12; Gu gūjrī 2

Kabīr has given up
all his weaving,
On his body he has written
the Name of Rām! *refrain*

Kabīr's mother
weeps in secret:
O God,
How will those children live?

As long as I went on
threading my shuttle,
So long the thread of Rām's Love
kept snapping!

(1) Basically, all following *pads* are found in the 'Rājasthānī' recension of Kabīr's Sayings, the *Kabīr-granthāvalī*. For the references in the *Gurū Granth* or in the *Bījak*, see App. 1: Concordances.

Says Kabīr,
O Mother, listen:
He who provides
is the Lord of the three worlds.

2[2]

KG2 24; Gu bhairaü 18.

If the soul stands firm,
can the body tremble?
My soul remained absorbed
in his lotus feet. *refrain*

Deep, fathomless
is the holy Gangā:
On its bank, in chains,
Kabīr was made to stand.

The waves of the Gangā
broke off his chains
And Kabīr emerged seated
on a deer skin.

Says Kabīr,
neither companion nor escort have I:
On land or in water, my sole Protector
is the Lord.

---

(2) This often-quoted *pad* and the following one allude to the alleged persecution of Kabīr by the Muslim ruler, Sikander Lodī.

3

KG2 23; Gu gauṇḍ 4

O You, my Lord,
the strength is Yours:
In vain did that Qāzī shout:
"Let loose the elephant!" *refrain*

Arms bound, I was cast down like a ball,
whilst to infuriate the beast
they beat him on the head.

But he ran away, that elephant, trumpeting loud:
to that holy beast[3],
I pay my homage!

"O Mahant! I'll cut off your head!
Apply the goad
and make him run forward!"

But the elephant won't move,
he is deep in meditation,
for in his heart dwells the Lord[4].

What harm had he done, that holy man,
to be thrown like a bundle
before the elephant's feet?

The elephant pays homage to the bundle -
but even then the Qāzī, in his blindness,
understands not!

---

(3) Lit.: 'to that *mūrti*: 'An Image, or a manifestation of God Himself'.

(4) *bhagavān*: the 'Adorable One', a Vaishnav name of God.

Three times did the Qāzī repeat the test:
so hardened was his heart,
he could not believe!

Says Kabīr: O my Govind!
You keep the soul of your devotees
on the Highest stage[5].

4[6]

KG2 46; Gu gaüṛī 15; Bī 108.

Now tell me, O Rām,
what will be my fate?
I had left Benares,
so foolish was I! *refrain*

Like a fish
out of water
I was bereft from the merits[7]
of my former life.

My whole life, I had spent
in the city of Shiva -
And now, at the point of Death

(5) The legend of Kabīr's rescue by a 'holy elephant' is very popular in India.

(6) This famous song is common to the *Gu* and *Bī* recensions. It is not found in 'Raj'. *KG2* gives the *Gu* text and adds the Bī text.

(7) Bereft from the merits acquired through austerities performed in his former life.

I've come to Magahar[8]!

So many years,
    I practised penance in Kashi -
Yet, at the point of death,
    I've become a citizen of Magahar!

Kashi or Magahar:
    what's the difference?
With so little devotion
    how could One be saved?

5[9]

Gu gaūrī 15; Bī śabda 108.

Now I have been born again, a fish in that water
    for, in my previous life, I had got mad on penance -
I had turned a Bairāgī at heart,
    I had deserted my people and I had clung to Rām. *refrain*

I had deserted Kashi, in my foolishness:
    O, Lord of my soul, tell me, what will be my fate?
Am I a bad servant or were You mindless?

---

(8) Magahar, near Kashi, a place of weavers, is known as a particularly wretched place.

(9) This second *śabda* is composed in the Maithili language, a dialect of Bihari. No provocation is implied, as it is in the *Gurū Granth* text, but a regret and lament on the part of 'Kabīr-dās', ('the servant Kabīr') is expressed. The comparison with another song on the same theme (see above: Autobiographical Verses, No. 6), suggests that the last two verses of *Bī* 108 may not be authentic. On the other hand, the first verse about Kabīr's former life as a 'Bairāgī' rings like a provocation.

Of the two of us, who is to blame?

I had come to seek refuge in You, O blessed Lord,
 yet nowhere could I see the feet of Hari.
I had come to seek your feet -
 but now the servant Kabīr has lost all hope.

6

KG2 200; Gu dhanāsarī 3; Bī śabda 103.

O People,
 you are fools!
If Kabīr leaves his body at Kashi,
 who will take refuge in Rām? *refrain*

Those who know of love and devotion
 should not wonder at this:
Like water poured into water,
 so he has merged and vanished, the Julāhā!

Says Kabīr, O people, listen:
 let no one err and forget:
What is Kashi? What is the barren land of Magahar
 if Rām dwells in your heart?

7

Gu dhanāsarī 3; Bī śabda 103.

O People, you are simple-minded!
As water mixes with water, so will Kabīr mix with dust.
refrain

If you are a true *Vyās* of Mithilā[10],
then you should die at Magahar!
Dying in Magahar, one becomes a donkey, they say[11]:
so, have you lost your faith in Rām?
Dying in Magahar, you won't know death,
dying elsewhere, you'll put Rām to shame!
What is Kashi? What is the barren land of Magahar
if Rām dwells in my heart?
If Kabīr gives up the ghost in Kashi,
what credit will that be to Rām ?

---

(10) Vyaś is famous as a great sage and savant, and Mithila is celebrated as a brilliant centre of learning.

(11) According to popular belief, people who die at holy Kashi obtain *mukti* 'liberation' from one's sins, whereas those who die at Magahar are re-born as donkeys. This is probably a dig at the Julāhās whose 'holy land' is Magahar.

2. SATIRES

1

KG2 181; Bī śabda 75

Puzzling indeed
are those distinguos:
What is Koran or Veda,
This-world and That-world[12],
man or woman? *refrain*

It's all one blood, one shit,
one skin, one flesh -
From a single drop[13] the whole creation emerged:
who is Brahman? Who is Shudra?

Spontaneously this body of clay took shape,
then *nād* and *bindu*[14] merged into one:
When there is no more, what name will you give it?
O fools! You got nowhere!

---

(12) *dīna aru duniyā* is the Persian equivalent of the Hindi expression: *lok-paralok* or 'this world and the other world'.

(13) KG2 gives the *Bī* reading: *eka būnda tai,* 'from a single drop'. The Raj (Dā) variant *eka joti tai* or 'from a single Light' refers to the Islamic belief in the world issued from the divine Light (Persian *nūr*).

(14) In the Tantric, especially the Sahajiyā tradition, *nād* or 'resonance' and *bindu,* 'drop' of energy or 'semen' are conceived as the two principles out of which the body is evolved. When both *nād* and *bindu* merge into each other, the body disappears and 'Vacuity' (*śunyatā*) equivalent to the *sahaj* state, is obtained.

Brahma is *rajas,* Shankar is *tamas*
and Hari is *sattva* - so they say[15]:
Kabīr, adore the One Rām:
there is neither Hindu nor Turk!

2

KG2 177; Gu bibhās 2; Bī śabda 97

O Allah-Rām,
present in all living beings
Have mercy on your servants,
O Lord! *refrain*

Why bump your head on the ground,
why bathe your body in water?
You kill and you call yourself 'humble' -
but your vices you conceal.

What's the use of ablutions, litanies, purifications
and prostrations in the mosque?
If you pray with a heart full of guile
what's the use of *Haj* and *Kaaba?*

Twenty-four times the Brahman keeps the eleventh-day fast[16],
while the Qāzī observes the Rāmzan:

(15) According to the Brahmanical tradition, the whole world is made of three *guṇs* or 'strands', called *sattva, rajas* and *tamas.* In the Buddhist Tantric tradition, the world has neither substance nor reality.

(16) All pious Vaishnavas fast on every *ekādaśī,* the eleventh day of each lunar fortnight, in honour of god Vishnu, that is 24 times a year, and the Muslims fast during the month of Rāmzan.

Tell me, why does he set aside the eleven months
  to seek spiritual fruit in the twelfth?

Hari dwells in the East, they say[17],
  and Allah resides in the West,
Search for Him in your heart, in the heart of your heart:
  there He dwells, *Rahīm-Rām*!

All men and women ever born
  are nothing but forms of yourself:
Kabīr is the child of *Allah-Rām*:
  He is my Guru and my Pīr.

3

KG2 182; Bī ra. 62

If the Creator
  had invented caste
Why didn't He mark the Brahmans at birth
  with the triple line[18]? *refrain*

A Shudra you were born,
  a Shudra you die!
Why do you befool the world
  with that contrived 'sacred Thread'?

---

(17) Allah's residence is said to be at the Kaaba in Mecca; the dwelling of Hari in the East probably alludes to the famous temple of god Jagannāth, at Puri in Orissa.

(18) Lit.: 'Why didn't you get the 'three lines' at birth?': the 'three lines' refer to the *triḍāndi* or *tripuṇḍa,* the three horizontal lines traced on the forehead of a Shaivite Brahman at the time of his initiation.

If you are a Brahman,
born from a Brahmani,
Why didn't you enter this world
through a different path[19]?

If you are a Turk,
born from a Turkini,
Why didn't God Himself
circumcise you in the womb[20]?

Says Kabīr,
there are no low-born:
This man alone is vile
who does not invoke Rām.

4

KG2 188; Gu āsā 26

"My tongue is Vishnu, my eyes are Nārāyaṇ
and Govind dwells in my heart" - so you boast!
When Death stands at your door, calling you to account
what's the use then to call 'Mukunda!'[21]? *refrain*

---

(19) Coming into the world through the impure channel of the vagina, head downwards, what an indignity for the so-called 'gods-of-the-earth'!

(20) Kabīr was strongly opposed to circumcision. The gibe at that Muslim practice suggests that low-caste converts to Islam such as the Julāhās resented the practice which orthodox Muslims tried to enforce on them. This is also implied in satire 11, see further.

(21) When Death comes near, the 'holy Brahman' loses his self-confidence and pitifully cries out to 'Mukunda' - a Vaishnav name of God - to help him out.

You are a Brahman and I, a mere Julāhā of Kashi.
listen to my own wisdom:
You keep begging from kings and princes,
while I meditate on Rām.

In my previous life, I too was a Brahman,
busy with mean business[22], devoid of austerity:
I had failed to take up the service of Lord Rām,
so I was caught and turned into a Julāhā[23]!

I am the beast and you, Reverend Sir, are the shepherd
who minds me from birth to birth -
Yet you never led me to good pasture;
how, then, are you my Master?

---

(22) This 'mean business' (*ochai karam*) is the ritualistic activity out of which the Brahman makes his living.

(23) In *Gu* the third verse is replaced by another one:

I, in my house, ceaselessly stretch the yarn on my loom,
yet the sacred thread is on your shoulder -
You keep reciting the Vedas and the Gāyatrī
but Govind dwells in my soul.

5

KG2 196; Gu rāmkalī 5; Bī śabda 17

You keep singing the Name of Rām
and exhorting others -
But you know nothing of Hari
and you wander all over. *refrain*

That one, mouthing away his 'Veda' and his 'Gāyatrī'[24],
he whose words bestow salvation,
That one to whose feet the whole world clings
that Pandit is a killer of living beings[25]!

Thinking yourself so high, you eat in low homes[26],
going through mean rituals to fill your belly -
At the time of eclipse or *amāvasyā,* you run around, begging[27]:
lamp in hand, you fall into the well[28]!

(24) The famous Vedic hymn which Brahmans should recite every morning.

(25) Allusion to the animal sacrifice which the Brahman performs once a year, dedicated to the Great Goddess, Kāli-Durgā.

(26) Ordinary Brahmans do perform rituals in the homes of 'vile' Shudras, for the sake of food and money.

(27) Moon eclipses and the moonless day of each month (*amāvasyā*) are considered unauspicious and dangerous. To counter evil influences, some auspicious acts, such as giving alms to Brahmans, must be performed. The Brahman won't miss the opportunity: at night-fall, lamp in hand, he starts on his round.

(28) The last half-line is a proverb, stigmatizing people who think themselves wise and pretend to enlighten others, whereas they themselves cannot see a step ahead.

6

Gu bilāval 2

The whole world is wise
I alone am a fool:
I have gone mad,
let no one else be distraught! *refrain*

Science, I don't study
of arguments, I know nothing -
Listening to Hari's praise
I've lost my head.

I didn't do it myself:
it was Rām who made me mad:
Burnt by the Satguru,
I got out of my mind.

I myself am distraught,
I've lost my head:
Let no one fall
in my folly!

7

KG2 191; Gu mārū 1

O Pande,
what foolishness is yours!
You don't call on Rām
you, wretched one! *refrain*

Carrying your Veda and Puranas, O Pande, you go along

like a donkey loaded with sandal-wood[29]-
The secret of the Name of Rām, you've never known
and so you come to shame[30].

You kill living beings and you call it 'Piety':
tell me, Brother, what then is impiety[31]?
Among yourselves, you address each other as 'Great Sage':
whom then, shall I call 'Butcher'[32]?

Blind of soul, dull of understanding,
how dare you preach others, O Brother?
For money, you sell all your 'Science'
and your human life is spent in vain.

"So spake Nārad", "So said Vyās"
"Go and ask Shukadev!"[33].
Says Kabīr, you'll get rid of your foolishness
only by merging in Rām.

---

(29) The Name of Rām is the very essence of all scriptures - but the Pande who recites them never understood the infinite power of the sacred Name - so he goes 'as a donkey loaded with sandal', a proverbial expression.

(30) 'Dust fall into your mouth': an expression meaning 'to be dishonoured'.

(31) Sacrificing animals to the Great Goddess is part of the *dharma,* or 'religious duty' of the Brahman - but this *dharma* is a heinous crime from the point of view of those who believe in strict *ahimsā.*

(32) *Kasāī* (Ar. *qassai*), lit.: 'a Butcher', is the worst possible insult thrown at the face of a Brahman priest.

(33) The names of great sages of old such as Nārad, Vyās and others, are ironically put in the mouth of the pompous, falsely erudite Brahman.

8

KG2 187; Gu āsā 14

The gardener's wife tears off leaves,
yet each leaf is alive -
But the idol for which she tears the leaves,
that idol is lifeless[34]! *refrain*

The sculptor had carved the idol,
putting his foot on the deity's chest:
Had the idol been alive,
would it not devour the sculptor?

With plenty of sweetmeats and delicacies,
man had performed a marvellous *pūjā* -
Then the Pujārī took off the oblations
and he threw dust into the god's mouth[35]!

The leaf is Brahma, the flower is Vishnu,
Mahādev[36] is both root and fruit -
For the three gods so manifested,
what cult has he performed?

---

(34) In the early morning, the *mālinī,* i.e. the gardener's wife, picks up and gathers flowers to be offered at the early morning *pūjā,* which consists in the 'Awakening' of the Deity.

(35) The greedy *pujārī,* in charge of the ritual awakening of the Deity, cares little for the god he is supposed to feed with the oblations: he takes away the sacred food, which ought to be resented as an offence by the deity.

(36) Mahādev: another name of god Shiva.

9

KG2 168; Gu āsā 20

In Rām, Rām, Rām,
steep yourself -
But mind you never talk
with the Shāktas! *refrain*

What's the use of reading
scripture to a dog?
What's the use of singing
Hari's praise before Shāktas?

Why feed camphor
to a crow?
Why pour milk
to a poisonous snake?

Why water a Nīm-tree
with nectar[37]?
Says Kabīr,
will their nature ever change[38]?

(37) The Nīm-tree is known for the bitterness of its juice. The general meaning is clear: 'Don't throw your pearls before swine'.

(38) After this verse, Raj (Dā, Sā) adds another verse (not found in KG 2) which is a proverb:

"The Shākta and the pig are brothers:
the one keeps slandering
while the other keeps grunting".

10

KG2 179; Bī śabda 40

O Pandit,
all your babbling is lies[39]:
If by crying 'Rām' the world is saved,
then by saying 'sugar' the mouth is sweetened!
refrain

By saying 'fire', is the foot burnt?
by saying 'water', is the thirst quenched?
If by saying 'food' hunger could be appeased,
then the whole world would be out of trouble!

Living with man, the parrot cries *'Hari'*!
but of His glory, he knows nothing -
Let him but fly away to the forest
and Hari he'll clean forget!

The Pandit's real craving is for pleasure and money,
for the devotees of the Lord, he cares not -
Says Kabīr, love takes no root in his heart:
in chains he'll go to the City of Death.

11

KG2 178; Gu āsā 8; Bī śabda 84

O Qāzī,
what is this book you are explaining?
Day after day, you kept reading it
yet of the true Path, you know nothing. *refrain*

(39) The Pandit here challenged is a 'Vaishnav' of kinds - in so far as he believes in the magic efficacy of the Vaishnav Name of God.

Sure of your right, you catch people
and you circumcise them -
but I'll have none of it, O Brother!
If God wanted me to be a Turk,
couldn't He do it Himself?

If it is circumcision that makes a Turk,
what then will you call your women?
A woman is a part of man's body, they say:
must she than stay a Hindu?

Hindu and Turk - where did those two come from?
Who had shown them the way?
Search your heart and let me know:
where did that 'Paradise' come from?

Give up that Book and worship Rām, O Qāzī!
What you are doing is just tyranny[40]-
Kabīr has taken his refuge in Rām
while the Qāzī keeps struggling in vain.

12

KG2 183; Gu bibhās 4

O Mullah,
You talk about the justice of God -
But such talk won't rid your soul

(40) *juluma* (Ar. *zalm*) 'oppression, tyranny': severely punished in the Islamic law. Kabīr ironically points out to the Qāzī his own infringement on the sacred Law he goes by.

from delusion[41]. *refrain*

Getting hold of living beings, you killed them -
yet what you sacrificed was but clay:
The Light Itself -their souls- eluded your grasp:
tell me, why then did you slaughter them?

Don't say that Veda and Koran are false[42]:
false is the man who does not think -
If you contemplate the One Being present in all,
why kill beings as if they were 'others'?

You keep slaughtering goats and fowls
and you talk of justice and right!
All living beings are dear to the Lord:
to whom will you appeal for salvation?

13

KG2 184; Gu āsā 17.

O Miyan[43],

---

(41) Addressed to the Mullah, a Master of Koranic law, this song is full of Arabo-Persian vocabulary: *bisamil* (P. *bismil kardan*: 'to slaughter an animal 'in the Name of God' (*bismillah*); P. *halāl kardan,* 'to slaughter an animal in the prescribed way (from Ar. *halāl,* 'lawful'); *hakka,* from Ar. *haqq* 'just, right', an attribute of God; *dila,* P. *dil,* 'the heart' in a spiritual sense; *pāka napāka* (P. *pāk napāk*: 'pure', 'impure'); *bhisati* (P. *bihisht,* 'heaven'); *dojaga* (P. *dozakh,* 'hell').

(42) Would not Veda and Koran, after all, contain some truth hidden from both Brahman and Mullah? Elsewhere, the Brahman carrying his holy scriptures is compared to 'a donkey loaded with sandal'.

(43) A Persian honorary title: 'Lord, Master'.

what you say is all wrong:
We are the humble servants of God
but you are fond of the trappings of kings! *refrain*

Allah, the Eternal, is the Protector of the poor,
He never ordered violence -
Tell me, your Murshid and your Pīr[44]:
where did they come from?

You keep the fast of the Ramzan and you do your prayers -
but the *kalimā*[45] won't earn you paradise:
He possesses seventy Kaabas within his own body
He who but knows.

Recognize the Lord, fill your soul with mercy,
renounce your craving for wealth -
Know yourself as the self of all the others:
this is paradise indeed.

(44) Ar. *murshid,* 'a spiritual Master'; P. *pīr,* 'an old man or a saint'. In Kabīr's language, *pīr* is often taken as an Islamic equivalent of the Hindu 'guru'.

(45) The Muhammedan profession of faith.

3. WARNINGS

1

KG2 174; Gu gaüṛī 4

Whether you go naked or clothed,
what's the use
If you have not recognized Rām[46]
who pervades all. *refrain*

If, by wandering in the nude,
one could achieve Yoga[47],
Would not all the deer in the forest
achieve salvation?

If by shaving one's head,
one could reach the goal,
Would not the sheep too
earn Paradise?

If by withholding your seed[48],
you could be saved, O my Brother,
Then, surely the eunuchs
would get to the highest heaven?

---

(46) *ātmarām*: or 'He who rejoices in Himself', 'He who is immanent in all'.

(47) *yoga,* here does not refer to yogic practices. It is taken in the sense of 'union' or 'reunion' of the created soul (*jīv*) with the supreme Reality: it is therefore taken as an equivalent of *mukti,* liberation or salvation.

(48) The retention of the seed is a practice enjoined upon the Yogī in the *Haṭh-Yoga* school, to which the Nāth-panthīs belong.

Says Kabīr,
O Brother, listen:
Without the Name of Rām
none ever achieved salvation!

2

KG2 170; Bī kaharā 7

Watch your step, be alert
I warn you solemnly!
If you haven't drunk deep of Rām
you have gambled your life away! *refrain*

Why sit proudly with a shaven head,
wearing chest-like ear-rings[49]?
Outside your body is wrapped up in ashes -
yet inside the house is plundered[50]!

That town you live in bears a pompous name,
but vile are the deeds you are doing:
When Yam casts his noose and drags you away,
what will your status be then?

Throwing away camphor, you collected poison -
from your capital, you never drew profit[51]!
Rām is the City of Fearlessness, there is my dwelling[52],

(49) Those enormous, heavy wooden earrings are the Nāth-panthī's *mudrā*.

(50) The Brigand 'Death' plunders the human body of that proud 'Nāth-panthī' who foolishly placed his confidence in a pellicle of ashes.

(51) The 'capital' here refers to the boon of a human birth.

(52) *abhai pad,* 'Fearlessness' is the supreme stage of absolute freedom.

says the Julāhā Kabīr.

3

KG2 198; Gu basant 2; Bī basant 10

They all went mad
none of them keeps awake,
While the Thief
is plundering the house[53]! *refrain*

The Yogīs went mad
with their concentration -
And the Pandits too,
reading their Puranas.

The ascetics went mad,
with their austerities -
And the Samnyasis
with their 'That-am-I'[54]!

God Shankar went mad,
serving the Lord's feet -
And in this Kali age,

---

(53) In the refrain and in vv. 1-2, various people are said to be *madimāte* or 'intoxicated, mad', in all the three recensions. In vv. 3 and 4, the Western tradition, Raj and Gu, substitute *jāge* ('awake') to *māte* ('intoxicated'). The thief symbolizes Death, as in Pad 28.2.

(54) *ahameva*: a Vedantic formula proclaiming the identity of the soul with the supreme Reality, the *Brahman-Ātman*.

Nāmā and Jaidev[55].

Full of impure desires
is that fickle Mind:
Says Kabīr,
worship the Name of Rām.

4

KG2 85; Gu sorathi 1

O Mind, this world
is a pit of darkness!
Already Yam's noose[56]
is seen over your neck! *refrain*

Worshipping ghosts, the Hindus died,
and the Turks, on their way to Mecca,
With their matted locks, the Yogīs too have died:
Your mystery, none has ever known.

Reciting poetry, poets died
and the Kapadis on their way to Kedar[57]-

---

(55) Nāmā (Nāmdev) and Jaydev are two famous saints of the 'Kali Age', i.e. of the age preceding Kabīr. Nāmdev is often quoted as a predecessor of Kabīr.

(56) *jama kā perā,* lit.: 'the tying rope of Yam'; *perā* is the tether used for tying a head of cattle to a pole. Kabīr sees every living being as a beast tethered to the pole of Death.

(57) The *kāpadī*s are the Kāpālikas, fearful Shaiva ascetics wearing garlands of skulls round their neck. Kedar (Kedarnath) is the famous Shaiva temple high in the Himalayas, a meeting point for such ascetics.

With shaven hair, the vow-keepers have died[58]:
none ever found salvation.

Piling up riches, the kings have died,
with their hoard of buried gold -
Reading and reciting the Veda, the Pandits too have died
and the women, mad on their own beauty!

Without Rām's Name, all sank to perdition,
see and ponder the fate of the body:
Without invoking the Name of Rām, none has ever been saved
says the Julāhā Kabīr.

5

KG2 83; Gu āsā 15

Crying 'Mine, it's Mine',
so you spent your life.
Your whole life has gone
and you didn't call upon Hari! *refrain*

Twelve years were wasted in childhood,
for twenty years you practiced no penance -
For thirty more years you didn't invoke Rām
then old age has come - and remorse!

Man builds a dam for a dried-out pond,
he keeps watch on a reaped-out field[59],

---

(58) The *Vratī* or 'vow-keepers', are those who have shaven their hair in order to keep a vow (*vrat*), on their way to a pilgrimage place.

(59) In India, once the crop is ready, the farmer keeps watch day and night until everything is harvested.

Once the Thief[60] has got in and stolen the horse,
that fool comes in to put on the snaffle!

His head, hands and feet tremble,
his eyes water endlessly,
His tongue talks haltingly,
and he thinks of gathering merits!

Says Kabīr, O Sants, listen:
hoarded riches no one can take along.
Once the summon comes from Gopālrāī[61],
man departs, leaving this house of Illusion[62].

6

KG2 102; Bī kaharā 8

"May Prosperity and happiness be yours,
may you have a peaceful life!"[63]
To whom did you wish all that?
As it comes and goes, twice robbed is the soul,
emptied of all substance! *refrain*

Gods and men, Munis and Yatis, Pīrs, Awliyas and Miras,

(60) The 'Thief' usually symbolizes Death. Here, it symbolizes both old age and Death, the one heralding the other. According to Kabīr, once the decaying process of old age has set in, salvation cannot be achieved.

(61) 'Gopālrāī' here apparently stands for 'Rām', not for the Cowherd-god.

(62) *māyā mandira,* or 'the temple of Māyā' is the body; here *māyā* means both 'illusion' and 'riches'.

(63) *kusala khema aru sahī salāmati*: the poet ironically juxtaposes the two formulas of salutation, the one used by Hindus and the other by Muslims.

the Lord created them all[64]:
Myriads of them, beyond all numbering -
and then He despatched them all.

Earth, sky and winds will pass away,
sun and moon too will pass -
Neither you nor I will remain, O my Brother:
Rām alone remains all in all.

With wishes of 'Welfare', the whole world went to its doom:
that 'welfare' is but a noose of Kal!
Says Kabīr, the whole word ends in nothingness,
Rām alone remains, the Eternal.

7

KG2 41; Gu mārū 7

O Bābā[65]! I won't stay
in this village no more -
Again and again, He keeps asking for my accounts,
that Accountant[66] called 'Conscience'! *refrain*

In the village of the Body, whose Headman is the Mind,

---

(64) Here again, the author juxtaposes two classes of 'holy men': Hindu sages, known as 'Munis' and 'Yatis', and Muslims called 'Pīrs' (saints, spiritual guides), Awliyas (plural of Wali, ' a slave of God'), and 'Miras', 'religious promulgators'; also 'Sayyeds', descendants of the Prophet.

(65) Persian *bābā,* or 'father', a familiar form of address, especially for an elderly man.

(66) *kāitha* (Skt *kāyastha*): a caste of scribes; though Hindus, the Kayasthas worked in the service of Muslim princes and big landowners as accountants. Dharmaraj is the 'Accountant' of the god of Death, Yam.

live five yeomen[67]:
Eyes, Nose, Ears, Tongue and Touch,
who listen to no one.

When Dharmaraj asked for the accounts
there were too many dues -
So the five yeomen ran away
and the soul was taken to Court, in chains[68].

8

KG2 111; Gu gaūrī 54; Bī śabda 15

O King Rām!
When the old Woman came to get her thread -
He left home and went away
that Weaver[69]. *refrain*

Of nine yards, ten yards, nineteen yards,
he stretched the warp,

---

(67) The five yeomen are the five senses or the five *prāṇ*, 'winds' or respiration. The name given to the fifth yeoman is 'Indrī' (Skt *indrīya*, lit. 'sense') which stands for the sense of Touch.

(68) The 'field' is the human body, the prisoner is the human soul, *jīv*.

(69) In this allegorical song, the 'Housewife' who brings her thread to be woven is *Māyā*, also called the 'Shrew' in v. 2. The Weaver is the human soul (*jīv*) or the mind (*manas*), busy weaving the endless cloth of Death and Life with the thread of Māyā. The seven threads allude to the seven *dhātus* or 'materials' out of which the human body is made; the seventy knots allude to the seventy-two articulations of the same. The harsh Master who bullies the poor Julāhā may be 'Kāl': 'Time' or 'Death'. The 'Three' refer to the 'three kinds of suffering', endured by the poor *jīv* in the endless cycle of *samsār*.

With seven threads, he tied the seventy knots:
what a big piece of cloth he made!

No yardstick could measure it, no scale could weigh it -
then five pounds of starch were added:
If but an ounce be missing,
the shrew would vituperate!

Ceaselessly his Master bullied him
and he was prey to all miseries -
So, leaving at home his bundle of wet thread,
in anger He went away, that Weaver.

Worthless was his shuttle,
for ever getting entangled in the warp:
O Fools! Leave that cloth-weaving alone
and adore Rām -
Kabīr warns you all!

9

KG2 128; Gu bhairaü 11

If He is the true Presence[70],
how could I say He's far off?
To make the frogs quiet
get hold of the Sundar[71]! *refrain*

---

(70) The 'true Presence': there is a pun on the work *hajūri* (Ar. *huzūr*), lit. 'presence', which is also a respectful way of address to Muslim dignitaries.

(71) There is a *double entendre*: 'Sundar' is the name of the shrew-mouse in the Bhojpuri dialect (spoken east of Benares). But 'Sundar'. lit. 'the

He is the true Mullah
who fights his own mind,
Who day and night
strikes Death with the discus.[72]

He is the true Qāzī
who passes judgment on his own body
And who burns it down
with the Yogic fire.[73]

He is the true Sultan
who shoots a double arrow,
Bringing back inside
that which goes out.[74]

He who pitches his camp
within the Cavern of the Void,[75]
That Sultan alone
holds universal sway.

Beautiful', may also mean God, whose presence silences the 'noisy frogs of vain thoughts'.

(72) The discus (*cakra*) is associated with god Vishnu, whereas, in the Yoga tradition, it is the *śabda* uttered by the Satguru which is supposed to 'kill' Death.

(73) *Brahmāgni,* the 'Fire of Brahman' is identified with the Yogic fire which destroys the impurities of body and mind and sets the Yogi free.

(74) Preventing the fall of semen and making it flow upwards is an important element of Haṭha-yoga practices.

(75) The Double Arrow symbolizes the movement of breath, which the Yogi should control and force within his own body.

The Jogi cries:
'Gorakh, Gorakh!'
The Hindu utters
the Name of Rām,[76]

The Mussalman repeats:
'God is One!'
But the Lord of Kabīr
pervades all.[77]

10

KG2 61; Gu gauṇḍ 1; Bī ra. 70

Why do you ask me
to speak, O Brother?
Talking, talking,
the Reality is lost. *refrain*

Talking and talking,
the obstacles increase:
Why don't you meditate
in silence?

Should you meet a saint[78],
exchange a few words,
Should you meet a sinner,
then keep quiet.

---

(76) The *gagan-maṇḍal* is an equivalent of *śūnya-maṇḍal,* the 'Circle of the Sky' or 'of the Void'.

(77) Gorakhnāth: the great Tantric Master revered by all Jogis.

(78) The *sant* is here opposed to the sinner or *asant*. The 'Sant' is not necessarily a 'holy man', but simply a good, honest person.

Conversation with a sage
  is a real boon -
Talking with fools
  is mere waste of time!

Says Kabīr, it's the half-empty pot
  that makes noise:
Once full,
  it's heard no more.

11

KG2 101; Gu āsā 5

Even if you be a Pandit, knowing all scriptures
  and all sciences and grammars,
And if you knew all treatises and spells and herb-balms[79]
  in the end, die you must. *refrain*

And if you possessed a kingdom, a throne and a canopy
  and many fair maidens for your pleasure,
And plenty of betel and camphor and sweet-smelling sandal -
  despite all, die you must.

An if you be a Yogī, a Yati, a Tapi or a Samnyasi[80],
  going on endless pilgrimages -
With shaven head or plucked hair, a silent One
  or One with matted locks,

(79) *tantra-mantra* or esoteric treatises full of magic spells are here associated with the science of *auṣadhi,* healing herbs.

(80) For a similar enumeration of various types of 'holy men', see above, song 9.

in the end, die you must.

Says Kabīr, I've thought and pondered,
watching the whole world:
none has ever escaped -
So I have taken refuge in You:
free me from that round of birth and death!

12

KG2 185, Gu bibhās 3

O People, my Brothers,
don't be led astray!
The Creator in His creation, creation in the Creator[81]:
He pervades all. *refrain*

In the beginning, Allah created light:
all creatures are slaves of His power -
From the One Light, He made the whole world.
Who then is noble? Who is vile?

Unfathomable is Allah's mystery -
but the Guru gave me a delicious sugar[82]:
Says Kabīr, I attained plenitude
as I contemplated the Lord in all beings.

---

(81) In this song, Kabīr makes use of Arabic vocabulary and addresses his Muslim brothers in the language of a Sufi, who sees the Lord (*Sāhib*) as immanent in all beings and the Creator (*khāliq*) as not distinct from the creation (*khalaq*).

(82) This 'sweet' is the Śabda imparted by the Satguru.

13

KG2 126; Gu basant 6

What can I do
with such a Trader[83],
whose stock keeps dwindling
while his debts increase? *refrain*

There was a Naik
with five Banjārās,
And twenty-five bullocks
loaded with shoddy goods.

He kept nine account-books
and ten load-sacks,
Which were tied
with seventy-two straps.

The three tax-collectors
set upon him -
And the Trader went away
empty-handed!

---

(83) The 'Trader' is the human soul, ensnared in the bonds of worldly life. That 'Trader' is depicted as a 'Naik' (*nāyak*), the leader of a caravan of Banjārās, a tribe of nomadic merchants who lead long files of pack-bullocks. The 'Naik' also symbolizes to Mind (*manas*) and the 'five Banjārās' are the five senses; the 'twenty-five bullocks' are the twenty-five *prakriti* ('natural properties'); the 'nine account-books' are the nine openings of the body; the 'ten sacks' are the ten senses (five *jñānendrīy,* plus five *karmendrīy*s), the 'seventy-two straps' are the seventy-two articulations of the human body; the 'seven threads' are the seven *dhātu*s, the 'materials' of the human body; the 'three tax-collectors' are the three kinds of sufferings.

His business came to an end,
  lost was his capital
And the ten-days caravan[84]
  went to naught.

Says Kabīr,
  vain indeed is this life!
So I gave up the load
  and I merged into the *Sahaj*.

14

KG2 129; Gu bhairaü 4

O Mullah,
  raise the call to prayer
Through the ten doors
  of the one Mosque[85]! *refrain*

Make your mind the Mecca,
  make your body the Qibla:
He who speaks inside
  is the supreme Guru.

In Allah's Name[86] kill Darkness
  kill Error, Impurity -

(84) The 'ten-days caravan' symbolizes the short span of a human life.

(85) The ten doors of the one 'Mosque are the ten openings of the human body within which salvation is to be achieved.

(86) *bisimili* (Ar. *bismillah*), 'in Allah's Name', is the formula used at the time of slaughtering an animal in the proper Islamic manner. Kabīr suggests that the Mullah should kill the error and impurity in his own soul instead of killing a living being; also that he should 'eat up' the 'Fives senses' rather

By eating up the Five senses
  only then will you find true Patience.

Says Kabīr,
  I have gone mad -
Silently that soul of mine
  has merged into the Sahaj[87]!

15

KG2 49; Gu gaüṛī 39; Bī śabda 36

Hari, the Thug[88],
  has tricked the whole world -
Yet, away from Him, I cannot live,
  O my Friend[89]! *refrain*

Who has a husband?
  who has a wife?
Think well about it
  and search your own soul.

---

than the flesh of innocent beings: in this way, he will find true *sabūrī* (Ar. *sabr*) or Peace of Mind, Patience.

(87) *sahaj*: or 'easy, natural', also means transcendental Oneness.

(88) Hari, i.e. God, has taken on the appearance of a *ṭhag* (Anglo-Indian *thug)*, one of those Indian highway-brigands, famous for their cunning and their cruelty. Through the power of Māyā, Hari (God) tricks the whole world; all family-ties belong to the world of Māyā who is also a Cheat.

(89) *māī,* lit.: 'mother', is also a familiar form of address from a woman to another (especially for an elderly woman). The woman speaker here stands for the wife-soul, complaining to her neighbour about having a cheat (or a 'Thug') as a husband - while revealing, in the last verse, that she herself (like Kabīr) has pierced the identity of the divine 'Brigand'.

Who has a son?
  who has a father?
Who is it who suffers,
  who is it who dies?

Says Kabīr, with that Thug,
  my heart is well pleased -
And the thuggery was over
  when I recognized the Thug[90].

16

KG2 87; Gu tilaṅg 1

O you, Servant of God,
  don't wander about in distress:
This world is like a town-fair,
  where no one will lend you a hand! *refrain*

Veda and Koran are false, O my Brother:
  do not worry in your heart -
If you but remain quiet for an instant,
  God, the Lord, will be present.

You keep reading lies with such gusto
  and you go on babbling nonsense -
He is the Truth, the Creator is in the creation, O Miyan[91],

(90) Once the wife-soul has recognized the Beloved, Rām, within her soul, the veil of Māyā is lifted and the wife-soul merges into the One.

(91) Addressed to a 'Miyan' (see above: Satires, 13) this song is composed in a fairly artificial language, saturated with Arabic and Persian vocabulary.

not in a dark-blue stone[92]!

It is in the River-of-the-sky, O Miyan,
  that He makes His ablutions -
Meditate on Him constantly,
  knowing He is everywhere present.

Allah is the Pure among the pure,
  but he who doubts sees something else -
Kabīr, he who acts like the All-merciful[93]
  he alone knows Him!

17

KG2 76

As to myself,
  I have known the One as One:
Those who speak of two will go to hell:
  they haven't known Him! *refrain*

One is the wind, one the water,
  which merges into the one Light -
One is the earth from which poets were made,
  One is the Potter.

By the tricks of Māyā, the whole world was fooled:
  O Men, why are you so proud?

(92) *śyām mūrti*, or 'a dark-blue idol': in this context, the 'dark-blue idol' does not refer to some Vaishnavite idol; it must refer to the Kaaba itself, the palladium of Islam, at Mecca.

(93) Allusion to the practice of *ahimsā*: a pious man should refrain from killing living beings.

Says Kabīr, listen, my saintly brothers[94],
why didn't you sell yourself into the Guru's hands?

4. DEATH

1

KG2 69; Gu kedār 4; Bī śabda 72

Why do you strut about
putting up such airs[95]?
In vain, you shut the nine hellish gates[96]:
the foul stench passes through. *refrain*

Burnt, your body turns into ashes,
buried, it's eaten by worms -
Or else it is food for pigs, dogs and crows:
what is it worth?

Blind are your eyes, your heart is unfeeling,
your mind devoid of understanding -
For lust, anger and burning desires,

(94) *bhāī sādhau* or 'saintly brothers', may allude to the so-called 'holy men' still ignorant of the spiritual path, a path which consists of a total surrender to the divine Satguru - or it may be taken ironically.

(95) *teḍhe teḍhe teḍhe,* lit.: 'with such contortions'.

(96) The 'nine hellish gates' are the nine apertures of the human body: the eight natural ones, plus the *brahmarandhra,* on the top of the head. Through *haṭh-yog* practices, the Yogī strives to close the natural nine apertures and to open the tenth, the *brahmarandhra,* which is supposed to be the Gate of salvation.

you are drowning without water[97]!

You don't invoke Rām, in your folly,
though Kāl is drawing near -
And you take endless pains for this body
which in the end turns into dust.

In a house of sand, they live,
unknowing, unaware -
Says Kabīr, failing to adore Rām
so many 'wise men' were drowned!

2

KG2 68; Gu soraṭhi 2; Bī śabda 73

Why do you flounce around
puffed up with vanity[98]?
Ten months, you spent head downwards:
did you forget? *refrain*

If burnt, your body turns into ashes,
if buried, it's eaten by worms -
Like an unbaked clay-pot filled with water,
such is your body's greatness!

As the bee keeps gathering honey,
you went on collecting wealth -
But once you're dead, they all cry: "Take it away!"

---

(97) The waterless ocean is the Ocean of *samsār*.

(98) *phūle phūle phūle;* lit.: 'all puffed up'. This song closely resembles the preceding one, both in subject and in style.

"Keep out the evil spirits!"[99]

Up to the threshold will your wife follow you,
  a little further may your good friends go,
Up to the burning-ground will your kith and kin come -
  ahead the soul will go alone[100].

You didn't merge yourself in Rām, fool as you are,
  so you are falling into the pit of Death -
Says Kabīr, man ensnares himself,
  like the parrot trapped on the bamboo branch!

3

KG2 62; Gu gaüṛī 35 & gauṇḍ 2;
Bī śabda 99

Why pride yourself
  on this foul body?
Once dead, it will not keep
  for a single moment! *refrain*

With rice pudding and molasses and butter,
  you have pampered this body of yours -
Yet, hardly has the breath gone
  it is cast away to be burnt.

---

(99) This refers to the Hindu dread of the *bhūt*s, which are supposed to take hold of the corpse immediately upon death. So all are in great hurry to drag the body out of the house.

(100) The word used here is *hamsa,* a beautiful bird, which symbolizes the human soul. In *sākhī* 14.3, the faithful Wife claims:

'O Burning-ground, O my Friend! All people, passengers, have gone:
You and I remain in the end.'

That head you used to wrap,
saucily, in a turban -
That same head, the crows
will decorate with their beaks!

Bones will burn
like dry wood,
Hair will burn
like dry hay.

Says Kabīr, even now,
man won't wake up -
Even as Yam's club[101]
is coming down on his head!

4

KG2 100; Gu kedār 6

Their fanfare[102]
lasted but four days!
Lifted from the stretcher, buried in the mud[103],
they couldn't take anything with them! *refrain*

Weeping, the wife sits on the door-step,

---

(101) Yam is the Lord of Death, who is represented carrying a club.

(102) Lit.: 'they played the *naubat*': the *naubat* is a musical performance given by a group of musicians in the service of a Muslim Grandee; the musicians play in a recess over the main gate of the palace called *naubat-khānā*. 'To play the *naubat*' also means: 'to display one's pomp and grandeur .

(103) The grandee is a Muslim, and the funeral is a burial.

up to the outer gate, the mother goes[104],
Down to the graveyard the kinsmen follow
then the soul departs alone[105].

Those sons of yours, those riches, that beautiful palace,
you'll never return and see them again:
Says Kabīr, unless a man prays devoutly
his life is spent in vain.

5. MĀYĀ

1

KG2 161; Bī kahār 12

That Māyā of Raghunāth
has gone hunting -
A shrewd Belle she is! She kills at will:
none will escape her who comes by. *refrain*

The Maunī and the Vīr and the Digambar[106], You struck down,
and the Yogī practicing his Yoga,
You struck the Jangam in the midst of the jungle
and You wander all over as You fancy.

---

(104) Women never follow a funeral.

(105) The *hamsa* refers to the soul; see above, song 2.

(106) The *Maunī*: he who has taken a vow of silence.
The *Vīr* (lit.: hero), in this context, may be a *Vīrashaiva,* an adept of the sect of that name, also known as *Jangams*.
The Digambar, (lit.: 'one clad in the cardinal points', i.e. naked) is an ascetic belonging to the Jain ascetic order of the same name.

You struck the Brahman reciting his Veda
and the Svami, engaged in worship[107],
You knocked down the Mishra[108] commenting on his text
and you threw your rope round their necks[109]!

Over the Shāktas, you rule supreme,
but You are the slave of the Saints -
Says Kabīr: O Sants, Listen!
Empty-handed She went away[110].

2

KG2 163; Bī śabda 59

Māyā is a great Swindler[111],
I know her well!
Holding in hand the noose of the three Qualities[112]
she wanders, speaking honeyed words. *refrain*

In Keshav's house, she sits as Kamlā,

---

(107) The Svāmī (Brahman) performing *sevā,* lit.: 'service' of a Vaishnav icon, which has to be served in the manner of a human King.

(108) The Mishra, member of a Brahman sub-caste, is held in high esteem for his scriptural learning.

(109) In the time-honoured manner of the famous brigands known as Thugs (see above, song 2.15).

(110) The true Sants (i.e. Saints) are beyond Māyā's power.

(111) *ṭhaginī* or 'a female Thug'; see above, song 4.1.

(112) The noose is one among the weapons held in the hand of the Great Goddess known as 'Kāli' and 'Durgā'. The three *guṇs* or 'qualities' are but illusory distinctions hiding the essential unity of being.

in Shiva's mansion, as Bhavānī[113],
In the Panda's house, she stands as his idol,
and she is the water in his sacred Ford.

In the Yogī's hut, she is a Yoginī,
in the King's palace, she is a Queen:
To the one, she appears as pure diamond,
to another, as a worthless shell[114].

To the devotee, she is a devout Lady,
to god Brahma, she is Brahmanī,
Says Kabīr, O Sants! Listen:
of her mystery, nothing can be told.

3

KG2 160; Bī śabda 44

O Ascetic, think hard
and figure it out:
Is it a male
or a female? *refrain*

She's neither married nor maiden,
yet she gives birth to sons -[115]
Blacked-haired or shaven, no man escapes her,

---

(113) There is a pun on the word *bhavan,* 'mansion' and 'Bhavānī', the name of the Great Goddess as god Shiva's consort.

(114) To the unenlightened one, Māyā appears precious as a diamond; to the saint, she appears as a worthless and ill-formed ('one-eyed') cowrie- shell.

(115) M.P. Gupta, in his edition of the *Kabīr-granthāvalī,* p. 265, interprets Māyā's 'sons' as *manovikār,* lit.: 'defects of the mind'; these 'sons' may also be interpreted as the lures of the world in general.

yet for ever she remains a virgin!

In the Brahman's house, she's Brahmanī,
in the Yogī's house, a disciple,
Endlessly repeating the *kalimā* , she's a Turkanī
yet, up to this Kali Age, she remains alone.

She lives in her mother's house, she doesn't go to her in-laws,
nor does she sleep with her husband -
Says Kabīr, that one will live from age to age
who gives up family, caste and lineage.

6. THE SUBTLE PATH

1

KG2 150; Gu āsā 36; Bī ra. 28

No one knows
the secret of that Weaver[116]
Who spread his warp
throughout the world[117]. *refrain*

In earth and in sky,
He dug the two ditches -
Of sun and moon,

(116) The Weaver, here called by the Hindu term *korī* (instead of the Persian 'Julāhā') represents both the *jīv,* the human soul and *manas,* the Mind.

(117) The loom is the human body; the 'sky' corresponds to the highest *cakra,* the *gagan-maṇḍal* or 'circle of the sky'; the 'earth' is the lowest *cakra,* the *mūlādhār-cakra* or 'circle of the base'.

He made his two spools[118].

With a thousand threads,
He filled his shuttle[119]-
Up to this day He's weaving,
yet the end is hard to reach[120]!

Says Kabīr,
it's a network of *karmas*
Joining good thread to bad thread, he keeps weaving
that good Weaver.

2

KG2 81; Gu gaüṛī 31

Mount the steed
of your own thought[121]
And place your foot
in the stirrup of the Sahaj[122]. *refrain*

With bit and bridle,

---

(118) The 'sun' and 'moon' are the *Iḍā* and *Pingalā nāḍī*s ('duct' or 'canal').

(119) The thousand threads filling the shuttle are the innumerable 'actions', or *karma*s, which bind the Jīv to the world of transmigration.

(120) In the last line, there are two different endings: We have preferred the *Bi* reading: 'Says Kabīr: He smashed his loom,
and he joined thread to thread, that Weaver!'

(121) Here, the 'thought' apparently alludes to the *kuṇḍalinī-śakti* of the Hath-yogic *sādhanā* or 'practice': the *kuṇḍalinī,* figured as a 'snake', should be made to rise so as to reach the 'sky'; see above, song 5.1.

(122) 'Sahaj' here seems to be both the way and the goal.

I'll curb my horse -
I'll saddle it with a fine saddle
and I'll spur it on up to the sky!

Come! It's to heaven[123]
I am taking you -
And if you falter, I'll lash you
with the Whip of Love[124]!

Says Kabīr,
only those are horsemen
Who keep away
from Veda and Koran.

3

KG2 127; Gu āsā 10

O my Friend[125], if you churn
then churn for Hari -
Let your churning be such
that the Essence is not lost[126]. *refrain*

Making your body the jar,
it is your mind you'll churn

(123) *baikunṭha* is the mythological paradise of god Vishnu, here symbolizing the supreme stage of *sahaj-samādhi*.

(124) *prem tājanai* (P. *tāziyanah,* or 'whip'); the image is an audacious one; *prem-bhakti,* the loving devotion advocated by the Vaishnavas is here strangely integrated in an allegory based on Tantric beliefs and practices.

(125) *sakhī,* a female friend, the woman's neighbour.

(126) Butter is 'the essence' of milk, as Hari (God) is the Essence of all beings.

Then, within the jar itself,
  the butter of Śabda[127] will collect.

Those three channels:
  Iḍā, Piṅgalā, Suṣumnā -
If you churn fast enough
  will strain the buttermilk[128].

Says Kabīr,
  that milkmaid[129] has gone crazy:
She has smashed her jar
  and vanished into the Light[130].

7. THE NAME OF GOD

1

KG2 22; Gu bhairaū 1

My only wealth
  is the Name of Hari:

---

(127) *Śabda,* lit.:, 'the word', here refers to the inner revelation provoked by the Perfect Guru, the *Satguru.*

(128) The three *nāḍīs* or 'channels' belong to the language of *Haṭh-yog. Buttermilk is the residue of the churning process after* the 'butter' has been extracted, and the mysterious *sahaj-samādhi* has been achieved within the body.

(129) The milkmaid here is called *Gujarī,* a woman of the Gujar pastoral caste, a wandering tribe.

(130) The action of the Gujarī milkmaid, breaking her jar after the 'Butter' has appeared, runs parallel to the action of the 'Weaver' smashing his loom in song 5.1.

I don't tie it in my belt
nor do I sell and spend it. *refrain*

Your Name is my field,
your Name is my orchard,
the object of my Love,
my only refuge.

Your Name is my fortune,
your Name is my capital -
Beside your Name
I know nothing.

Your Name is my kith and kin,
your Name is my Brother -
On the last day, your Name will be
my sole Companion.

I cling to your Name
as a poor wretch finds a Treasure -
Says Kabīr, as a tramp
grabs sweetmeats!

2

KG2 21; Gu gaürī 33

Invoking Rām,
my body was consumed -
In the Name of Rām,
my spirit has merged. *refrain*

He Himself is the Fire,

He Himself is the Wind -
If the Lord[131] Himself sets you afire,
who will protect you?

Whose is this body?
Who loses what[132]?
He plays like a clown
That Lord Sāraṅgpāṇi[133]!

Says Kabīr,
repeat the Two Syllables:
If there be a Rām[134],
He will protect you.

3

Bī śabda 35

Rām is my Husband,
I am His little wife[135],
Rām is great,
and I, so small! *refrain*

---

(131) The word here used is the Persian *khasam,* 'Lord'.

(132) The body itself is just 'Māyā': Illusion.

(133) A Vaishnav epithet of God.

(134) *hoigā rāma* (variant 'Lord', P. *khasam*) may be interpreted as: 'If there is a Rām' or 'wherever He [Rām] may be, He will save you'. In the Vaishnav tradition, God Vishnu-Hari is so fond of his devotees that He feels the obligation of rushing to the rescue of all those who invoke His Name in distress - as shown by the well-known legends of Ajāmīl, Gajendra and the Harlot.

(135) The 'little wife' is the Servant of God. *Sadgranth Bījak,* p. 289, Varanasi, 1969 A.D.

Fixing the four pegs,
and the two thread-holes
Easily, she has set
the wheel in motion.

For six months she has spun
and she rolled up the thread for twelve days -
So people say:
'How well she's spun, that poor little one!'

Says Kabīr,
beautiful is the thread she's spun -
But the Giver of salvation
was not her wheel.

4

KG2 58; Gu gaūrī 68

O you, foolish Mind,
stop fluttering about!
The Wife has resolved to die on the pyre,
holding the *sindūr*-box[136] in hand. *refrain*

Fearlessly, she dances in a trance,
free from Desire and Error:

(136) The soul which has taken the way to the supreme Stage is compared to the *Satī,* the heroic wife who has made up her mind to be burnt on the pyre with the dead body of her Husband. As she departs in the procession, all decked with her ornaments, she holds in her hand the bowl containing *sindūr,* the red powder which the married woman applies to the parting of her hair as a symbol of fidelity up to death.

Could a true Warrior fear Death?
  Could a *Satī* care for the household-pots[137]?

World and Veda and family Pride,
  all are but nooses around your neck -
Whoever goes half-way and then turns back
  is the laughing-stock of all.

This world is nothing but dirt,
  only those who invoke Rām are saved:
Says Kabīr, hold fast to the Name,
  though you fall and stumble, you'll reach the summit.

8. IN PRAISE OF THE SAINTS

1

KG2 51; Gu gaüṛī 12.2 & 13.4

If there be a saint in whose heart the bliss of Sahaj[138] is born,
  I'll give Him all litanies and penance as brokerage:
Let He but give me a single drop of Rām's Liquor[139]

---

(137) Literally: 'A Sati does not gather pots and pans': She has no care for worldly things. Like the Warrior (*sūr*) with whom she is associated, she has a pact with Death. Cf. *sākhī* 11. 13; 14. 23-24; 41 *et passim*.

(138) *sahaj-sukh*, or 'the Bliss of Sahaj' is identical with *mahāsukh*, or 'perfect bliss' which pertains to the supreme stage of *sahaj samādhi*.

(139) *rām-ras*, or 'the Liquor of Rām' is identical with *mahāras* or *amrit-ras*. It alludes to the Liquor of Immortality concocted by the Yogīs addicted to alchemy (*rasāyan*). See below: The Enigma,3. Here, the saint's progress towards the ultimate state of *sahaj-samādhi* through merging into the Ultimate (Rām) is compared to the distillation process of country-liquor, as done

as the Liquor-girl pours out a drink! *refrain*

For the sake of money, that Liquor-girl of the body
had taken the Guru's Word as sugar:
Greed, lust, anger, envy and pride, she's ground them fine
and used them as toning up.

From the fourteen worlds, she made her still
and she lit the Fire of Brahman:
In the vat sealed with *mudrā*[140], the sound of the Sahaj rose up,
Sushumnā itself was the worm.

The spring flowed, ambrosia oozed out,
on such a drink, the Prince[141] got drunk -
Says Kabīr, such a flavour is hard to find:
the all-knowing Guru alone masters the art!

2

KG2 30; Gu gaürī 26

Pure is he who sings
the praise of Rām, the Pure:
He is a true devotee
and dear to my soul. *refrain*

---

in India by the *Kalāl* (liquormaker) and his wife, the *Kalālī*. The parallel already appears in the Buddhistic *Caryā-gīti*.

(140) The body itself is the vat; *mudrā*, here, refers to the Yogic exercise consisting of closing all the natural apertures of the body so as to force the *kuṇḍaliṇī-śakti* upwards through the channel known as the *suṣumnā-nāḍī*, here compared to the worm of the still.

(141) The 'Prince' (*rāval*) is the Yogī, drunk with *mahāras*.

To those devotees
who invoke the Name of Rām,
I offer myself
in sacrifice.

To those men whose bodies
overflow with Rām's presence,
May I be the dust
of their feet.

By caste a mere Julāhā,
but steadfast of soul -
Joyfully Kabīr steeps himself
in the Lord's praise.

3

KG2 27; Gu gaüṛī 42; Bī śabda 112

O Rām,
settle this quarrel,
If you really care
for your devotees! *refrain*

Who is greater? God Brahmā,
or He where he came from?
Who is greater? The Veda,
or that from which it came?

Which is greater? The heart,
or that it believes in?
Which is greater: Rām
or the Knower of Rām?

Wandering all over,
Kabīr has lost heart:
Is the holy spot greater
or is it the devotee[142]?

4

KG2 29; Gu gaürī 10 & Bairaü 16

They all talk
about going there -
But I do not know
where that Heaven[143] can be! *refrain*

They have not covered
a single league on the road -
Yet they keep explaining and talking
about Heaven!

As long as the Mind
yearns for Heaven,
It won't find rest
at Hari's feet.

It's nothing but hear-say:
how can one believe it?

---

(142) *hari kā dās,* or 'the servant of Hari', does not seem to fit in the *Bī* reading: *tīrath dās* should not be interpreted as 'the servant of the pilgrimage', but as the 'devotee' or 'saint' who is himself the sanctifying *tīrth.*

(143) *baikunṭha* or the Paradise of delights which is supposed to be the residence of god Vishnu.

Unless and until
  one has reached There?

Says Kabīr,
  whom shall I tell?
The company of the Saints[144]
  that's the real Heaven.

9. PRAYER

1

KG2 45; Gu bilāval 7

Exhausted, I stand at your royal Gate[145]:
  but for You, who will remember me[146]?
Allow me to see Your face,
  open the door! *refrain*

None is so rich and generous as You,
  may my ears be filled with the sound of your praise!
Whom else shall I beg from? All are just broke:
  You alone are my salvation.

---

(144) *sādha samgati;* or 'the company of the holy' is heaven on earth, and also a way to salvation.

(145) *darabārī* (P. *darbar*): a King's audience or a Court of Justice.

(146) *surati* here clearly stands for *smriti,* or 'remembrance', and has an esoteric meaning.

To Jaydev and Nāmā and to the priest Sudāmā[147],
didn't You grant marvellous favours?
Says Kabīr, You alone are the all-powerful Giver,
Who can grant me all boons at once.

2

KG2 36

O Mādhau,
when will you have pity on me?
Lust, anger and pride are set upon me
and Māyā won't leave me alone! *refrain*

From the day I was formed from a drop of semen,
I have never found peace:
I had taken to the company of five Brigands[148]
and with them, I've ruined my life.

The Wife[149], like a snake, bites my body and soul,
of quarrels, there is no end -
Unless the snake-charmer[150] comes to my help,
the deadly poison will spread all over.

Says Kabīr, to whom shall I tell my misery?

---

(147) The priest Sudāmā is famous in Vaishnav lore: he was a poor Brahman and a close friend of Lord Krishna; his simple devotion was rewarded by the gift of miraculous wealth.

(148) The 'five Brigands' are the five senses.

(149) That 'wife' whose bite is deadly like that of a poisonous snake is Māyā.

(150) The *garuḍī* is a magician who heals snake-bites with the help of appropriate *mantras*: that 'Garuḍī' is the Guru Himself.

there is none to understand my sorrow -
Grant me your Vision[151], rid me of my own fancies,
then only will my soul find Peace.

10. PANGS OF SEPARATION

1

KG2 47; Bī śabda 108

Today, how can I
win the Vision of Your Face?
Yet, deprived from that Vision,
my soul cannot find peace. *refrain*

Am I a wicked servant
or are You forgetful?
Which of us two
is to blame, O Lord?

They say that You are
the Master and King of the three worlds -
You are He who fulfills
all the soul's desires:

Prays Kabīr, O Hari,
show Yourself to me!
Either call me to Yourself
or else come to me.

(151) The Persian word *dīdār* refers to spiritual enlightenment.

2

KG2 37; Gu āsā 12

Hari, You are my Mother
and I am your child:
Why couldn't You forget
all my faults? *refrain*

However often,
a son commits a fault,
Every time his mother
will forgive and forget!

Should he catch hold of her hair
and deal her blows -
Even then, his mother
won't cease loving him[152]!

Says Kabīr,
that much only I know:
If the child is in pain,
won't his mother feel pain too?

3

KG2 13

O Beloved,

(152) In the Vaishnav Bhakti tradition, which takes its source in the *Bhāgavat-Purāṇ,* god Vishnu-Hari is described as *bhakta-vātsalya,* i.e. loving his devotees like a mother-cow loves her calf. The motherliness of God, and the pangs of separation He Himself endures for his distance from his Bhaktas has been especially emphasized in the Maharashtrian *abhaṅga* literature, beginning from Nāmdev.

come to my house:
Away from You,
my body aches! *Re!*[153] *refrain*

They all say I am Your wife
but I have my doubts -
If we don't sleep together on one couch
what kind of love is that? *Re*!

I've no taste for food, sleep deserts me,
neither at home nor in the wilderness,
I don't find peace:
As woman is dear to the lecher, as water to the thirsty,
so are you to me! *Re*!

Will there be anyone so kind
to go and bring my message to Hari?
So great is Kabīr's distress,
for not seeing You, he is dying - *Re*!

4

KG2 9

Away from Rām,
my body burns for ever -
In water itself
a blaze has broken out! *refrain*

You are the Ocean

(153) This song has the form of a folk-song on the Virah theme; it is put in the mouth of a *virahiṇī,* a deserted wife, who is Kabīr. As usual in folk-songs, each line ends with a meaningless syllable, such as *'Re'*.

and I, the fish in the water:
In water I live,
yet for water I pine.

You are the Cage
and I your parrot -
And that Cat, Death,
can do nothing to me.

You are the Perfect Guru[154]
and I your little disciple -
Says Kabīr, may I meet You
at the last moment!

5

KG2 19; Gu āsā 35

I beseech You,
turn Your face towards me, my Beloved[155]!
Why do you kill me
by turning away? *refrain*

Rather a saw on my neck
than Your turning away[156]-
I cling to your neck,

(154) The *satguru,* which cannot be apprehended, but at the time of 'merging' into the One.

(155) The wife-soul is portrayed as a young woman who, lying on the conjugal bed, cannot attract the attention of her husband and reproves him in anguish.

(156) There is a pun on *karavaṭ,* 'a saw', and *karvaṭu* 'the act of turning round' (on a bed).

listen to my prayer!

Between You and me,
there was never anyone else:
You were my Husband
I was always Your wife[157].

Says Kabīr,
Listen, you people:
I have no faith left
in You, any more[158].

6

KG2 70; Gu sūhī 2; Bī śabda 106

The night is over
and the day too passes in vain[159]:
The black-bee has flown away
now the white crane has come[160]. *refrain*

---

(157) The wife-soul is a *satī*, a faithful wife, from birth to birth wedded to the same Husband.

(158) The last verse is not very clear. The implication seems to be that the wife-soul, even when slighted by her divine Husband, will nevertheless cling to Him and take no account of all human creatures. The verse is probably a late addition.

(159) The 'night' alludes to the ages during which the unfortunate *jīv*, the soul, has been blindly wandering from womb to womb; the 'day' is the human birth the soul has attained at last: its one and only chance to achieve salvation.

(160) The blackbee symbolizes black-haired youth, the white crane, white-haired old age.

She shivers and trembles
  the little girl-soul:
'How am I to know
  what my Husband will do with me?'[161]

In the raw pot of clay,
  water won't stay -
Once the Hamsa-bird has departed,
  the body dries up[162].

Putting crows to flight,
  my arms are aching[163]-
Says Kabīr,
  that's the end of the story.

7

KG2 139; Bī śabda 37

That Thug[164] keeps swindling

---

(161) The human soul is here compared to the little Hindu child-wife, on the night following the *gaunā,* when she is brought for the first time to her husband's house: Will he take her to Himself or discard her?

(162) The 'raw clay-pot' symbolizes the human body, unable to hold the fluid of life and doomed to decay as soon as the *Hamsa-bird,* i.e. the *jīv,* the soul, has left.

(163) In Indian folklore, the crow figures as a messenger, especially between a village-girl and her far-away husband or lover. 'Putting crows to flight' is also a popular pastime with village-girls who seek an omen: the direction in which the crow will fly away is supposed to indicate the direction from which the awaited Husband or lover will come.

(164) The wife-soul complains of the waywardness and deceit of her divine Spouse, calling Him a *ṭhag* or a highway-brigand; see above: Warnings, 15.

roaming the whole world!
He left me and went off
without telling me a word. *refrain*

From my childhood days
were You not my Friend?
Why did You forsake me
and stay away from me?

Are You not my Husband,
Am I not your wife?
Your waywardness weighs on me,
heavier than stone!

This body is but clay,
these limbs are but air -
Kabīr is terrified
by the tricks of that Thug[165].

8

KG2 109; Bī śabda 54

To my Father-in-law's house,
as a new bride[166], I came,
But I couldn't unite with my Lord
and my youth passed in vain! *refrain*

---

(165) The implication is that the human body, through which alone salvation can be achieved, will soon dissolve. The wife-soul is terrified at the thought that Death will overcome her before she has achieved union with the divine 'Thug', God.

(166) The girl-soul came as a *gauhanī,* one brought over to the father-in-law's house in the *gaunā* ceremony, a kind of inthronisation.

The Five[167] erected the wedding-canopy,
  the three fixed the marriage's date,
My girl-friends sang the wedding songs
  and smeared my brow with the turmeric of Joy and Sorrow.

Clad in motley array , I circled the sacred Fire,
  the knot was tied, true to my father's pledge:
Without a Bridegroom, I entered wedlock -
  on the marriage-square I stood as a widow
    by my Lord's side!

My Husband's face, I've never seen,
  yet people urge me to be a perfect wife.
Says Kabīr, I'll raise a pyre and I'll die on it:
  clinging to my Spouse, I'll cross over,
    playing the trumpet of Victory!

9

Gu āsā 30

Rām is my Husband,
  I am his little wife:
Rām is very big

---

(167) The 'Five' are the five 'elements' (*tattva*) which compose the human body, here symbolized by the wedding-canopy; the 'Three' are the 'strands' (*guṇs*) out of which the whole creation is made. The *sakhī-sahelī* are young women of the bride's party, whose duty it is to sing the auspicious songs' (*mangal-gīt*) at the approach of the Bridegroom and to apply turmeric paste to the bride's forehead. But the Bridegroom - God - remains invisible. As a *Satī* the bride-soul will immolate herself on the pyre and meet Her true Husband: God.

and I so small! *refrain*

For our meeting,
I had decked myself,
But I didn't find Hari,
the Lord of my soul.

The Lord is my beloved,
For Him, I live -
One is the couch
but the meeting is hard to find!

Blessed be that Wife
who could please the Husband:
Says Kabīr,
She won't be born again.

11. THE JOY OF UNION

1

KG2 5; Gu āsā 24

O young Wives,
sing the wedding-songs[168]!
For He has come to my house -
my Spouse, King Rām! *refrain*

(168) *mangalācār* (equivalent to *mangal-gīt*), the auspicious songs sung at an Indian wedding.

Having dyed my body red, I'll dye my soul too[169],
the five Elements will be the Bridegroom's party[170]-
The Lord Rām has come to stay in my house,
I am drunk with the spirit of Youth!

In the lake of my body, I'll set up the altar,
god Brahma Himself will intone the Vedic hymns.
Together with Lord Rām, I'll circle the fire,
Ah! Blessed, blessed am I!

Thirty-three myriads of gods have come to see the marvel
and so have eighty-eight thousand sages[171]:
Says Kabīr, I was well and truly betrothed
to the One, the eternal Spouse!

2

KG2 6

After so many days,
my Beloved has come -
So great is my fortune:

---

(169) Red is the colour of Love. On the wedding-day, the hands and feet of the bride, as well as her forehead, are decorated with henna, and her lips are reddened with the juice of the betel-leaves.

(170) God being the Master of the Universe, the divine Bridegroom's attendants are the five 'Primordial Elements', out of which the universe is made: it is they who composed the marriage-procession, the *barāt*.

(171) The bride's family takes pride in the large number of distinguished guests who come to attend the wedding. Here, the mysterious 'wedding' of the bride-soul is attended by a crowd of deities and great *muni*s (divine Seers) who compose 'the hosts of Heaven'.

sitting at home, I found Him[172]! *refrain*

In the joy of the wedding-song,
my soul is enraptured
And my tongue savours
the life-giving nectar of Rām[173].

I who had lost hope
found the Nine Treasures!
What merit do I have?
The glory is all yours.

Says Kabīr,
I have done nothing:
It's Rām who has given me
the conjugal Bliss of the Sahaj[174].

3

KG2 7

Now I won't let You go,
O Rām, my Beloved:
So long as You please
may You be mine! *refrain*

After a long separation,
I've found Hari -

---

(172) The bride-soul found her Lord within her own soul.

(173) *rām-rasāiṇ* (*rasāyan*) or the Liquor of Immortality.

(174) *sahaj suhāg,* the *'suhāg'* (*saubhāgya*: Bliss of Love) of the Sahaj. Here, *sahaj-suhāg* is an equivalent of *sahaj-sukh,* 'the bliss of Sahaj', enjoyed by the perfect Yogī who has attained to the *sahaj-samādhi*.

So great is my blessing:
I just sat at home and He came!

Clinging to His feet,
I do Him service
And I keep Him entangled
in the bonds of my Love.

Stay, O stay,
in the pure mansion of my heart -
Says Kabīr,
do not betray me with another!

12. OF SIMPLE LOVE

1

Gu gaüṛī 21

O Rām, your Love
is a sharp arrow:
He who is stricken,
he alone knows the pain! *refrain*

Searching on my body,
I could not find the wound,
How then could I apply
the healing herbs?

When all women
look alike,
Who knows which one

is the Lord's Beloved?

Says Kabīr,
That one with the mark on her brow,
Renouncing all,
that one alone obtains Union.

2

Away from Rām,
my body is afire,
In water itself
a blaze has burst off. *refrain*

You are the Ocean
I am the fish in it:
In water I live,
yet for water I pine!

You are the Cage,
and I am Your parrot
And that Cat, Death,
can do nothing to me!

You are the Perfect Guru,
and I your little novice:
May I meet You at the last moment,
So prays Kabīr.

3

Gu bhairaü 18

When the heart doesn't flinch,
  what would the body fear?
My soul remained immersed,
  in the Lotus of His feet. *refrain*

Deep, bottomless was the holy Gangā,
  by its side, Kabīr stood bound in chains -
A wave of the Gangā broke his chains
  and Kabīr was seated on a deer skin!

Says Kabīr,
  I have neither helper nor companion:
On land and on water,
  the Lord is my Protector.

13. THE GOAL

1

KG2 123; Bī gyān cautīsā

In such a way
  worship Narhari[175]
that your soul
  may be rid of all doubts. *refrain*

(175) This long didactic song appears as an attempt to reconcile the concepts of the Tantric yoga with a theistic point of view, the supreme stage of *sahaj* or *śūnya* being identified with the supreme Being, here called 'Narhari'.

Where there is Nothing[176],
find something -
Where there is Nothing,
learn to recognize!

At the tenth Gate[177],
purify your mind
And meditate at the confluence
of the Gangā and Yamunā[178].

Is *nād* in *bindu*
or *bindu* in *nād*?
Where *nād* and *bindu* have merged,
there is Govind[179].

Though the Self is without attributes
beyond all qualities -
Even so, the world, deluded,
sees the rope as a serpent!

Do away with the bark
get hold of the pith -
Then you'll contemplate
infinite treasures.

---

(176) Here, 'nothing' or 'Nothingness' corresponds to the Void (*śūnya*) or the 'Cavern of the Void' (*śūnya-maṇḍal, gagan-maṇḍal*).

(177) The tenth Gate is the *brahmarandhra*: a secret 'Opening'.

(178) Those two rivers symbolize the two *nāḍī*s (secret channels) 'Iḍā' and 'Piṅgalā'; together with the third *suṣumnā,* all three merge within the sixth *cakra,* situated between the Yogī's eyebrows and called the *Triveṇī,* lit.: 'three Strands'.

(179) 'Govind' here stands for the Ultimate Stage.

Says Kabīr,
  Infinite is the Guru's wisdom:
Meditatc on Him
  in the Cavern of the Void.

2

Gu bhairaü 19

If the soul absorbs itself
  in the Name of Rām,
Old Age and Death give up
  and Error scurries away. *refrain*

Inaccessible, impregnable is that Fortress[180]
  where He makes His dwelling -
There shines
  the perfect Light.

No bright colours are found there,
  no deep blue or golden yellow -
No joyous tumult
  and no songs[181].

No other sound is heard
  than the Unsounded Sound[182]-

---

(180) The fortress is the *śūnya-maṇḍal.*

(181) The blue colour evokes god Vishnu-Hari's dark-blue hue and yellow is the colour of his garment (*pītāmbar*); the joyous tumult and songs allude to the singing of His praise in the *kīrtan* musical performance.

(182) *anāhat-sabad* is identical with *anāhat-nād,* or 'the Sound of the Anāhat'.

In that place where
sits the all-powerful Lord.

Like a Kadali flower[183],
with a lamp shining within,
Is the Lotus of the Heart[184]
where He dwells.

Between above and below
is an empty space -
In that Cavern of the Void
He spreads His radiance.

Neither finding or losing,
neither sunshine nor shadow -
neither day nor night
is anything to Him.

He neither shrinks nor wards off,
he no longer comes nor goes away -
For ever He remains absorbed
in the *Sahaj-śūnya*[185].

He whose mind
is firmly fixed on that light,
that one has achieved Salvation,
says Kabīr.

---

(183) A mysterious flower which is supposed to grow in the 'Kadali forest', associated with sensual desires.

(184) The empty space is 'the Lotus of the Heart' or *anāhata-cakra,* which is god Vishnu's residence.

(185) The *sahaj-śūnya* or the Ultimate State, of which nothing can be said.

3

KG2 125; Gu gaūrī 29; Bī śabda 79

Tell me, O Brother,
on what prop does the sky rest?
Happy is he
who has pierced the mystery! *refrain*

On that canopy of the sky,
stars appear:
Who is the clever artist
who painted them?

Him whom you seek
is not up there -
He has His dwelling
in Immortality[186].

Says Kabīr,
He alone will know Him
Who has Rām in his heart
and Rām on his lips.

(186) Lit.: *amar-pad* or the state of Deathlessness, which is identical with the *sahaj* state.

4

KG2 52; Gu gaürī 43[187]

See, O my Brothers,
a gale of Wisdom has swept -
All the screens of Error, it has blown away,
all the bolts of Māyā, unbolted - *Re*! *refrain*

The poles of Two-mindedness[188] were flung to the ground,
the Ridge-pole of Delusion was broken -
The Thatch of Desire fell crashing down,
the Jar of Wickedness was smashed to pieces - *Re*!

After the storm, there was a rain-shower
so that Your servant was soaked through:
Says Kabīr, light dawned on me,
when I recognized the rising Sun - *Re*[189]!

5

KG2 50; Gu āsā 28

Now I can
no longer dance:

---

(187) This song is composed in the style of a folk-song, with the meaningless syllable 'Re' placed at the end of each line.

(188) *gyān kī āmdhī,* lit.: 'a storm of Knowledge', which is spiritual enlightenment. The mystical experience *paracā* (*paricay*) is compared to a sudden, devastating tornado.

(189) The rain-shower, which follows the gale apparently symbolizes the enlightenment which pervades the body and soul of Kabīr and allows him to have a glimpse of the mysterious Light which is God.

The dancing drum[190] in my mind
no longer can play! *refrain*

What once was empty is now filled to the brim,
the clay-pot of Desire[191] has burst apart -
The tunic of Lust[192] is torn to shreds
and all wanderings are over.

Whatever disguises I had put on, I've given up:
from now on, no more comedy[193]!
All my attires I've put away, all my companions I've left
through the power of Rām's Name.

All that was moving has now been stilled
all arguments are over -
Says Kabīr, I found Plenitude[194]
when I obtained the grace of Rām.

6

KG2 151; Bī śabda 65

---

(190) *mandariyā* is a kind of elongated dancing-drum of the *mridanga* type, which is an accompaniment to folk-dances.

(191) *gāgarī*: a large clay-pot which also serves as a kind of drum, whose mouth is bound with skin.

(192) *colnā*: a kind of tunic donned by a dancer or *mridanga* player: here, it symbolizes the body assumed by the *jīv*: a body full of impure desires.

(193) A comedian is known as a *bahurūpi,* lit.: 'one who assumes many forms' (or disguises). In the same way, the soul assumes may disguises, as long as it wanders in the Ocean of *samsār*. Once enlightened, the soul won't assume more appearances or forms: it will no longer be reborn.

(194) *pūr,* 'the Full', designates the supreme Being, Rām, who is Plenitude.

That Jogiya is gone,
departed for the sky[195]:
There he remains entranced
free from the five women[196]! *refrain*

He has gone to another land,
one none could tell about:
Never will that Jogiya
come back to his cave.

Burnt is his patched robe
torn is his flag,
Broken his staff,
smashed his begging bowl[197]!

Says Kabīr,
that Jogiya has found the trick[198]:
He went off to the sky -

---

(195) 'Jogiya' is a familiar, rather derogatory form of the word 'Jogī': it suggests a lonely wretch living in a hole or a little shed, begging. Here, the Jogiya symbolizes the human soul, the *jīv*.

(196) Popular esteem of the 'Jogiya' is low. He is sometimes accompanied by some female beggar, the disreputable 'Joginīs'. Here, the 'five women' symbolize the five senses. Once the Jogiya has departed for the 'sky' (*gagan*), such as *gagan-maṇḍal* or *śūnya-maṇḍal*), he is free from all mortal attachments and desires as he reaches the mysterious stage of *sahaj* or *śūnya-samādhi*.

(197) The Jogi's paraphernalia: his parched cloth (*kanthā*), his flag (*dhvaj*), his staff (*dānḍa*) and his begging-bowl (*khapar*) symbolize the material body: a mere appearance.

(198) *juguti* (*yukti*) or 'the trick' leading to the supreme stage of *sahaj samādhi*.

all his wanderings are over[199].

14. THE ENIGMA

1[200]

KG2 120; Bī śabda 95

Who could be
the sheriff of such a Fort?
There, meat is on display
and the Watchman is a vulture! *refrain*

The bullock calves,
the cow is barren,
And they milk the calf
three times a day.

The rat is the boatman,
the cat plies the oars
The frog is asleep,
the snake keeps watch.

Again and again,
the jackal attacks the lion -

---

(199) Lit.: 'He neither comes nor goes': he is free from the endless round of birth and death, and the Ocean of *samsār* which he has now crossed over.

(200) This short poem is a *ulṭabāmsī* or an paradoxical song composed in the form of a riddle, in the style of the Buddhistic *Caryāpads*. As noted by S. Dasgupta, this song - but for the first verse - is almost identical with Caryā XXXIII, attributed to the Master *Dhendhana-Pā* in: Atindra Majumdar, The *Caryāpads* (Shahidullah, No. 33; Sen No. 41).

That song of Kabīr
  few will understand!

2[201]

KG2 114; Gu āsā 6

Spicy indeed
  are Hari's fritters:
Only He who knows
  can eat them! *refrain*

The dove beats the drum[202], the bullock plays the rebeck,
  the crow claps the hands,
Dressed in a billowing skirt, the donkey dances
  while the buffalo leads the dance.

The lion[203] sits mincing the betel-nuts
  while the big rat spreads the lime -
The poor little she-rat sings the festive song[204],
  while the tortoise blows the conch.

---

(201) This song is a specimen of *ulaṭ* or 'upside-down' language. The introductory verse is not clear; another version gives:

gyāna aceta phirai nara loī, tāthai janami janami ḍahakāe

'Devoid of knowledge, men roam endlessly,
wandering from birth to birth'.

(202) This strange feast is a 'wedding' feast, celebrating the merging of the wife-soul into the divine Spouse.

(203) Both the lion and the rat are engaged in making *pān-supārī,* a mixture of minced betel-nut and spices, rolled in a fresh betel-leaf spread with lime.

(204) The *mangal-gīt,* here sung by the she-rat, is one of the auspicious songs to be sung at the time of the wedding.

Says Kabīr, O Saints, listen:
  the sheep has eaten the mountain -
The Chakvā bird is eating hot coals
  and the Ocean has run off to the sky!

3

KG2 133; Gu siri 2

King Rām
  plays the violin of the Anāhad
in which all sounds
  are stilled. *refrain*

O you, Pandit, listen to the strange tale!
  Now there is nothing more to say:
That Yogī has duped men, gods and Gandharvas
  and bound the three worlds with a single chain!

He made his own skull the furnace,
  he made his whistle the funnel,
  and He got a jar of pure gold -
In the jar, a stream of pure Liquor is flowing
  which the tongue enjoys within.

A marvellous thing has occurred:
  with his own breath He made a cup:
In all the three worlds, there's only One like Him:
  tell me, who is He, what King of Yogīs?

So was the knowledge of the Great Being[205] revealed
  Says Kabīr, I was dyed in the colour of Love -

(205) *purakhotam* (*puruṣottam*).

While the rest of the world went astray in error,
  I got drunk on the Liquor of Rām[206]!

4

KG2 138; Bī śabda 19

O Creature! Call on Rām, the one Reality,
  ponder the unutterable mystery:
He who is truly devoted to Hari[207]
  stays awake day and night. *refrain*

The hellcat casts her net, the she-god stalks around[208],
  the tiger prowls in the forest -
The Five warrior-clans are on the war-path,
  fiercely beating their drums.

In the forest, the *nīlgāy* and the hare are[209] surrounded
  but the Hunter's arrow can't reach them -
Fire sweeps the Ocean, the whole forest is ablaze,
  yet fish and game keep frolicking!

---

(206) *rāma rasāina*; *rasāyan* is a magic fluid, taken as an equivalent of *amrit,* the Liqour of Immortality. See above: In Praise of the Saints, 1.

(207) The one who has *bhāv* (i.e. *bhāv-bhakti*) or 'a tender devotion' to Rām.

(208) The hellcat ((*dāin, dākinī*), a female demon or ghoul, and the she-dog symbolize Māyā, who hold sway on the human body, symbolized by the 'forest'. The tiger may be *man* or the 'Mind', or Kāl (Death); the five clans are the five senses.

(209) Nīlgāy and hare, fish and game symbolize the soul (*jīv*) or souls which have attained the supreme state of *sahaj,* in which both the body and the world (*samsār*) are abolished. The 'Hunter' is Death.

He alone is a true Pandit, he alone is a Knower[210],
who understands that song of mine -
Says Kabīr, that one is my Guru,
who saves Himself and saves me too!

5

KG2 107; Gu gaūrī 17

Now I have taken
all things in good part:
My soul has found peace
when I recognized Govinda! *refrain*

My body was prey
to a thousand miseries -
Which all have turned
into the bliss of the Sahaj[211]!

Now for me Death
has turned into Rām:
All pain is gone,
joy and peace are mine.

The foes I had
turned into friends
And the Shāktas
changed into noble souls!

---

(210) That true 'savant', that Knower of Reality (*tattva*), can only be the perfect Yogī (*siddha*) or the perfect Saint (*santa*).

(211) Lit.: 'Reversing', became *sahaj samādhi*: the whole song is built on the repetition of the word *ulaṭi,* or 'turning back', alluding to the Haṭh-yogic process of 'reversal'.

Reversing, the self
  knew itself as the Self -
And the three forms of suffering
  were gone.

Says Kabīr, I've dissolved
  into the Bliss of Sahaj,
So I live free from fear
  and cause fear to none.

6

KG2 53; Bī kaharā 10

I am in all, all are in me,
  I am in each and every one - Ho!
Let one call me 'Kabīr',
  let another call me 'Rām-Rāī' - Ho[212]! *refrain*

Neither a child nor an old man am I,
  nor a father of young children - Ho! -
Sent away, I don't go, sent for, I don't come:
  easily[213], I remain in the whole world - Ho!

All I wear is a loin-cloth
  and people say it's whole - Ho!
Yet the Weaver couldn't weave it whole:

(212) This song, in the form of a folk-song, alludes to the supreme stage of the soul; Now, He who comes and goes is no longer Kabīr, but a mere appearance.

(213) *sahaji*: 'Easily' refers to the Sahaj state.

So he tore it in ten places[214]- Ho!

Since I merged into that Fruit which is Quality-less[215],
my Name is 'Rām-Rāī' - Ho!
I see the world, the world does not see me:
that little bit Kabīr has secured - Ho!

7

KG2 180; Bī śabda 67

If God
is in the form of a seed[216],
Then, O Pandit,
what more can you ask? *refrain*

Neither body nor mind has He,
nor ego,
Nor the three Qualities
of *sattva, rajas* and *tamas*[217].

Fruits appear in plenty,
either poisonous or life-giving -

---

(214) The loin-cloth torn in ten places in the human body with its ten apertures. The 'Weaver' who wove it so, here refers to the Creator.

(215) *phal,* the 'Fruit' or 'Reward' which is said to be *nirguṇ,* 'Quality-less', is the Sahaj state itself; Kabīr has been resorbed into the One Reality, 'Rām' - so that his name has changed into 'Rām- Rāī' (*rājā-rām*).

(216) As the whole tree is said to be contained in the seed, so the whole created world is said to be contained in the supreme Being, here called 'Bhagavān', 'The Adorable One'.

(217) *sattva, rajas* and *tamas,* are the three *guṇs* (strands) out of which the *prakriti,* lit.: 'nature', is said to be made.

But the Veda and the sages proclaim
there is but One Tree.

Says Kabīr,
with that One, I am well pleased -
Who was ever released?
Who was ever bound[218]?

---

(218) When the *jīv* has reached the ultimate stage of *sahaj* in which all duality is abolished, there is no one left to say who it was that was saved - if ever there was any One?

Part Five

Śloks of Kabīr in the Gurū Granth

[A Selection][1]

2
Kabīr, that caste of mine
is a joke to everyone[2]:
Blessed indeed be such a caste
which makes me invoke the Creator!

3
Kabīr, why are you afraid?
why let your soul be shaken?
Drink the nectar of Rām's Name,
of Him who is the Lord of all joy.

5
Kabīr, few indeed are those men,
who, whilst living, are as if dead:
Free from fear, they're absorbed in Rām's praise:
wherever they look, they see but Him.

(1) *Gurū Granth,* pp. 1364-1377.

(2) An allusion to popular jokes about the 'vile' Julāhās.

6

Kabīr, on the day I died,
  was my joy born:
My Master embraced me
  He, Govind[3] who loves His friends[4].

7

Kabīr, I am the worst of all,
  they're all better than I:
He who thinks this way
  He's my true friend!

8

Kabīr, Māyā approached me,
  dressed in so many garbs -
But the Guru protected me
  so she made obeisance and went away!

12

Kabīr, the Bamboo was ruined by its haughtiness -
  let no one follow its way:
Though he dwells by the side of the Sandal-tree
  the Bamboo can't enjoy its fragrance.

14

Kabīr, wandering all over,
  I saw a great many places -
Yet, without the One, Rām,
  all, to me, was a desert.

---

(3) 'Govind' is one of the Vaishnav names of the supreme Lord.

(4) The 'companions' (*samgi*) are the true devotees of God.

15
Kabīr, pleasant is the saint's humble hut,
but the village of the wicked is a burning oven -
May that palace be set on fire
where Hari's Name is not invoked!

16
Kabīr, when the saints die, why lament?
They are going home:
Cry over the miserable Shākta
who is sold from market to market[5].

17
Kabīr, the infidel
is like a dinner of garlic.
You may eat it in a corner
yet, in the end, it will be found.

21
Kabīr, this world holds no happiness
for Him who keeps many friendships -
Those whose hearts are bound to the One,
they obtain constant joy.

22
Kabīr, that Death which people fear
is joy to me:
Those whose heart is steeped in the One,
they obtain constant joy.

---

(5) The market is the world of transmigration.

23
Kabīr, having found the Treasure of Rām,
O Kabīr, don't open your purse[6]:
For it has neither house nor assayer,
nor purchaser and no price!

25
Kabīr, attach yourself to the One,
get rid of Duality -
Then keep your hair long
or shave it as you please!

26
Kabīr, the world is a pit of soot
and they fall blindly into it -
I am a sacrifice[7] to those people
who, having entered, came out!

27
Kabīr, this body of ours is going,
never to return -
Naked they departed those people,
owners of lakhs and crores!

29
Kabīr, dying, dying, the world died
but none knew how to die:
Let man die such a Death

---

(6) *gānṭhi na kholha,* lit.: 'don't open the knot': actually a piece of cloth in which the money is folded at the waist, to serve as a purse.

(7) *balihārī,* lit.: 'I offer myself in sacrifice to', here means: 'I admire', 'I will be damned if'.

through which there is no rebirth!

30
Kabīr, a human life is hard to gain
and it comes but once:
The fruit fallen on the ground
will not return on the branch.

34
Kabīr, that one wears beautiful clothes
and he chews betel-leaves -
Yet, without Hari's Name
in chains he'll go to Yam's hell.

35
Kabīr, the boat is rickety,
pierced in a thousand holes:
The light ones found an escape,
the heavy ones were drowned.

36
Kabīr, the bones burn like firewood
and the hair burns like fodder -
Seeing the whole world aflame,
Kabīr lost heart.

37
Kabīr, don't be so proud,
you are bones in a bag of skin:
Those with fine horses and umbrellas
at last are buried in the ditch.

39
Kabīr, don't be so proud,
do not deride the poor:
Today your boat is in mid-ocean
who knows what will happen to it?

40
Kabīr, don't pride yourself
on the fairness of your body:
Today or tomorrow, you'll leave it and go
as the snake sheds its skin.

41
Kabīr, if you can plunder, then plunder:
let Rām's Name be your booty -
Or else you'll repent later
when you breathe your last.

43
Kabīr, Will this one sell me his son?
will that one sell me his daughter[8]?
Those who've become Kabīr's partners
will trade only of Hari!

46
Kabīr, those wretched people squander
as they have not found Wisdom -
But those drunk with the Liquor of Rām
have taste for nothing else.

---

(8) This *ślok* has been given diverse interpretations, none of which is convincing. More likely, for Kabīr, love of God frees the soul from all human attachments.

47
Kabīr, the wanderer's skirt
caught fire on all sides -
the tattered garment was burnt to ashes,
yet the flame spared the waist-string.

48
Kabīr, when the flame arose, the wallet was burnt up
the begging-bowl broke to pieces -
The Jogi[9] who was there had disappeared,
ashes alone keep the posture.

49
Kabīr, O dull-witted Fish,
the Fisherman has cast his net:
In a shallow pond, there is no escape,
if you can, take refuge in the Ocean[10].

50
Kabīr, don't leave the Ocean,
however brackish its taste:
Searching for ponds and pools,
won't get you anywhere.

52
Better the bitch of a Vaishnav
than the mother of a Shākta:

(9) The 'stranger' and the 'Jogi' have met God: 'burnt to ashes', they have passed beyond; now their mortal frame is just an appearance.

(10) The Fisherman is a predator; the enlightened 'Fish' should merge into the Ocean, i.e. God.

The one keeps listening to Hari's praise
while the other runs to buy sin[11]!

53
Kabīr, the deer is lean,
despite the greenery round the pond:
For a single life, there are thousand hunters,
how long can he hope to escape?

56
Kabīr, turmeric is yellow
and lime is white by nature[12]-
But when Rām, the Generous, is found,
both lose their colour.

58
Kabīr, the door of salvation
is tiny as a mustard-seed[13]
and Mind is a huge elephant:
how can it go through?

60
Kabīr, neither roof have I, nor shed,
neither home nor village:
Let Hari not ask who's that one
who is lying at my door?

---

(11) The 'Vaishnav' is seen as vegetarian and non-violent; the 'Shākta' is seen as 'a killer of living beings', also addicted to hard drink and meat-eating. Though a Muslim by birth, Kabīr strictly adheres to vegetarianism.

(12) Turmeric (safran) and lime stand for low-caste and high-caste: turmeric is deep yellow, while lime is pure white.

(13) The mustard-seed is the tiniest of all seeds.

62
Kabīr, I have done nothing and nothing can I do,
this body of mine can't do a thing:
I don't know what Hari has done
to make Kabīr 'Great'[14]!

63
Kabīr, for that one who, even in dream,
keeps muttering the Name of Rām -
Let the skin of my own body
be shoes for His feet!

64
Kabīr, we are puppets of clay,
bearing the name of 'Men' -
We're just guests of five days,
taking so much room!

69
Kabīr, dead is the physician, dead is the patient,
dead is the whole world -
Kabīr alone is not dead,
over him none shall weep.

74
Kabīr, I am the dog of Rām,
'Mutiya' is my name[15]-

(14) There is a pun on 'Kabīr', which was the given name of our Kabīr: *kabīr* means 'Great'.

(15) *Motī,* lit.: 'pearl': *mutiyā,* derived of *motī,* is common as a dog's name. But 'Mutiya', here, is a pun on *mukti*: 'salvation'.

There is a leash on my neck,
  wherever He takes me, I go.

76
When the Snake of Separation enters the soul
  no spell can control it:
He who is separated from Rām shall not live
  or, if he lives, he'll get mad.

80
Kabīr, that *naubat* of yours[16],
  take and beat it for ten days:
This world is like meeting on a boat
  people you'll never meet again.

81
Kabīr, were I to make the seven oceans my ink,
  the trees of the forest, my pens -
Were I to make the earth my paper,
  still I couldn't write God's Greatness.

85
Kabīr, climbing the pyre, the Satī[17] cries out:
  'Hear, O Lord of the burning-ground!
All those people, mere travellers, have gone away -
  You and I remain in the end'.

---

(16) *naubat*: festive music.

(17) The heroic woman who burns herself on the pyre with her dead husband.

87
Kabīr, Him whom I was seeking,
I found just here,
That One, I recognized
that I had called 'Another'!

88
Kabīr, I die of evil company,
like the plantain by the wild caper -
This one wavers and is pierced by that one's thorns:
avoid the company of the Shākta!

90
Kabīr, the standing forest-tree,
burning, cries aloud:
May I not fall into the hands of the Smith
to be burnt again in his forge!

100
Kabīr, associating with the saints,
the love of God day by day increases -
But the Shākta's black blanket
won't ever turn white by washing!

101
Kabīr, you've not shaved your heart,
what's the use of shaving your hair?
What was done was Mind's work
what's the use of shaving the head?

103
Kabīr. we play the instrument,

but all the strings are broken:
What can the poor instrument do
when the Player has departed?

111
Kabīr, fortunate that family
in which a servant of God is born:
Fruitless as the *ḍhak*-tree
is that family without a servant of God.

113
Kabīr, I have roamed through the whole world,
with my drum on my shoulder:
I have seen and searched all:
nobody has any one!

115
Kabīr's family was ruined
when his son, Kamāl, was born:
He gave up the service of God,
and he brought wealth into the house.

123
Kabīr, the Kulang bird pecks its food,
pecking, pecking, he ever remembers its young:
As its young is dear to the Kulang
so is worldly love to the mind.

125
Kabīr, the Sheldrake bird, at night, is separated from his mate
yet, at daybreak, they are reunited -
But he who is separated from God,

finds him neither morning nor evening.

127
Kabīr, what are you doing, sleeping?
Wake up and lament your fate:
He whose dwelling is the grave,
how can he sleep in peace?

132
Kabīr, you have not thought of Rām
and old age had come upon you:
Once the door of the house is on fire,
what can be taken out?

137
Kabīr, they built a prison made of books,
with doors made of ink!
Stones have drowned the world,
Pandits have wrecked the road.

143
Kabīr, a pig is better than a Shākta,
for he keeps the village clean,
Once the wretched Shākta is dead,
no one will remember him.

144
Kabīr, cowrie by cowrie[18],
People have amassed lakhs and crores -
Yet, when departing, they keep nothing:
stripped of all, up to their loincloth!

---

(18) The cowrie is a small shell, which represents the smallest value.

146

Kabīr, be the broken stones on the road,
putting aside pride of mind -
If such a servant there be,
he shall meet the Lord.

147

Kabīr, of what avail, those broken stones?
Wouldn't they hurt the traveller's feet?
O God, let thy servant be
like the dust of the earth.

148

Kabīr, of what avail, that dust?
It flies and falls on men's bodies -
O God, thy servant ought to be
like water, to wash all limbs.

149

Kabīr, what's the use of water?
It gets too cold or too hot -
The servant of God ought to be
like Rām Himself.

154

Kabīr, I have seen a strange thing:
a diamond was displayed in a shop -
But, without a purchaser,
it was sold for one cowrie!

157
Kabīr, when I met the True Guru,
He shot a single Word at me -
When His Word struck me, I fell to the earth
and a wound opened in my heart.

170
Kabīr, the Lake[19] is filled to the brim,
yet few can drink the water -
By great good fortune, you found it:
drink it in handfuls, says Kabīr.

172
Kabīr, that house made of wood
is on fire on all sides[20]:
All the Pandits perished in the fire
the illiterate escaped.

176
Kabīr, this world is the Creator's play
which none can understand,
But for the Master Himself
or the slave at his Court.

178
Kabīr, having collected dust,
God made them into little packets[21]-

---

(19) The Lake is God's bountiful mercy.

(20) The house of wood is the human body; priding in their knowledge, the Pandits go to hell.

(21) The little 'packets' [of medicines prepared by the Physician], represent human bodies, which are nothing but dust in the end.

It was just a four-days show:
  in the end, nothing but dust!

184
Kabīr, O Mullah, why do you climb to the minaret?
  The Lord is not deaf!
Search within your heart for that One,
  for whose sake you throw the call to prayer.

185
If the Shaykh is devoid of kindness
  what's the use of going to the Kaaba pilgrimage?
Kabīr, he whose heart is not firm,
  how can he find God?

187
Kabīr, to use force is tyranny,
  and you call it 'lawful'!
When your account is called for at God's office
  what will be your plight?

188
Kabīr, khichrī makes a good meal[22],
  seasoned with a little salt:
Who would cut his own throat
  to eat meat with his bread?

194
Kabīr, when the brave true Guru
  shot his arrow at me,
Stricken, I fell on the ground -

(22) *khichrī*: a plain meal, made of rice and pulse.

my heart was pierced.

197
Kabīr, I was going to a pilgrimage to the Kaaba,
when I met God on the way.
The Lord scolded me, saying:
Who ordered you to go there?

200
Kabīr, to use violence is tyranny,
God will take you to task:
When the Clerk produces your account
you'll be beaten on the mouth!

202
Kabīr, in earth and in heaven,
there are two beggar's pipes[23]:
The six religious systems tumbled down
together with the eighty-four Siddhas!

216
Kabīr, the Mind knows all,
yet, knowingly, it commits sin:
What advantage is that to him?
Lamp in hand, he falls into the well!

225
Kabīr, God's Name is the Jewel, the Mouth is the Purse -
open it before a true Assayer:
If a good Purchaser be found,

(23) The 'beggar-pipes' probably refer to the competition and struggle between the various religious systems, which lead nowhere.

he may take it at the highest price[24]!

229
Kabīr, plant the seed of a tree
that shall bear perennial fruit -
Whose shade be cool, whose fruit be abundant,
in which birds shall play[25].

237
Kabīr, the Brahman is the guru of the world,
but he is not the guru of the saints:
And he worries himself to death
over the perplexities of the four Vedas!

236
Hear, my friends, my soul dwells in my Beloved,
or my Beloved in my soul:
I know not whether my soul is in my heart
or my Beloved dwells in my soul!

(24) He may give up his life for it.

(25) The 'Birds', here, represent holy men.

Part Six

Śloks of Sheikh Farīd

The Indian tradition knows at least of two 'Shaykh Farīd': the great 13th century 'Ganj-i-Shakar' of Ajodhan and Pakpattan, known as 'Bābā Farīd', and his grand-son, Shaykh Farīd Brahm or Ibrahīm. Two hymns attributed to the second Farīd are preserved in the *Ādi-Granth,* in *rāg āsā* and *rāg sūhī:* both appear rather flat. In the *Ādi-Granth,* 'Shaykh Farīd' is given as the author of four hymns and a hundred and twelve *ślok*as - but there is no certitude about his identity. Specialists of old Panjabi literature, such as D. Matringe, believe that the mysterious 'Farīd' was 'capted' by the Sikh Gurus themselves.

"The fact is that the Sikh Gurus tended to consider that such a great Chishti saint as Bābā Farīd was a natural choice for the Sikh Gurus". According to the same author, "concerning Shaykh Farīd's verses, the most remarkable remains the very fact of their inclusion in the Sikhs's sacred Book". Though Kabīr himself could not have known Shaykh Farīd, there is a strange resemblance between the two mystics. Like Kabīr, Farīd rejects both Hinduism and Islam:

"I am neither Hindu nor Muslim -
  Let us sit in the spinning party and abandon pride".

"Since the Lord dwells in every heart.
  I have renounced to be either a Hindu or a Turk".

This meets Kabīr's utter contempt for 'the Two Religions'.

[A Selection]

1

For that young girl's marriage
the day was fixed in advance:
Now the Angel of Death she has heard about
has come, open-faced!

The soul is the bride, Death is the bridegroom:
He'll marry her and take her away -
With your own hands you gave away your soul:
to whom, then, will you run for an embrace?

Finer than a hair is that Bridge of *Salāt*[1]:
didn't you hear of it before?
Farīd, its hellish cries you can already hear:
Hasten, lest you be robbed of your soul!

2

Farīd, hard it is to become a Darvesh at His Door -
and you went on walking the way of the world:
That burden which you've tied to your own head,
how will you ever cast it off?

---

(1) *salāt,* Ar. *sirāt*: according to Muslim belief, an extremely narrow bridge to pass over the inferno of hell: the 'Just' alone can pass - the others fall into it.

3

I understand nothing, I know nothing,
  this world is a smouldering fire:
The Lord Himself protected me
  or else I too would have been burnt!

4

Farīd, had I known that my sesame seeds were so few,
  I would have spent them sparingly[2]-
Had I known that my Lord was so young,
  I wouldn't have been so proud[3].

6

Farīd, if you be possessed of fine wisdom
  don't pen black accounts of others.
Rather bend your own ear
  and look beneath your shirt-collar!

8

Farīd, when it was time for you to earn,
  you were engrossed with the world -
So Death has strengthened its grip on you:
  once your sack is full, you'll be packed away!

---

(2) Allusion to the Indian custom of sprinkling sesame seeds (*til*) at the time of marriage: the *til* seeds here symbolize the days of a human life.

(3) The bride-soul should not have shown pride, refusing to give herself up to her impatient Husband· Life is short and God does not wait.

10

Farīd, see what has come about:
sugar has turned into poison[4]-
Your sorrow, to whom can you tell
but to the Lord Himself?

11

Farīd, the eyes got weary of seeing,
the ears weary of hearing[5]:
As it ripens, the crop
takes on a different colour.

12

Farīd, she who didn't enjoy Her Spouse when black-haired,
will she enjoy Him when grey-haired?
Love the Lord with such a Love
that your hair's colour will never change!

13

[Guru Amardās, replies:][6]
Farīd, whether man's hair be black or grey,
the Lord is ever present, if one but remembers Him.
True love doesn't come from man's own desire:
That cup of the Master's love
He himself gives to whomever He pleases!

---

(4) Worldly pleasures at last revealed their true nature, and now the soul is full of bitterness.

(5) With the oncoming of age, eyes and ears weaken, and the body withers.

(6) Note the change of style and expression when the Sikh Gurus interfere.

14
Farīd, those eyes I have seen
that once captivated the world:
In such eyes, too delicate to bear collyrium,
birds are now hatching their young! 16
Farīd, if you long for the Lord of all beings,
be like grass on the pathway:
When one breaks you and another tramples you,
then you'll enter the Court of the Lord.

17
Farīd, revile not dust:
there is nothing like it -
When we are alive, it's under our feet,
when we are dead, it's over our head!

19
Farīd, why wander from jungle to jungle,
trampling thorns under foot?
God dwells in your heart:
why seek Him in the forest?

20
Farīd, on those stick-like legs of mine,
I once scoured hills and deserts -
But today, that prayer-jug of mine[7]
appears a hundred miles away.
21
Farīd, endless are the nights,
my sides are burning with pain:

---

(7) The Prayer-jug, *kuza,* is a small earthenware for ablutions before *namāz,* the Muslim prayer.

Cursed be the life of such men
who sought anything but God!

23

That Jāt[8] peasant sows Kikar,
hoping to harvest sweet Bijaur grapes -
He keeps spinning rough wool
hoping to wear a silk garment!

24

Farīd, the lanes are muddy, far is the house
of Him whom I love so much:
If I go, I'll wet my blanket,
if I remain, our love shall be severed.

25

Let the blanket be soaked through,
O God, let it rain ever so much:
Go I must to meet my Lord
for fear our Love be severed!

28

Farīd, my bread is made of wood,
and hunger is my condiment -
Those people who eat buttered bread,
envy them not!

35

(8) The Jāt is a simpleton. The thorny *kikar* (*babūl*) and the rough wool symbolize bad actions: the sweet grapes of Bijaur (in Svat, on the northwest frontier of Pakistan) and the silk garments stand for the benefit of good deeds, i.e. the grace of God.

Farīd, anxiety is my bed, suffering is my bed-strings,
   the pain of separation, my mattress and my coverlet:
Such is my condition:
   O my true Lord, look upon me!

36
They all keep saying: 'Virah, Virah' -
   but Virah is a King[9]:
Farīd, that body in which Virah isn't born
   is nothing but a burning-ground!

41
Shaykh Farīd has grown old,
   his body has come to tremble -
Would it live a hundred years,
   this body will turn to dust in the end.

43
With the axe on the shoulder and a jar on the head,
   you go to the forest, O Blacksmith:
Farīd, it's the Lord I am seeking,
   but all you want is charcoal!

44
Farīd, some have too much flour
   and others don't even have salt:
When they all have gone, it will be known
   who'll get the harsh punishment.

47
Farīd, your patched coat is stitched all over [10-]

_____

(9) *virah* is the torment of separation endured by the human soul, yearning
for God. But that torment itself is the true Path to God.

but there are no stitches on your soul:
One after the other, they departed,
all those Mashaikas and Shaykhs[11]!

48

Farīd, though the two lamps were alight,
the Angel of Death came in and sat down:
He conquered the fortress and plundered it,
then he put off the two lamps and went away[12].

50

Farīd, on the shoulder they carry a prayer-mat
and they wear rough wool,
but they have a dagger in their heart,
and they tell lies:
However bright they may appear,
in their heart, the darkness of night!

54

Farīd, in early youth, the little bride couldn't enjoy her Spouse,
grown in years, she died:
In the grave, her soul is wailing:
'O Lord! I haven't found union with You!'

61

(10) The quilt or patched coat of the Sufi is made of a number of rags carefully stitched together - yet the soul remains 'unstitched', i.e. loose: any time it will depart.

(11) Doomed are all those 'Saints and Sadhus of yours!'

(12) The 'two lamps' are the eyes. Forcing open the fortress of the body. Death takes hold of it and 'plunders' it at leisure.

Farīd, black is my wear,
black is my attire[13]:
Full of sins, I wander about -
yet people still call me 'Darvesh'!

64
By the bank of a brackish water-pond,
the Hamsa birds have alighted[14]:
They dip their beaks, but they drink not,
yearning to fly away.

67
Farīd, a brick is your pillow, earth is your bed,
worms feed on your flesh:
How many ages will you pass in this way,
lying on one side[15]?

68
Farīd, the decorated pitcher is broken,
its fine rope has snapped[16]:
In which house will the Angel Israel
come as a guest tonight[17]?

---

(13) Black is the colour of the Muslim ascetic - but simple people are easily deluded by the garb of the black-souled 'holy man'.

(14) The brackish water-pond symbolizes the impure pleasures of the world; the Hamsa-birds are the Saints, who yearn only for God.

(15) According to Muslim belief, the souls should remain imprisoned in the grave until the day of Judgment.

(16) The gaily decorated pitcher refers to the human body, and the fine rope to breath.

(17) Israel Farishta, one of the four main Angels, is the heralder of Death.

77
My teeth to chew, my feet to walk, my priceless eyes,
my ears to hear: all have now left me -
This body of mine cries out loudly:
'Where have all my companions gone?'

79
Farīd, the birds are just passing guests
in the beautiful garden of the world:
At dawn, the drum resounds:
'Prepare for departure!'

81
Farīd, I thought I alone was in grief,
but the whole world is grieving -
From my house-top, I looked and saw:
all the houses are afire!

85
Farīd, my days have passed in pain,
and my nights on a bed of thorns:
Now the Boatman calls aloud[18]:
the Boat is in the jaws of the storm!

90
Farīd, my dry body has turned into a skeleton,
crows peck at my soles:
Up to this day, O God, you have held me by the hand -
see your servant's misery!

92

(18) *patani,* the Boatman, symbolizes the Guru.

O Crows, peck not at this cage of my body,
just sit on it and fly away:
For in this cage, my Lord dwells -
do not eat the flesh!

93
Farīd, the wretched tomb calls out:
'Homeless one, come home!
At the end you'll come to me:
do not fear death'.

96
That tree grown on the river-bank,
how long can it hope to stand?
Farīd, that water stored in an unbaked clay-pot,
how long can it remain?

101
Farīd, I am a sacrifice to those birds
whose dwelling is in the jungle:
Picking pebbles, staying in desertic stretches,
they never leave God's side[19].

103
Farīd, tear your silk garment,
put on a rough woollen blanket -
Assume whatever garb
that may bring you nearer to the Lord.

[Guru Amardās replies:]

---

(19) The 'birds' are the ascetics who have chosen to live in the wilderness, relying on God's mercy.

Why tear your silken garment?
  What's the use of wearing a rough blanket?
Nānak, while sitting at home,
  you'll find the Lord, by purifying your mind.

[Guru Arjan Dev says:]
Farīd, those who took praise in their greatness,
  in wealth and in the pleasures of youth, they went away
from the Lord,
  as bare as a hillock after rain!

110
Farīd, the human heart clings to love of the world,
  though this world be worthless -
Hard indeed is the way of the Faqirs:
  the fruit of previous merits!

112
The first watch of the night is the blossom,
  the last watch brings out the fruit:
The Lord's blessing is upon those
  who keep vigil in prayer.

119
My body is oven-hot,
  my bones burn like firewood:
If my feet fail me, I'll walk on my head
  to meet my Beloved.

[Guru Nānak speaks:]
Don't heat your body oven-hot,
  burn not your bones like firewood,

What harm have your head and feet done?
Rather behold the Beloved within your soul!

[Guru Rāmdās speaks:]
I keep searching for my spouse[20],
but my Spouse is within me:
Nānak, the Unknowable[21] can't be seen
but the Guru[22] can make him seen.

128
Those who, wise, pass as ignorant,
who, strong, pass as weak,
Who, having not, share all they have -
those are true saints.

129
Do not utter a single bad word,
for the true Lord dwells in all men -
Do not pain a single heart,
for all hearts are priceless jewels.

130
All human hearts are jewels:
it is wrong to hurt them:
If you hanker after the Beloved,
don't distress a single heart!

---

(20) *sajan,* lit.: 'noble Person'; in the mouth of a wife, *sajan* refers to her own husband.

(21) *alakh* 'that which can't be perceived': the supreme Reality, God.

(22) *gurumukh,* lit.: 'One who is facing God'; in the Sikh tradition, 'a Man of Faith'. It is the Guru who can grant the vision of God.

Part Seven

The Bhagats

1. KABĪR'S FORERUNNERS

RĀMĀNAND

Gu basant

How could I go, tell me?
  I am happy at home:
My spirit won't move,
  my mind is crippled[1]!

One day, I felt inspired to go:
  Grinding sandalwood and aloes and all kinds of perfumes,
I went some place to worship Brahman
  but the Guru showed me Brahman within my own soul.

Wherever one may go, there's nothing but water and stones[2]:
  You alone fill all, present in all -
In vain I searched all the Vedas and Puranas:
  Go and search over there, if He is not here!

---

(1) This *pad* takes the form of the poet's reply to an interlocutor who has advised the saint to go on a pilgrimage (*tīrth-yātrā*). This 'Rāmānand' is probably distinct from the Vaishnav reformer of the same name.

(2) Such as the objects of cult in all *tīrth*as (sacred spots).

O Satguru, I am a sacrifice unto You
who have done away with all my doubts and wanderings -
Rāmanand's Lord is the all-pervading Brahman,
the Guru's word[3] abolishes millions of sins.

---

(3) The divine Word: *śabda.*

NĀMDEV

1

Gu āsā 2

You brought a pitcher of water
to bathe the Lord:
Fourty-two lakhs of beings live in that water:
why do you pollute Vitthala[4]?

Wherever I look,
there is Vitthala:
In perfect Joy
He sports for ever!

You brought flowers and you wove a garland
as an offering to the Lord -
But the Blackbee had sipped the nectar already:
why do you pollute Vitthala?

You brought milk and you prepared sweet rice,
as an offering to the Lord -
But the calf had already lapped the milk:
why do you pollute Vitthala?

Vitthala is here, Vitthala is there,
no place in the world where He is not!
In every and each spot, Nāmā renders Him homage -
everywhere He is present in plenitude.

---

(4) *Viṭṭhala,* or *Bithūla* is a name of God in Maharashtra; for Nāmdev, God is everywhere: those who worship Him as an idol are the polluters.

2

Gu āsā 3

With the mind as my measure-tape,
  with my soul as my scissors,
Measuring, measuring,
  I keep cutting the bonds of Death!

  What do I care
    for caste and for lineage?
  Day and night,
    I invoke the Name of Rām.

What should be died, I dye,
  what should be sewn, I sew[5]-
Without the Name of Rām,
  I could not live half an hour!

With heartfelt devotion,
  I sing Hari's praise,
From morning to night,
  I meditate on my Lord.

Of gold is my needle,
  of silver is my thread.
Nāmā's soul
  has melted into God.

(5) Nāmdev or 'Nāmā' was a tailor (*chīpā*) by caste. What is to be 'dyed' is the Mind, which should imbibe the 'colour' of Love; what is to be sewn is the soul, which should 'melt' in God.

3

Gu āsā 4

As a snake sheds off slough,
  but not its venom,
As the crane stands still in water,
  pretending to meditate - so he is[6]!

  What's the use
    of meditation,
  What's the use of litanies,
    with an impure heart?

A man who feeds
  on the food of lions,
You may well call
  the Kings of Thugs[7]!

Nāmā's Lord
  has settled the quarrel:
Drink the elixir of Rām's Name[8],
  you, Cheat!

---

(6) This *pad* is addressed to the wicked Shākta, hypocritically assuming the stance of a holy man. The crane is a Cheat.

(7) The meat-eater, who feeds on bleeding flesh, eats 'the food of lions': he is no better than the famous brigands known as *Thugs,* who used to drink the blood of their victims.

(8) *mahāras,* in Haṭh-Yoga language, means the elixir of immortality, but in the context of left-hand Shāktas, it means strong liquor.

4

Gu āsā 6

If you but recognize the Parabrahman[9],
you'll feel no other desire -
If you but stick to the Love of Rām
your mind will remain free from care.

O my Soul! How shall you cross over
that Ocean of Existence, full of poison?
At the sight of false riches,
you were befooled, O my Soul!

In a poor calico-printer's home I was born
but I got the Guru's instruction:
Thanks to the Sants' grace,
Nāmā has met God.

5

Gu gujrī 2

What can be said of Him?
Who could understand?
Ramaiya pervades all,
O my Friend!

Like the trace of a bird
on the firmament,
Like the path of a fish in the Ocean,
He cannot be seen.

Like the mirage water,
in the sky

(9) Parabrahman: The supreme Being.

Such is Nāmā's Lord, Vitthala,
who pervades the three worlds.

7

Gu dhanāsarī 3

As water is dear to the desert traveller,
as the creeper is dear to the camel,
As music at night ravishes the deer,
so is Ramaiya dear to my heart.

Beautiful is your Name,
beautiful is your form,
Beautiful is your hue,
O Ramaiya!

As Indra's shower is dear to the earth,
as the flower's perfume to the bee,
As the mango-tree to the Kokila bird,
so is Ramaiya dear to my heart!

As sunshine is dear to the Chakva bird,
as the Mansarovar to the Hamsa-bird,
As the husband to the young wife,
so is Ramaiya dear to my heart!

As milk is dear to the babe,
as the rain-shower to the Chatak bird,
As water is dear to the fish,
so is Ramaiya dear to my heart!

The Sadhakas and Siddhas and all the Sages seek Him
yet very few have found Him:

As your Name is dear to all the worlds,
so is Vitthala's Name to Nāmā's heart!

8

Gu ṭoḍī 1

Some say He is near
some say He is far -
As if the water fish
could feed on a palm-tree[10]!

Why do you keep talking
such nonsense?
Those who have found God
keep mum about it.

Those learned Pandits
keep discoursing on the Veda -
Poor Nāmdev is a fool:
he knows nothing but Rām.

11

Gu gauṇḍ 2

As a deer bewitched by the hunter's song
gives up his life rather than break his rapture -
In such a way, O Rām,
in such a way, I keep gazing at You.

My soul will not part with Rām
to wander elsewhere.

(10) A proverbial expression: the Pandits are fond of arguing about the supreme Being - but they get nowhere.

As the kingfisher
  gazes at the fish,
As the goldsmith intently fixes the gold
  while carving it,

As the debauché stares
  at another man's wife,
As the gambler intently fixes the dice
  as he throws it,

In such a way, wherever I look,
  I see but You, O Rām!
For ever Nāmā meditates
  at God's feet.

12

Gu gauṇḍ 4

Like a lonely cow
  away from her calf
Enduring the torment
  of separation,

Like a fish out of water,
  writhing in pain,
So is poor Nāmā
  without the Name of Rām!

As the little calf,
  as soon as untied,
Starts sucking its mother's teats,

enjoying the butter[11].

In this way did Nāmā
meet the Lord:
Meeting the Guru,
he recognized the Unknown[12].

As the passion of the lustful man
for another man's wife,
Such is the love of Nāmā
for Murari[13].

As the body endures the burning
of a fierce sun,
such is poor Nāmā's torment
without the Name of Rām!

13

Gu rāmkali 1

With paper, the child makes his kite
and lets it fly in the sky:
He keeps chatting with his mates,
yet his eyes remain fastened on the string.

My soul is threaded
on the Name of Rām,
As the goldsmith's mind

---

(11) The butter is supposed to be hidden in the milk as its 'essence': here it symbolizes the spiritual ambrosia distilled by the repetition of the Name of Rām.

(12) *alakha,* 'the Unseen' or 'the Unknown' refers to the supreme Being.

(13) Murāri: a name of God.

on his gold.

The Princess's maid brings her pitcher to the well
and fills it with water:
Though chatting and laughing with her companions
she never looses sight of her pitcher.

All the cows from the big city with ten gates
were let out to graze:
However far they may wander,
they'll keep their calf in their heart.

Says Nāmdev: O Trilochan, listen:
Having laid her child in the cradle,
The mother busies herself with her work, in and out -
but her heart remains ever fixed on her child.[14]

20

Gu bhairaü 6

Full of happiness
I entered your Temple -
But as I was worshipping You,
they took hold of me and threw me out!

Low is my caste,
O Lord of Yadavas! Why was I born
a calico-printer?

Taking my blanket,
I went back,

(14) The love of God for his children is here expressed as *vātsalya,* the love of the mother-cow for her young.

And then I sat down
  behind the temple.

While I, Nāmā, was singing
  the praise of the Lord,
Lo! the temple turned round
  towards its devotee!

22

Gu basant 2

Waves of greed rushing up
  sound like a cataract:
In them, I am drowning,
  O Keshava!

O Govind! Make me cross over
  the Ocean of Existence
Float me over,
  O my Father Vitthala!

In such a gale,
  I can't steer my boat:
I can't reach your shore,
  O Vitthala!

Says Nāmā,
  I can't even swim -
Lend me your arm, lend me Your arm,
  O Vitthala!

26

Gu malār 2

Forget me not, forget me not,
Forget me not, O Ramaiya!

When I entered the temple[15],
they all went mad after me:
Shouting 'Shudra! Shudra!' they beat me and threw me out:
what shall I do, O my Father Vitthala?

If you grant me salvation after death,
who will know about it?
When those Brahmans called me 'Ḍheḍh'[16],
was it not a blow at your Honor?

You are known as the Merciful, the Compassionate One,
all-powerful is Your arm!
Then the temple itself turned round towards Nāmā
and turned its back on the Brahmans!

---

(15) Like *Gu* Bhairaü 6 (*supra,* 20), the *pad* alludes to the famous miracle of the turning temple.

(16) *Ḍheḍh* is the name of an untouchable caste, closely related to, and often identical with the 'Mahār' caste, whose main duty is to drag away and dispose of carcasses. The word 'Dheḍh', like 'Mahār', is an insult - here thrown at the *Chīpā* Nāmdev by the infuriated Brahmans.

TRILOCHAN

Gu gujrī 1

Without cleansing your soul from filth,
 you have donned the garb of an *Udāsī* -
But within the lotus of your heart, you've not recognized Brahman:
 how then have you become a *Sannyāsī*[17]?

O Jay Chand[18]!
 you are wandering in error:
Never, never did you find
 your Paramanand!

Eating in each and every house, you've fattened your body,
 wearing a patched garment and an ascetic ear-ring for gain!
In vain, you rub on yourself the ashes of the cremation-ground:
 without the Guru, you never found the Essence.

What's the use of your litanies and penance?
 Why do you keep churning water?
O you Seeker of Nirvana! Invoke that One
 who created the eighty-four lakhs of beings!

---

(17) This *pad* is a condemnation of all kinds of wandering 'holy men' and ascetics, whatever their garb and denominations: 'Udāsī', 'Sannyāsī', 'Nirvānī' or 'Kapāḍiyā' (Kapālika). According to Trilochan, all their pretensions are vain, since they never got the 'corn', i.e. the experience of God within their soul, necessary to 'redeem the pledge' and obtain final release from the bonds of mundane Existence.

(18) The 'Jay Chand' mentioned in the refrain is a high sounding name meaning 'Moon of Victory', apparently used ironically.

O you, Kapālika[19]! What's the use of carrying that gourd-pot,
of wandering to the sixty-eight holy spots?
Says Trilochan: 'O living beings, listen:
without the corn, there is no redeeming the pledge!'

(19) The *Kapālika* is a wandering ascetic carrying a human skull, here ironically called 'gourd-pot'.

SADHNĀ

Gu bilāval 1

To obtain a king's daughter,
a man had assumed Vishnu's own garb[20]-
Though he had done it out of selfish desire
God redeemed his pledge!

If you don't erase my *karma*
what's your worth, O Guru of the world?
What's the use of seeking the protection of the lion
if we fall prey to the jackal[21]?

For a single drop of rain,
the Chatak-bird endures torment[22].
But once his life-breath is gone,
a whole ocean would be of no avail!

Now my life is ebbing out
just hovering a little more:
Once the man is drowned, what's the use of a boat?
There is none to rescue then[23]!

---

(20) This alludes to a story about a carpenter's son who decked himself like god Vishnu, complete with four arms and weapons, to win a king's daughter. When the fraud was found out and his life was in danger, he called on Vishnu for help - and Vishnu rescued him.

(21) The lion stands for God (Hari-Vishnu), the jackal for Yama (Death).

(22) In the torment of separation from the rain-drop, the Chatak bird is supposed to eat live-coals.

(23) Salvation can only be achieved in this human life.

I am nothing, I am nothing,
  nothing is mine:
In this dire conjecture, take care of Your honour:
  for Sadhnā is your servant!

2

Kabīr's Contemporaries

RAVIDĀS

1

Gu gauṛī 1

Vile is my company[24],
  such is my despair day and night -
Degrading is my trade[25],
  low is my birth.

  O my Lord Rām[26],
    You are the life of the living -
  Do not forget me,
    your servant!

Do away with my misery,
  give me the heart of a true devotee -
I won't leave your feet,
  should I lose my life tomorrow!

Says Ravidās, I have come
  to take refuge in Your court:

---

(24) Ravidās's natural company is that of the filthy, untouchable Chamārs, whose behaviour reflects the degraded status which caste Hindus have imposed on them.

(25) *karamu* (*karma*) here refers to Raidās's hereditary occupation as a leather worker. In the Sants' view, such an occupation is not only socially despicable but also morally wrong, since it is connected with the skinning of carcasses.

(26) *rāma gusaia* 'Gosāin Rām', in a Vaishnav context, may refer to a holy man, with the meaning of 'Reverend', or to God Himself.

Make haste to meet Your servant,
do not tarry!

2

Gu āsā 3

You are the sandal-tree
and I the poor castor-oil plant by your side:
From a mean shrub, I turned into a noble tree
when my foul smell was pervaded by your fragrance!

O Mādhav! I take refuge
in the company of Your saints -
I am worthless
but you are bountiful!

You are like the white and golden silk
and I am the poor silk-worm[27]-
Let me ever remain in the company of saints, O Mādhao,
as the bee sticks to the honey.

Vile is my caste, vile is my lineage,
vile is my birth -
For I did not serve King Rām[28],
says Ravidās the Chamar.

---

(27) Slowly, the miserable silk-worm is transformed into silk, i.e. God Himself.

(28) The implication seems to be that, if Ravidās was born a Chamār, it was due to his lack of devotion in his former birth.

6

Gu āsā 6

That puppet of clay[29],
how well it dances!
It looks and looks and listens
it rums and spins around!

If man acquires anything,
he gets proud -
If he looses his wealth,
he begins to weep.

His whole mind and soul
is engrossed in pleasure -
And then he is gone:
nowhere to be found!

Says Ravidās, O my Brother,
this world is just a magic show -
But I've fallen in love
with the Magician.

8

Gu sorathī 5

If You be a sacred hill[30],
then I am your peacock -
If You be the moon,
then I am your Chakor-bird!

---

(29) The puppet of clay is man.

(30) *girivara,* lit.: 'an excellent hill' is also the name of the famous *Govardhan* or *Giriraj* hill in Braj - the hill itself being identified with the Lord of the Hill, Krishna-Gopāl.

O Mādhao, if You don't break with me,
I won't break with You -
If I broke with You
to whom would I cling?

If you are a Lamp,
then I am your wick -
If You are a holy spot,
then I am your pilgrim.

Between You and me,
such a bond of love -
Once I united to You
I broke all other friendships.

Wherever I go,
I remain at your service -
You alone are my Master[31]
I have none else, O God!

Worshipping You alone,
I got free from Yama's[32] bonds -
For the sake of pure devotion
Ravidās sings your praise.

9

Gu soraṭhī 6

Walls of water, props of air

(31) *Thākur* means a Master, or a Krishnaite idol, object of continuous 'service' (*sevā*).

(32) Yama is the god of Death.

mortar of semen and blood -
In that cage made of bones, flesh and veins,
the poor bird-soul must dwell[33].

O you Mortal!
What's mine, what's thine?
The bird's dwelling
is on the tree.

You dig foundations
and you fix props -
But your real size
is just three and a half cubit[34]!

You curl your hair
and wear a turban jauntily on one side -
Yet, that body of yours
will turn into a heap of ashes.

Lofty mansions you own
and beautiful women -
But without Rām's Name
you've lost the game!

Vile is my caste and my lineage,
low is my birth -
But I have taken refuge in You, O King Rāmchand[35],
says Ravidās the Chamār.

---

(33) The 'cage' is the human body.

(34) Such is the size of a grave.

(35) Rām or 'Rāmchand' is here identified with Rāmachandra, the hero of the *Rāmayaṇ* Epic; Rām is divinized as a *avatār* of God Vishnu-Hari.

13

Gu mārū 1

But for You, my beloved
who could do such a thing?
O Protector of the poor, O my Master,
you've placed the royal umbrella over my head!

From my polluting touch, the whole work shrinks,
yet You bent Yourself towards me -
You exalt the lowly, O my Govind,
and You fear no one!

Nāmdev, Kabīr, Trilochan, Sadhnā and Sain[36]:
all of them, You've saved:
Says Ravidās, listen, O Sants:
Hari can achieve anything He wants!

15

Gu malār 2

Neither Lakshmī's Husband[37]
nor the Lord of Kailāsh
Can be reckoned as equal
to Hari's devotees!

He remains One
present in so many
In each and everyone
He dwells in plenitude.

---

(36) All those five great saints are known to have been low-born. In their achievements, Ravidās the Chamār rejoices.

(37) The Husband of Lakshmī is Vishnu, the Lord of Kailāsh is Shiva.

He who was known as a holy man[38]
  who was all devotion -
By birth was nothing but
  a wretched calico-printer!

He whose family observed 'Id Bakri',
  butchered cows, revered Sheikhs and Pirs -
Whose father did so, the son following him
  in such family was Kabīr born,
    revered as a Siddha in the three worlds[39]!

He whose family
  used to drag dead cattle over Varanasi -
Before that one bowed Brahmans and Acharyas,
  before Ravidās, the slave of slaves!

---

(38) The epithet *bhāgavat,* here attributed to Nāmdev, the calicoprinter, shows the author's preference for the Vaishnav religion, though Nāmdev, a workman, was surely born Shaiva.

(39) The author, Ravidās, insists on the fact that Kabīr was born a Muslim - neither Shaiva nor Vaishnava. Kabīr here is clearly held as a 'perfect Yogi', a *Siddha-* and not a 'Sant'. The Siddhas are credited with magical powers.

PĪPĀ

Gu dhanāsarī 1

Within the body is the god, within the body, the temple,
within the body, all the Jangamas[40]!
Within the body the incense, the lamps and the food-offerings
within the body the *pūjā*-leaves[41].

After searching so many lands
I found the nine Treasures within my body:
Now there'll be no further going and coming,
I swear by Rām!

That which pervades the universe lies within the body[42]:
He who searches will find it there:
Says Pīpā, there is the supreme Reality
which the Perfect Guru reveals.

---

(40) *jangama jāti,* lit.: 'the Jangama breed': *Jangam,* literally 'One who is ever on the go', refers to a Virashaiva sect, whose members are itinerant *sādhus*, visiting Shaiva shrines. Pīpā himself, before his conversion to Vaishnavism, is said to have been a staunch Shaiva.

(41) The incense and the lamps are needed for the *ārati*; the food offerings (*naivedya*) and the *bilva* leaves are necessary for the *pūjā* to god Shiva.

(42) Lit.: 'Both the *'brahmaṇḍa'*, lit.: 'the Universe', and the *'piṇḍa'*, 'the body', are one; both have no reality besides the supreme Reality which pervades all.

DHANNĀ

Gu āsā

In Govind, Govind, Govind
was Nāmdev's heart immersed:
A calico-printer worth half a penny
became a millionaire[43]!

Giving up all his stretching and weaving,
Kabīr took to the love of God's feet -
He, a low-born Julāhā,
see what great fame he won!

Ravidās, who dragged away dead cattle,
gave up all attachment to worldly things -
And lo! He took his place in the company of the saints
and obtained the vision of Hari!

And Sain, the barber, a mere village-servant,
his story is told in every house -
The supreme Being dwelt in his soul
and he was counted among the great devotees[44]!

So have I heard - and I, a simple Jāṭ[45],
took to the practice of devotion -
And the Lord revealed Himself to me:
great indeed was Dhannā's fortune!

---

(43) A *lākhpati,* i.e. a millionaire - but his riches were spiritual ones.

(44) He became a 'Gosain', cf. Ravidās, 1, note 3.

(45) A Jāṭ is a peasant from the North-Western frontier.

BHĪKHAN

Gu sorațhī 2

The priceless Jewel of the Name
must be the reward of some past merits[46]-
Though I took great pains to keep it in my heart,
never could I hide it!

The greatness of Hari
is beyond words!

My tongue relishes the Name, my ears delight in it,
my mind rejoices in meditating over it -
Says Bhīkhan: It is the delight of my eyes:
wherever I look, it is Him that I see.

---

(46) A way of saying: 'I do not know how I got such a boon'.

PARAMĀNAND

Gu sārang 1

O Man! What did you achieve
by listening to Puranas?
You did not take to prayer,
nor did you feed the hungry[47].

You didn't forsake lust or anger,
You didn't get rid of greed, you 'god'!
You never ceased to slander others
and all your worshipping went in vain!

By highway robbery and house-breaking[48],
you filled your body, you, sinner -
And you fell into that very ignorance
which will make you infamous even in the next world!

Violence[49] never left your heart,
on creatures you had no pity:
Says Paramānand, you never sought the saintly
nor conversed on holy things.

---

(47) This *pad* is a condemnation of the Brahmanical view of 'holiness', as opposed to the religious ideal of the Sants. The man here ironically apostrophed as a ***dev,*** lit.: 'god', is a Brahman, a 'god-of-the-earth', is a ritualist, a greedy and brutal fellow who does not recoil from animal sacrifice.

(48) The knavery and lack of scruples of the ritualistic Brahman in his dealings with his clients are ironically alluded to highway-robbery and house-breaking.

(49) *hiṁsā,* 'violence' is the opposite of *ahiṁsā,* the highest virtue in the eyes of the Sants.

You search, you search, O my friend,
But Kabīr has disappeared:
The drop has merged into the ocean,
How can it be found?

You search, you search, O my friend,
But Kabīr has disappeared:
The ocean has merged into the drop,
How can it be found?

Appendix 1

Bibliography[1]

Editions and translations of Kabīr's verses

I. Principal editions

A. The *Bījak*

1. *Bījak* with 'Pākhaṇḍakhaṇḍinī' commentary (litho.), Light Press, Benares, 1868.
   This lithographed edition gives an incomplete version of the *Bījak,* together with a commentary which Kabīr himself is supposed to have dictated to the Rājā of Bhagel (i.e. the Rājā of Rewah). The commentary is based on *saguṇ upāsanā,* the cult of the 'qualified' or visible Guru.

1a. Ibid., printed edition, Nawal Kishore Press, Lucknow, 1872.

1b. Ibid., Venkateshwar Press, Bombay, Vi.S. 1961 (A.D. 1906).
   The printed edition, together with its commentary, is known as the 'Rājā of Rewah edition'; the Bombay re-edition adds a life of Kabīr in verse and some extra *pad*s, *sākhī*s, and

(1) This critical Bibliography does not purport to be exhaustive; it merely lists the most ancient and the most important editions of Kabīr's verses. A number of these editions are popular ones, which have been reprinted many times, together with their commentaries. A chronological order has been kept, so as to acquaint the reader with the development of the printed words of Kabīr in India, though, even now, his utterances are mostly handed over by word of mouth.

ramainīs, plus a genealogy and history of the royal lineage of the Rājā of Rewah.

2. *Bījak Śrī Kabīr Sāhab,* with 'Trijyā' commentary by Purandas, Ganga Prasad Varma Press, Lucknow, 1872.
The Purandas or Puran Sahib commentary is said to be composed from the *nirguṇ upāsanā* point of view, i.e. the cult of the 'non-qualified' or invisible Guru, as opposed to the *saguṇ upāsanā* point of view adopted in the commentary found in the Rājā of Rewah edition (cf. above, A. 1). The Purandas edition has been often reprinted; it appears to be the standard text for the Kabīr Chaurā branch of the Kabīr-panthīs: a 1968 reprint *Bījak saṭīk,* was found in the use of the Mahant of the Kabīr Chaurā Maṭh at Benares in 1970. A Gujarātī translation of the Purandas commentary was published in Baroda in 1937.

3. *Kabīr kā pūrā bījak,* ed. Prem Chand, Calcutta, 1890.

4. *Satayśabda ṭaksār arthāt bījakmūl,* with a commentary by Swami Yugalanand, Lucknow, 1892.

5. *The Bījak of Kabīr,* ed. Ahmed Shah, Baptist Mission, Cawnpore, 1911.

6. *Sant Kabīr kā bījak,* ed. Sivavrat Lal (3 pts.), Gopiganj, 1914.

7. *Kabīr Sāhib kā bījak,* Belvedere Press, Allahabad, 1926.

8. *Kabīr Sāhab kā bījak,* with a commentary by Vicardas Shastri, Allahabad, Vi.S. 1983 (A.D. 1926).
The Vicardas Shastri edition is said to be based on five manuscripts preserved at the Kabīr Chaurā Maṭh, Benares, but no variants are given in the edition itself.

9. *Bījak* with 'Śisubodhinī' commentary by Hanumandas (3 pts.), Baroda, 1926.

9a. Ibid. with Sanskrit commentary, Kabīr Press, Baroda, 1939.

9b. Ibid., Gujarātī edition (2 pts.), Baroda, 1933.

The Hanumandas edition corresponds to the version of the *Bījak* which P.N. Tiwari calls the 'Fatuhā branch' of the work (*Bīfa*).

10. *Bījak-mūl* with 'Sarvāṅgapadaprakāśikā' commentary by Raghavadas, Benares, 1946.

10a. Ibid without commentary, Benares, 1946; repr. 1948.

11. *Mūl-bījak,* ed. Mahant Methi Gosain Sahib, Chapra, 1937.

11a. *Bījak, Bhagavān Gosāin Sāhab kā pāṭh,* Saran, 1938.

This edition, established at the 'Mānsar Gaddī' of the Kabīr-panthīs, Daudpur, Chapra, is known as the 'Gosāin Bhagavān Sāhibwālā pāṭh' of the *Bījak.* According to P.N. Tiwari, it represents the 'Bhagatāhī branch' of the work (*Bibha*).

12. *Kabīr Sāhab kā bījak,* ed. by Hamsdas Shastri and Mahabir Prasad, Kabīr Granth Prakashan Samiti, Barabanki, Vi.S. 2007 (A.D. 1950). This often-reprinted edition is known as 'the Barabanki edition'. It contains an Index of difficult words and a list of symbols found in the *Bījak,* with interpretations. It is so far considered as the standard edition of the *Bījak* (*Bī*).

13. *Sadgranth Bījak* with 'Parakh-prabodhinī' commentary by Abhilashdas Shastri of Shri Kabīr Mandir, Gonda, Benares, 1969.

14. *The Bījak of Kabīr* was elegantly rendered in English by Linda Hess, North Point Press, San Francisco, 1983. Shukdev Singh, unfortunately, does not give his sources and text criticism is absent.

B. The *Gurū Granth* collection.

1. *Ādi Śrī Guru-granth Sāhab Jī* (Gurumukhi script), ed. Bhai Mohan Singh Vaidya, Amritsar, n.d.
This was the early edition used by E. Trumpp, see further II.B.5.

1a. Ibid, Nāgarī script edition, Vi.S. 1984 (A.D. 1927).

2. *Śrī Gurū Granth Sāhab,* Shiromani Gurudvara Prabandhak Samiti, Amritsar, 1952: (a) Gurumukhī script (b) Nāgarī script.
The Nāgarī edition is here referred to as *Gu.*

3. *Kabīr-pada-sangrah,* ed. Kishandas Udasi Niranjani, Nirnay Sagar Press, Bombay, 1876.
This is the first collection of Kabīr's verses as found in the Guru Granth.

4. *Śrī Guru Sahab,* Sarva Hind Sikh Mission, Amritsar, 1937.

5. Varma, R.K., *Sant Kabīr,* Allahabad, 1947.
After a fairly long Introduction dealing with the life, times, and works of Kabīr, the author gives the text of Kabīr's verses as they appear in the *Guru Granth* : (a) *padas* classified according to the *rāg* and (b) *saloku* (i.e. sākhīs) numbering 243 in all. Appendixes 1 and 2 respectively give approximate renderings of the padas and salokus into modern Hindi prose; appendix 3 gives an interpretation of a number of symbols appearing in Kabīr's verses; appendix 4 is a short lexicon (*śabda-koś*) of obsolete or difficult words, with interpretations; the work also includes a synopsis of similar padas found in the *Guru Granth* and in the *Kabīr-granthāvalī* collections of Kabīr's verses; at the end, an Index of *incipits* is found.

C. *The Kabīr-granthāvalī* (i.e. the Rajasthani tradition [Raj])

1. *Kabīr-Granthāvalī,* ed. S.S. Das, Kashi Nagari Pracharini Sabha, Benares, 1928.
This first edition of the *Kabīr Granthāvalī* has been reprinted a number of times.

2. *Kabīr Granthāvalī,* ed. P.N. Tiwari, Hindi Parishad, Allahabad, 1961. *(KG)*.
This edition, without a commentary, is the first critical edition of Kabīr's words. The Appendix includes an alphabetical list of incipits, an alphabetical list of the variants discussed in the Introduction, and a bibliography. The edition forms the basis of most of the research work which has been done on Kabīr in India since 1961.

3. *Kabīr Granthāvalī saṭika,* ed. Pushpalal Singh, Delhi, 2nd edn., 1965.
This edition closely follows the S.S. Das text, with some additions; it includes a general Introduction in Hindi, but no critical apparatus. Each verse is followed by an interpretation of difficult words and a paraphrase in modern Hindi.

4. *Kabīr Granthāvalī,* ed. L.B. Anant, Delhi, 1968.
This edition is also based on the S.S. Das text. It includes an Introduction and a Commentary in modern Hindi.

5. *Kabīr Granthāvalī,* ed. M.P. Gupta, Agra, 1969.
This edition is an improvement on the S.S. Das text; the author has made use of one more important manuscript belonging to the same tradition (i.e. the Rajasthani or Dādū-panthī tradition) and he has closely compared the readings within this tradition itself and also with the reading found in the Guru-Granth collection. The edition includes a critical Introduction in Hindi and each verse is followed by a translation into modern Hindi; some interesting variants

are also discussed. An Index of difficult words and an Index of *alamkārs* (figures of speech) are found in the Appendix.

D. *Main compilation of Kabīr's Sākhīs*

1. *Upadeś-ratnāvalī* (225 sākhīs from the *Bījak*) (Litho.), ed. Shri Totaram Varma 'Bharatbandhu' and Motilal Kapinvis, Bharatbandhu Yantralay, Aligarh, Vi.S. 1882 (A.D. 1825).
2. *Kabīr kā rekhta,* 'The Rekhtus of Kabīr's, in W. Price, *Hindee and Hindostanee Selections,*
3. *Bayaz-i-sākhī Kabīr,* 'Album of the sākhīs of Kabīr', (date ?). A copy of this compilation is mentioned in the manuscript Catalogue of the books of Farzada Culi, a catalogue belonging to the Royal Asiatic Society, London (and mentioned by Garcin de Tassy, *HLHH,* i.p. 130).
4. A collection of 243 'slokas' of Kabīr as found in the Guru-granth in Gurumukhī characters, ed. with a Panjabi translation and commentary by Nihal Singh Gyani, Lahore, 1896.
5. *Satya Kabīr Sāhab kī sākhī,* ed. Swami Yugalanand (2 pts.), Lucknow, 1899; reed. Venkateshwar Press, Bombay, 1908 (numerous reprints).
6. *Kabīr Sāheb kā sākhī-sangrah* (2 pts.), Belvedere Press, Allahabad, 1926.
7. *Sadguru Kabīr Sāhab kā saṭīka sākhī-granth,* ed. Maharaj Raghavadas Ji, Benares, 1950.
8. *Sadguru Kabīr Sāhib kā sākhī-sangrah,* ed. with commentary by Vicardas Shastri, Baroda, 2nd edn., 1950.
9. *Kabīr-sākhī-sudhā,* ed. with commentary by R.C. Srivastava 'Candra', Agra, Vi.S. 2010 (A.D. 1963).
10. *Kabīr-sākhī-sār,* ed. with commentary by Ram Vashishth and Taraknath Bali, Agra, 6th edn., 1968.

E. *Other compilations or selections of Kabīr's verses*

1. *Kabīrdas-kṛt ramainī,* Benares, 1819.
(Mentioned by Garcin de Tassy *HLHH*, i, p.139.)
2. *Kabīr-darpan,* A collection of verses of Kabīr on 101 different subjects in Gujarātī script, Bombay, 1898.
3. *Kabīr Sāhib kī śabdāvalī* (4 pts.), Belvedere Press, Allahabad, 1907.
Numerous reprints.
4. *Kabīr* (3 pts.) ed. Kshiti Mohan Sen, Calcutta, 1910.
In Bengali characters, with an Introduction and a paraphrase in Bengali.

4a. *Kabīr ke pad* (4 pts.), ed. Kshiti Mohan Sen, Shantiniketan Series, 1920.
5. *Kabīr vacanāvalī,* ed. Ayodhyasingh Upadhyay 'Hariaudh', Kashi Nagari Pracharini Sabha, Benares, 1st edn. (?); 9th edn., Vi.S. 2004 (A.D. 1947).
Numerous reprints.
6. *Kabīr vacanāvalī*; ed. S.S. Das, Kashi Nagari Pracharini Sabha, Benares, Vi.S. 1982 (A.D. 1925).
7. *Kabīr Sāhib kī baṛī aur choṭī śabdāvalī,* ed. Sadhu Lakhandas Kabīr Chaurā, Benares, n.d.
8. *Satya-Kabīr śabdāvalī arthāt Kabīr bhajanāvalī,* ed. Sadhu Amritdas Ji, Kabīr Chaurā, Benares, 1950.
9. *Kabīr padāvalī,* ed. R.K. Varma, Allahabad, Vi.S. 2011 (A.D. 1954).
10. *Kabīr-saṅgrah,* ed. P.N. Tiwari, Allahabad, 1952.
This is a small selection of 60 padas, 5 ramainīs, and 151 sākhīs, the readings being those of the critical edition of the *Kabīr Granthāvalī* by the same author (cf. above, C 2).
A detailed commentary of the same selection has been published separately by the author:

10a. *Kabīr-saṅgrah-samjīvanī,* Allahabad, 1965 *(KSS).*

11. Shankar Haribhai, *Samudāy santanivāṇī,* 1888: A Collection of poems of Kabīr and other Vaiṣṇava poets.

A number of short selections of Kabīr's verses are found included in several works, such as:

12. H.P. Dvivedi, *Kabīr* (see below, III B), Appendix 2, *Kabīr-vāṛī.*

13. P. Chaturvedi, *Sant-kāvya,* Allahabad, Vi.S. 2009 (A.D. 1952).

14. Viyogi Hari, *Sant-sudhā-sār,* New Delhi, 1953.

F. *Sectarian works attributed to Kabīr*

Several large compilations published by Kabīr-panthī authors contain a number of a apocryphal works attributed to Kabīr such as:

1. *Kabīr-sāgar tathā bodh-sāgar,* ed. Swami Yugalanand Ji, II vols., Venkateswar Press, Bombay.
This huge compilation includes 40 works attributed to Kabīr.

2. *Ambu sāgar,* ed. Swami Śrī Nanhelal Murlidhar, Sarasvati Vilas Press, Narsinghpur.

3. *Anurag-sāgar,* Narsinghpur, 1930 ed. Swami Yugalanand, Venkateshwar Press, Bombay, 1948, refs. Baroda, ViS. 2003 (A.D. 1946).

A number of apocryphal works are fairly popular and are also found printed separately, such as:

Akharavati, Belvedere Press, Allahabad, 1946.

Kabīr-Gorakh-guṣṭi, ed. Sadhu Lakhandas, Kabīr Chaurā, Benares, Vi.S. 1983 (A.D. 1926).

Kabīr-Kṛṣṇa-gītā, Sarasvati-Vilas Press, Narsinghpur.

Surati-śabda-samvād, ed. Gurusampati Sahib, Jodhpur, Vi.S. 1934 (A.D. 1874).

Kabīr-Niranjan-goṣṭi, (by Dharam-das?), Sarasvati-Vilas Press, Narsinghpur, 1926.

II. TRANSLATIONS OF KABĪR'S VERSES

A. *Indian Languages*

(a) Bangālī

1. Sarkar, Yogendranath, *Kabīr,* Calcutta, 1893.
   Biography of the poet in Bangālī, with a Bangālī translation of some verses.
2. Bhattacharya, P., *Kabīr,* Calcutta, 1890.
3. Mukhopadhyay, U., *Dohāvalī,* Calcutta, 1901.
   Religious verses by Kabīr and others with a Bangālī translation.
4. Sen, K.M., *Kabīr,* cf. above, I E 4 and 4a.

(b) Panjābī

Cf. above I D 4.

(c) Sindhī

Kabīr Sāhib Jī kā ślok, with a Sindhī translation; Hyderabad (Sind), 1924.

(d) Tamil

Mohanram Singh, *Kabīr-Kamāl dāsakīrta naigal,* Kundur, 1897.

B. *European languages*

(a) Italian

Padre Marcus a Tumba arrived in India 1758; Italian translation of 'Mulapanci' in Mines de l'Orient, vol. iii; published by Angelo de Gubernatis.

(b) English

1. Wilson, H.H., *Religious Sects of the Hindus* (RSH)

(Extracts from the Bījak).

2. Jhabwala, J.H., Translation from the original Hindi into English, Bombay (date ?).
3. Prem Chand, *A translation of Kabīr's complete Bījak into English,* Calcutta, 1911.
4. Ahmed Shah, *The Bījak of Kabīr,* Hamirpur, 1917; (*AS*).
5. Trumpp, E., *The Ādi-Granth,* London, 1877.
   The translation includes part of Kabīr's poems in the Granth, i.e. the two first rāgas, Gaūrī and Āsā.
6. Lala Kanoo Lal, *One hundred and seventy-five Moral Sayings of Kabīr selected and translated into English,* Madras, 1923.
7. Macauliffe, M.A.,
   The Sikh Religion, 1st edn., 1909, repr. Delhi, 1963, vol. vi (*SR*).
8. Tagore, Rabindranath, *One hundred Poems of Kabīr,* with an Introduction by Miss E. Underhill, London, 1914.
9. Machve, Prabhakar, *Kabīr,* with a foreword by H.P. Dvivedi, Sahitya Akademi, New Delhi, 1968.
   A small selection of Kabīr's poems.
10. Uniyal, J.P., *Kabīr,* New Delhi, 1968.
   A small booklet translated from the *Kabīr-sangrah* published by P.N. Tiwari; cf. above, *I.* E 10.

(c) French:

1. Mirabaud-Thorens, *Cent Poèmes de Kabīr,* traduits de l'anglais, Paris, Gallimard, 1922; repr. in 'La Fugitive', Collection du Monde entier, Gallimard, 1969. The French translation is from *One Hundred poems of Kabīr* by Rabindranath Tagore.
2. Vaudeville, Ch., *Kabīr Granthāvalī, Dohā,* with Introduction and notes, Institut Français d'Indologie; Pondichery, 1957.

A French translation of the complete collection of Dohās or 'Sākhīs' as found in the S.S. Das edition of the *Kabīr-Granthāvalī,* cf. above, I C 1.

3. Vaudeville, Ch., *Paroles de Kabīr,* Collection UNESCO d'oeuvres représentatives, Paris, Gallimard, 1959; reprinted. An Anthology of the poems of Kabīr (padas) borrowed from the three main traditions and classified according to the themes.

(d) German

Glasenapp, H. von, *Indische Geisteswelt,* Baden-Baden, 1958. A few translations of Kabīr's verses into German are found in vol. i, pp.258 ff.

(e) Russian

Lipkin, S.I., *Lirika,* poems translated from Hindi into Russian, Moscow, 1965.
Includes a few poems of Kabīr translated into Russian; the translations are of a popular character.

Appendix 2

Concordances

SĀKHĪS in KG (Raj.), Gu, Bī.

I		
1.5	158	321
1.6	-	154
1.7	-	88
1.8	-	160
1.9	157/194	-
1.10	67	-
1.11	161	-
1.12	193	-
II		
2.1	76	97
2.2	-	99
2.3	124	
2.4	125	
2.5	48	
2.6	126	
2.7	-	67
2.8	-	72
2.9	-	270
2.11	-	118
2.12	-	193
2.13	-	Bībhā 55
[2.14]	-	310
III		
3.1	127	-
3.3	41	-
3.4	223	-
3.5	109	-
[3.24]	204	153
IV		
4.1	11	-
4.2	174	-
4.3	150	-
4.4	14	-
4.5	164	-
4.6	192	-
4.7	169	-
4.8	141	-
4.9	111	-
4.10	159	-
4.11	160	-
4.12	181	-
[4.13]	63	-
4.14	197	-
4.15	-	54
4.16	-	98
[4.17]	-	167
[4.18]	-	172
V		
5.1	42; 83	-
5.2	332	-
VI		
6.1	74	-
6.3	51	-

VII		
[7.10]	[122]	
VIII		
8.1	62	-
8.2	81	-
8.3	97	-
IX		
9.2	121	-
9.3	177	-
9.4	87	-
[9.41]	-	57
X		
10.1	-	241
10.2	-	33
10.3	-	266
[10.6]	-	52
10.7	152	-
XI		
11.1	95	-
11.2	21	-
[11.3]	-	81
[11.4]	-	51
[11.5]	-	268
[11.6]	-	317
XII		
[12.10]	-	121
XIII		
13.1	-	33-9
13.2	-	217
XIV		
14.1	71	-
14.2	22	-
14.3	85	-
14.4	182	-
14.5	183	-
XV		
15.1	-	102
15.2	- Bībhā	268
15.3	80	-
15.4	178	-
15.5	30	115
15.6	-	113
15.7	36	174
15.8	153	209
15.9	-	291
15.10	-	206
15.11	-	29
15.12	-	12
15.13	-	248
[15.14]	-	27-3
[15.15]	-	219
[15.16]	-	334
[15.17]	-	330
15.18	-	70
15.19	-	226
15.21	-	28
15.22	-	40
15.23	-	38
15.24	-	37
15.25	-	117
15.26	-	34
15.27	-	35
15.28	-	166
15.30	-	113

15.30	-	113
[15.31]	-	44
[15.32]	-	7
[15.33]	-	155
[15.34]	-	243
[15.35]	-	9
[15.87]	-	Bī. sā 246
[15.88]	-	Vipramatīsī dohā 1
XVI		
16.1	103	297
16.2	90	71
[16.3]	53	18
16.4	-	133
[16.5]	-	129
[16.6]	-	295
[16.7]	-	231
[16.8]	-	229
16.9	-	230
[16.10]	49	-
16.11	-	227
[16.12]	218	
16.13	132	
[16.14]	64	
[16.15]	208	
XVII		
17.1	175	349
17.3	229	-
XVIII		
18.1	162	169
18.2	154	-
18.3	114	-

[18.4]	23	-
[18.10]	-	289
[18.11]	-	194
[18.12]	-	170
XIX		
19.1	29	324
19.2	69	-
[19.3]	16	-
19.4	33	-
[19.5]	61	-
19.6	146	-
[19.7]	148	-
[19.9]	149	-
19.10	55	-
XX		
20.1	120	-
[20.2]	-	86
20.3	56	-
20.4	165	31
20.5	69-15	255
[20.6]	-	189
20.7	-	138
XXI		
21.1	98	311
21.3	76.2	188
21.4	237	-
21.5	187/199	-
21.6	200	-
21.7	185	-
21.8	54	-
21.9	96	-
21.10	52	-

21.11	172	-
[21.12]	143	-
[21.13]	142	-
[21.14]	-	180
21.15	-	151
21.16	-	215
XXII		
22.1	-	337
22.2	-	162
[22.3]	-	161
[22.5]	-	197
XXIII		
23.1	-	46
XXIV		
24.1	195	-
24.2	88	242
24.3	86	-
24.4	232	-
[24.5]	24	-
[24.6]	99	-
24.7	-	226
[24.8]	-	227
24.9	240	280
24.10	-	207
XXV		
25.1	25	-
25.2	145	-
25.3	101	-
25.8	-	46
25.9	-	155
XXVI		

26.1	126	-
26.2	137	-
[26.3]	184	-
[26.4]	-	214
26.5	-	216
XXVII		
27.3	68	-
XXXVIII		
28.1	190	-
28.6	-	21
XXIX		
29.1	58	-
[29.2]	224	-
29.3	-	219
29.4	-	128
XXX		
30.1	17	-
XXXI		
31.1	-	142
31.2	-	141
31.3	156	140
XXXII		
32.1	-	219
32.2	-	168
XXXIII		
33.1	-	173
33.2	-	45
[33.6]	-	Bī. ramainī dohā
33		

SĀKHĪ [SALOKU]

Gu - KG2

7	15.32	49	16.10	98	21.1
9	15.35	51	6.3	99	24.6
11	4.1	52	21.10	101	25.3
13	15.29	53	16.3	103	16.1
14	4.4	54	21.8	106	15.19
16	19.3	55	19.10	109	3.5
17	30.1	56	20.3	111	4.9
21	11.2	58	29.1	113	15.30
22	14.2	61	19.5	114	18.3
23	18.4	62	8.1	117	15.25
24	24.5	63	4.13	120	20.1
25	25.1	64	16.14	121	9.2
26	24.7	67	1.10	122	7.10
27	15.21	68	27.3	124	2.3
28	15.20	69	19.2	125	2.4
29	19.1	70	15.18	126	2.6
30	15.5	71	14.1	127	3.1
33	19.4	74	6.1	132	16.13
34	15.26	76	2.1	136	26.1
35	15.27	80	15.3	137	26.2
36	15.7	81	8.2	141	4.8
37	15.24	83	5.1	142	21.13
38	15.23	85	14.3	143	21.12
40	15.22	86	24.3	144	15.8
41	3.3	87	9.4	145	25.2
42	5.1	88	24.2	146	19.6
44	15.31	90	16.2	147	19.7
45	33.2	95	11.1	148	19.8
46	23.1	96	21.9	149	19.9
48	2.5	97	8.3	150	4.3

152	10.7	174	4.2	201	21.2
153	15.8	175	17.2	202	20.5
154	18.2	177	9.3	203	6.2
155	15.33	178	15.4	204	3.6
156	31.3	181	4.12	208	16.15
157	1.9	182	14.4	216	29.8
158	1.5	183	14.5	218	16.12
159	4.10	184	26.3	219	32.1
160	4.11	185	21.7	223	3.4
161	1.11	187	21.5	224	29.2
162	18.1	190	28.1	226	15.19
164	4.5	192	4.6	227	16.11
165	20.4	193	1.12	229	17.3
166	15.28	194	1.9	232	24.4
168	32.2	195	24.1	237	21.4
169	4.7	197	4.14	240	24.9
172	21.11	200	21.6	243	15.34
173	33.1				

Pads in KG2 (Raj.), Gu, Bī.

KG2	Gu	Bī.
5	Āsā 24	-
8	Gaüṛī 21	-
9	Gaüṛī 2	-
10	Gaüṛī 55	-
11	Āsā 30	sab. 35
12	Gūjrī 2	-
[19]	Āsā 35	-
20	Dhanāsarī 5	-
[21]	Gaüṛī 33	-
22	Bhairaü 1	-
23	Gauṇḍ 4	-
24	Bhairaü 18	-
25	Bhairaü 17	
26	Basant 12	
27	Gaüṛī 42	sab. 112
28	-	sab. 38
29	Gaüṛī 10	-
	Bhairaü 16	-
30	Gaüṛī 26	-
31	Bilāval 12	-
32	Kedārā 1	-
37	Āsā 12	-
38	Gaüṛī 22	-
39	Bilāval 3	-
40	Rāmkalī 8	-
41	Mārū 7	-
42	Bhairaü 15	-
43	Basant 5	-
[44]	Bilāval 6	-
[45]	Bilāval 7	-
[46]	Gaüṛī 15	sab. 108
		[Bībha 48]
47	-	sab. 108
48	Gaüṛī 36	sab. 92
49	Gaüṛī 39	sab. 36
50	Āsā 28	
51	Rāmkalī 1	
52	Gaüṛī 43	
53	-	Kaharā 10
54	Mārū 5	
55	Gaüṛī 64	
56	Rāmkalī 2	
57	Mārū 4	
58	Gaüṛī 68	
60	Āsā 23	sab. 89
61	Gauṇḍ 1	ra. 70
62	Gaüṛī 35	sab. 99
	Gauṇḍ 2	
63	Bhairaü 9	
64	Gaüṛī 25	
65	Āsā 16	
66	-	sab. 26
67	Āsā 27	sab. 60
		[Bībha 3]
68	Soraṭhi 2	sab. 73
		[Bībha 107]
69	Kedārā 4	sab. 72
		[Bībha 106]

70	Sūhī 2	sab. 106	108	-	sab. 24
		[Bībha 66]	109	-	sab. 54
71	Bhairaü 14		110	-	sab. 68
72	Soraṭhi 7		111	Gaüṛī 54	sab. 15
73	Sārang 1		112	Rāmkalī 6	
[74]	Mārū 11		113	Gaüṛī 52	
[77]	Gaüṛī 6		114	Āsā 6	
78	Gaüṛī 8		[115]	Rāmkalī 10	
79	Gaüṛī 11		116	Āsā 22	
80	Gaüṛī 73		117	Bilāval 11	
81	Gaüṛī 31		118	Soraṭhi 6	
82	Gaüṛī 63		119	-	sab. 16
83	Āsā 15		120	-	sab. 95
84	Āsā 37		121	-	sab. 87
85	Soraṭhi 1		122	-	sab. 2
86	Soraṭhi 3		125	Gaüṛī 29	sab. 79
87	Tilang 1		126	Basant 6	
88	Sūhī 11		127	Āsā 10	
89	-	sab. 85	128	Bhairaü 11	
		[Bibha 26]	129	Bhairaü 4	
[90]	-	sab. 91	130	Gaüṛī 19	
[97]	Gaüṛī 57	Cāmcar 2	131	Gaüṛī 66	
99	Āsā 21		132	Āsā 1	
	Bhairaü 2		133	Sirī 2	
100	Kedārā 6		134	Gaüṛī 47	
101	Āsā 5		135	Āsā 25	
102	-	Kaharā 8	136	-	sab. 35
103	-	sab. 45	137	-	sab. 111
		[Bībha 63]			[Bībha 111]
106	Gaüṛī 12.2		138	-	sab. 19
	Gaüṛī 13.4				[Bībha 18]
107	Gaüṛī 17		139	-	sab. 37

[140]	-	sab. 100
[150]	Āsā 36	ra. 28
[151]	-	sab. 200
[152]	-	sab. 114
153	Dhanāsarī 1	
154	Gaüṛī 70	
155	Bhairaü 20	
156	Gauṇḍ 3	
[157]	-	sab. 23
159	Gaüṛī 36	
160	-	sab. 44
161	-	Kaharā 12
162	Gauṇḍ 7	
[163]	-	sab. 59
166	Bhairaü 5	
167	Gaüṛī 44	
168	Āsā 20	
169	-	sab. 39
170	-	Kaharā 12
171	Soraṭhi 8	
172	Bilāval 8	
173	Mārū 2	
174	Gaüṛī 4	
177	Bibhās 2	sab. 97
178	Āsā 8	sab. 84
179	-	sab. 40
180	-	sab. 67
181	-	sab. 75
182	-	ra. 62
183	Bibhās 4	
184	Āsā 17	
185	Bibhās 3	
186	Gaüṛī 67	
187	Āsā 14	
188	Āsā 26	
189	Bhairaü 6	
190	Bilāval 2	
191	Mārū 1	
192	Basant 7	
[196]	Rāmkalī 5	sab. 17
[197]	Sūhī 1	
198	Basant 2	Basant 10
199	Gaüṛī 51	sab. 38
200	Dhanāsarī 3	sab. 103

Pads in KG2 (Raj.) Gu

1	-	32	Kedārā 1
2	-	33	-
3	-	34	-
4	-	35	-
5	Āsā 24	36	-
6	-	37	Āsā 12
7	-	38	Gaüṛī 22
8	Gaüṛī 21	39	Bilāvalu 3
9	Gaüṛī 2	40	Rāmkalī 8
10	Gaüṛī 55	41	Mārū 7
11	Āsā 30	42	Bhairau 15
12	Gūjrī 2	43	Basant 5
13	-	44	-
14	-	45	-
15	-	46	Gaüṛī 14
16	-	47	-
17	-	48	Gaüṛī 36
18	-	49	Gaüṛī 39
19	Āsā 35	50	Āsā 28
20	Dhanāsarī 5	51	Rāmkalī 1
21	Gaüṛī 33	52	Gaüṛī 43
22	Bhairaü 1	53	-
23	Gauṇḍ 4	54	Mārū 5
24	Bhairaü 18	55	Gaüṛī 64
25	Bhairaü 17	56	Rāmkalī 2
26	Basant 4	57	Mārū 4
27	Gaüṛī 42	58	Gaüṛī 68
28	-	59	-
29	Gaüṛī 10	60	Āsā 23
30	Gaüṛī 26	61	Gauṇḍ 1
31	Bilāvalu 12	62	Gaüṛī 35

	Gauṇḍ 2	94	-
63	Bhairaü 9	95	-
64	Gaüṛī 25	96	-
65	Āsā 16	97	Gaüṛī 57
66	-	98	-
67	Āsā 27	99	Āsā 21. 1, 2, 3
68	Soraṭhi 2		Bhairaü 2. 3; 5
69	Kedārā 4	100	Kedārā 6
70	Sūhī 2	101	Āsā 5
71	Bhairaü 14	102	-
72	Soraṭhi 7	103	-
73	Sāraṅg 1	104	-
74	Mārū 11	105	-
75	-	106	Gaüṛī 12. 2
76	-		Gaüṛī 13. 4
77	Gaüṛī 6	107	Gaüṛī 17
78	Gaüṛī 8	108	-
79	Gaüṛī 11	109	-
80	Gaüṛī 73	110	-
81	Gaüṛī 31	111	Gaüṛī 54
82	Gaüṛī 63	112	Rāmkalī 6
83	Āsā 15	113	Gaüṛī 52
84	Āsā 37	114	Āsā 6
85	Soraṭhi 1	[115]	Rāmkalī 10
86	Soraṭhi 3	116	Āsā 22
87	Tilaṅg 1	117	Bilāvalu 11
88	Sūhī 4	118	Soraṭhi 6
89	-	119	-
90	-	120	-
91	-	121	-
92	-	122	-
93	-	123	-

124	-
125	Gaüṛī 29
126	Basant 6
127	Āsā 10
128	Bhairaü 11
129	Bhairaü 4
130	Bhairaü 19
131	Gaüṛī 66
132	Āsā 1
133	Sirī 2
134	Gaüṛī 47
135	Āsā 25
136	-
137	-
138	-
139	-
[140]	-
141	-
142	-
143	-
144	-
145	-
146	-
147	-
148	-
149	-
150	Āsā 36
151	-
152	-
153	Dhanāsarī 1
154	Gaüṛī 70
155	Bhairaü 20
156	Gauṇḍ 3
157	-
158	-
159	Gaüṛī 36
160	-
161	-
162	Gauṇḍ 7
163	-
164	-
165	-
166	Bhairaü 5
167	Gaüṛī 44
168	Āsā 20
169	-
170	-
171	Soraṭhi 8
172	Bilāvalu 8
173	Mārū 2
174	Gaüṛī 4
175	-
176	-
177	Bibhās 2
178	Āsā 8
179	-
180	-
181	-
182	-
183	Bibhās 4
184	Āsā 17
185	Bibhās 3
186	Gaüṛī 67
187	Āsā 14

188	Āsā 26
189	Bhairaü 6
190	Bilāvalu 2
191	Mārū 1
192	Basantu 7
193	-
194	-
195	-
196	Rāmkalī 5
197	Sūhī 1
198	Basant 2
199	Gaüṛī 51
200	Dhanāsarī 3

Pads Gu KG2

Sirī	
2	133
Gaüṛī	
2	9
4	174
6	77
8	78
10	29
11	79
12	
13	106
14	46
17	107
21	8
22	38
25	64
26	30
29	125
31	81
33	62
36	159
38	48
39	49
42	27
43	52
44	167
47	134
51	199
52	113
54	111
55	10
57	97
63	82
64	55
66	131
67	186
68	58
70	154
73	80
Āsā	
1	132
5	101
6	114
8	178
10	127
12	37
14	187
15	83
16	65
17	184
20	168
21	99
22	116
23	60
24	5
25	135
26	188
27	67
28	50
30	11
35	19
36	150
37	84
Gūjrī	
2	12
Soraṭhi	
1	85
2	68
3	86
6	118
7	72
8	171
Dhanāsarī	
1	153
3	200
5	20
Tilaṅg	
1	87
Bilāvalu	
2	190
3	39
8	172
11	117
12	31
Gauṇḍ	
1	61
2	62
3	156
4	23
7	162

Rāmkalī

1	51
2	56
5	196
6	112
8	40
10	115

Mārū

1	191
2	173
5	54
7	41
11	74

Kedārā

1	32
4	89
6	100

Bhairaü

1	22
2	99
4	129
5	166
6	189
11	128
14	71
17	25
18	24
19	130
20	155

Basant

2	198
4	26
5	43
6	126
7	192

Sāraṅg

1	73

Bibhās Prabhāti

2	177
3	185
4	183

Index